VEDIC MEDICINE

Dr. Rita Singh

ANMOL PUBLICATIONS PVT. LTD.
NEW DELHI - 110 002 (INDIA)

ANMOL PUBLICATIONS PVT. LTD.
4374/4B, Ansari Road, Daryaganj
New Delhi - 110 002 (India)

ISBN 81-7488-836-5

First Edition 1998

PRINTED IN INDIA

Published by J.L. Kumar for Anmol Publication Pvt Ltd, New Delhi - 110002 and Printed at Tarun Offset Printers 518/14, Mauzpur, Delhi-53,

Contents

Preface

Indian medicine seems to have been evolved from prehistoric period. There is evidence that certain parts of India were occupied by human beings as early as the Middle Pleistocene. Stone implements constitute the sole memorial of the men of this age. The writings of the tablets and seals excavated from the sites of Indus Valley have yet to be deciphered. Their medicine to be inferred from the relics of the Indus Valley, their surviving relics in the Atharvaveda and from a study of the medicine of the contemporaneous civilization of Mesopotamia and Egypt. Scanty references to diseases and their cures are found scattered in the Rigveda. It is to the Atharvaveda, we are indebted to our knowledge of Vedic Medicine.

Vedic medicine, however was not primitive medicine. There are two types of medicine-primitive and magico-religious medicine. In primitive medicine, magical, religious and emperico-rational elements are inextricably combined, whereas, in magico-religious medicine, though these elements are frequently combined, a separation takes place. In Vedic Medicine, we have noticed this separation between the magical and religious elements and the emperico-rational elements. The medicine of Mesopotamia and Egypt were magico-religious. It is though that the medicine of Indus Valley must have evolved into magico-religious.

The Atharvadeda is a compendium of medicine in its various stages of evolution and contains the most primitive as well as highly advanced stages of therapy. It is a record of psychosouratic technique of healing by a combined procedure of charms, prayers, incantations, amulets and drugs. The yogic concept of the bodily functions was primarily evolved from introspection, whereas, the modern approach to elucidation of bodily functions is experimental, in which the function is recorded in one or more physical parameters.

The aim of the present work is to critically the Vedic medicine in all spheres of life. The subject matters have been treated in seven chapters-initiating with an introduction to the history of Indian medicine. Continuing in the next chapter, the work deals with the medical heritage of ancient India. IN the third and fourth chapter I have given in detail about sciences in the Vedas and origin of Vedic Medicine. Ayurveda, *i.e.* the Old Indian Medicine is the oldest medical science of the world. The history has distinctly shown that the Western Medicine is the offspring of Ayurveda. This interesting as well as important topic has been clearly discussed from all angles in the same chapter. In the fifth chapter I have tried to focus on the concepts of universe which influenced the ancient ideas about the body functions. In the sixth chapter, the lore pneuma, vata, wind, airs or breath which dates back to early vedic times has been discussed. The last chapter deals with the western school of thought about Indian medicine and how they have interpreted Atharvaveda as the veda of spells, and charms. They think that Atharvaveda is a veda which contains a whole series of magic, incantation and exorcisms.

To complete this book, I have taken help from all possible sources of informations. All along the book I have tried to avoid the scientific jargon so as to make it easily readable for all classes of people. I am thankful to the members of the National Medical Library, Indian National Scientific Documentation Centre (INSDOC), Delhi, for their sincere help in supplying relevant materials.

I acknowledge my deep gratitude to my husband Dr. N.K. Singh who painstakingly went through the entire manuscript. My sincere thanks is due to my publisher Mr. J.L. Kumar for bringing out this book in record time.

DR. (Mrs.) RITA SINGH
Director,
AIDS PREVENTION SOCIETY.

1

Introduction to the History of Indian Medicine

Indian Medicine: From Ancient Times to 1200 AD

Indian medicine seems to have been evolved from prehistoric period. To study ancient Indian medicine, let us divide the period into prehistoric period comprising the Stone Age and the duration of the Indus Valley Civilization (2500-1500 B.C.) and the historic period (1500 BC – 1200 AD) or in other way we can say that the whole period is comprised the Prehistoric, the Vedic and the Classic periods.

The Prehistoric Period

This comprehends the Palaeolithic, the Neolithic and the period of the Indus civilization. Though writing was known and employed in India in the third and the second millenium BC the peculiar script of the Indus civilization has not yet been deciphered. So the period of the Indus civilization has to be included in this period.

The Palaeolithic and the Neolithic Ages

There is evidence that certain parts of India were occupied by human beings as early as the Middle

Pleistocene. Stone implements constitute the sole evidence of the men of the Stone Age. These stone implements are classified into Paleolithic, Mesolithic and Neolithic. There are two varieties of Paleolithic implements viz., the Madrasian and the Sohan, including the pre-Sohan. The pre-Sohan implements occur in the Boulder Conglomerate of the Sohan valley and belong to the early Paleolithic and are referred to the Middle Pleistocene. The Mesolithic implements are represented by the microliths, which are widely distributed in India and Pakistan. Neolithic implements are more abundant than the Paleolithic ones and are found mostly in the Ballary district of the Madras State[1].

No authentic fossil remains of the men of the Stone Age have yet been found in any part of India or Pakistan. Racial anthropologists inform us that there is no particular race of men belonging to ancient India but about six races have, from time to time, migrated into India from outside and have become characterized in India. Of these the Proto-Austroloids and the Dravidians seem to have been the earliest and these still survive in good many aboriginal tribes of India, although more or less mingled with other people. The aboriginal tribes of India fall into two great classes viz., that of the Kolarians, who speak the Munda language, a branch of the Austric family of languages and that of the Dravidians, a type of the Mediterranan. The chief representatives of the Kolarians are the Kolas, the Koches, the Santhals and the Savaras and of the Dravidians the Khonds and the Ghonds of the middle peninsula, together with the Oranos and the Todas of the extreme south.[2]

Though we have no fossil remains of the men of the Stone Age, we have in the existing primitive tribes, what may be considered as "living fossils" of these men. By a study of the customs and beliefs of these "living fossils" field anthropologists have given us an insight of the sort of beliefs and culture to which these aboriginal tribes have risen to. All these tribes believe in the existence of souls and their survival after death. They also believe in many nature-spirits. They perceive among the nature-spirits great gods who rule the universe. The Khonds believe in a rain-god. Most tribes believe in a sun-god. Besides the sun-god, some tribes worship the moon-goddess. The Khonds worship an earth-goddess and besides they have a river-god, hill-god, and a god of small-pox. The Ghonds and Kholes worship snakes and trees. Some tribes have their totems. The Oraons have the "mouse totem" and the Santhals the "goose totem". Birth rites, marriage-rites, funeral-rites, human sacrifice, taboos, witch-craft, worship of ancestors, divination and demonology are almost universal among the tribes[2]. The culture of the primitive tribes of India closely resembles that of other aboriginal tribes in other parts of the world. Taylor who laid the foundations of modern anthropology has given to these beliefs the name of "animism".

Primitive thought saw in every illness not readily susceptible of explanation, where the sequence of effect upon cause was not immediate, as in most illnesses, the influence of a strange malevolent will or a demonic power. Thus he arrived at the conception that all not-readily explanable diseases were the creation of super-natural powers and thus came to formulate the most ancient theory in medicine viz., demonism. These supernatural powers he conceived under two categories viz., those beyond his powers of control and those amenable to his control. By religious rites like prayers, incantations and propitiation, he tried to appease the first group and by magic he tried to influence the second group and bring them under his control. Thus the medicine of the men of the Stone Age consisted of religion and magic. Demonism formed their theory of medicine and magic their practice.

The Indus Valley Civilization (2500-1500 B.C.).

The archaeological discoveries at Harappa, Mohenjo-daro, Chanhu-daro and other sites in the lower Indus valley have disclosed that at the dawn of history there existed in the plains of lower Indus an extensive, highly evolved, chalcolithic culture named the Harappa culture or more comprehensively the Indus civilization. This civilization was in full flower in the time of Sargon of Agade (in Mesopotamia) whose date is now placed a little before 2300 B.C. This civilization came to an abrupt end by its destruction by the Aryan invaders in 1500 B.C., which is the date generally accepted today as a reasonable approximation of the Aryan invasion. Wheeler estimates that the period 2500-1500 B.C. is likely to have comprised to material available.[3]

We do not know with certainty who the author of this civilization were. "The sum of the evidence from the skulls discovered at Mahenjo-daro and Harappa shows that in the Harappa culture there was at first the aboriginal Proto-Austroloid type (the Austric speaking people), perhaps then as now, ranking among the under-dogs of the social systm; second the predominant Mediterranean (the Dravidian speaking people) presumably the main contributor of the agricultural and urban features of the whole prehistoric world and with them probably the short-headed Alpine element."[4]

"Before the discovery of the Indus civilization, it was assumed, that the Aryan invaders encountered a rabble of aboriginal savages, who could have contributed little, save a few animistic beliefs, to Vedic thought and nothing to the structure of the latter Indo-Aryan society"[4] "Our knowledge that the Indus civilization was flourishing in northern and western India, at the beginning of the second mellennium, centered on cities with strongly fortified citadels and containing among its population a large proportion of Proto-Austroloids, with dark skin and flat noses and that the cities came to a sudden and violent end, makes the identification of the *dasyus* and *dāsas* with the inhabitants of Harappa and Mohenjo-daro something near to a certainty."[4]

Though this civilization came to an abrupt close by its conquest by the Aryans, its influence persisted for centuries after. "Clearly after the first drastic 'Aryanisation' of the Punjab, some sort of modus vivendi was arrived at; if not there, eastwards in the Gangetic basin, as the frontiers receded eastwards. Harappa ideas permeated the religious thought of the Brahmins."[4] That such a permeation did actually take place is evident from a study of the *Rg-Veda* and the *Atharva-Veda*. "The *Atharva-Veda* came into existence considerably later than the *Ṛg-Veda*. In form it is similar to the *Ṛgveda* but in spirit it is entirely different from it and represents a much more primitive stage of thought. Whilst the *Ṛgveda* deals, almost exclusively, with the higher gods as conceived by a comparatively advanced and refined sacredotal class, the *Atharva-Veda* is, in the main, a book of spells and incantations appealing to the demon-world and teems with notions current among the lower grades of the population and derived from an immemorial antiquity."[5] The hymns of the *Ṛgveda* may be taken to reflect the civilization of the Aryan people at different periods of antiquity before and after they had come to India; whereas the hymns of the *Atharva-Veda* may be taken to reflect the civilization of the prehistoric non-Aryan inhabitants of India i.e., the inhabitants of the Indus civilization. There is also evidence that the above mentioned permeation continued to take place to the non-Aryan inhabitants of the Gangetic Valley down to the sixth century B.C. Thus in the Buddhist Canon, the *Śīlas,* we are told of palmistry, divination of all sorts, auguries drawn from the celestial phenomena, prognostications by interpretation of dreams, repeating charms, laying of ghosts, snake charming, astrology, the power of prophesy, incantations, oracles, and many other of the same kind.

Unfortunately we have no means of ascertaining the medical beliefs of the Indus civilization, as their script has not yet been deciphered. These beliefs have to be conjectered from a study of medical beliefs prevalent in the contemporary civilizations of Mesopotamia and Egypt, with which the Indus civilization had close contacts and about whose medical beliefs we have written records. The medicine of Mesopotamia was magico-religious. It was ancillary to religion. Here the art of divination attained a high degree of development. Astrology formed an important aid to prognostication of diseases. Oracles were sought on all occasions and the doctrine of the stars influenced deeply all phases of popular thought and religion. Egyptian medicine was magico-religious. Magic, incantations, spells, and prayers were freely employed in treatment. We have seen that in the *Atharva-Veda* and the Buddhist Canon, the *Śīlas,* divination of all sorts, astrology, oracles, auguries drawn from celestial phenomena and other signs, magical rites, incantations, spells, and charms were very prevalent. It is resonable to suppose that these beliefs were derived, as a result of permeation of these beliefs, from the Indus civilization, who shared these beliefs with contemporary civilizations of Mesopotamia and Egypt.

The question naturally arises from whence the Indus civilization derived these beliefs. There are many possibilities. They might have evolved from the primitive medicine of the people of the Stone Age. They might have been borrowed from the older civilizations of the ancient world with which Indus civilization was in close communion. Finally the possibility that these beliefs were common to the older civilizations and Indus civilization shared these views with them. Medicine, based on an animistic hypothesis, has followed the same pattern of evolution all the world over. It either remains as primitive medicine or evolves into magico-religious medicine. The medicine of Mesopotamia and Egypt were magico-religious. So also the medicine of the Indus Valley must have evolved into magico-religious. The final answer to this question must wait till we know something more definite about the Indus civilization medicine.

But on one point the excavations at Harappa and Mohenjo-daro provide positive, evidence *viz.*, hygiene and sanitation. These two cities between them represent the oldest samples of town-planning in the world. In those cities were baths, lavatories, drains, manholes with covers, fresh-water tanks, and handsome interior court-yards, comfortable bed-room etc. Their whole conception shows a remarkable concern for sanitation and health, without parallel in the Orient in prehistoric past or at the present day.[4]

The Vedic Period (1500-800 B.C.)

It is now considered that the hymns of the *Ṛg-Veda* were composed between 1500-1200 B.C. and that the collection of the Vedic hymns in the present form was completed by 800 B.C. Scanty references to diseases and their cures are found scattered in the *Ṛg-Veda.* It is to the *Atharva-Veda* we are mainly indebted to our knowledge of Vedic medicine.' The oldest name of the *Atharva-Veda,* in Vedic literature, is *Atharvāṅgirasah,* i.e., the *Atharvans* and the *Aṅgirasah.* The two words denote two different species of magic formulae; *atharvan* is holy magic bringing happiness and *aṅgiras* is hostile or black magic. The former included among others, formulae for healing of diseases, while the later included curses against enemies, rivals. malicious magicians etc." "The hymns of the *Atharva-Veda* comprise incantations against demons sorcerers, enemies; of charms for expelling diseases wrought by demons or sent by gods as punishment of man's sins; of incantations intended to impart health, longevity, success and victory, sex-attractiveness and mainly vigour. In the Vedas these hymns are supplemented by amulets, medicines, philters and other devices of witch craft and magic."[6] In the *Atharva-Veda,* religion and magic, reign supreme.

Vedic medicine, however, was not primitive medicine. Sigerist distinguishes between primitive and magico-religious medicine. In primitive medicine, magical, religious and emperico-rational elements are inextricably combined, whereas in magico-religious medicine, though these elements are frequently combined, a separation takes place. In Vedic medicine we notice that separation between the magical and religious elements and the emperico-rational elements. Thus we read in A.V.11.9.3., that there are hundreds of medical practitioners and thousands of herbs but what can be done by these can be effected by binding an amulet with the particular charm of this verse. Thus it would appear that the practice of pure medicine by professional medical men, apart from the priest-physicians, has already begun. Again in A.V. 11.9.5. the *Atharvan* who binds the amulet is described as the best of all the doctors. In A.V.VIII. 7.20, we read, in how many herbs the human physicians finds a remedy, so many, all remedial do I bring to thee. This would imply that even at the time of the *Atharva-Veda* there were physicians and an elaborate pharmacopoeia treating diseases with drugs. The praise of the Atharvan as the physician *par excellence,* being superior to all remedies prescribed by the other physicians, implies the existence of two contending systems of medicine viz., the system of charms prescribed by the Atharvan, the priest-physician, and the system of drugs prescribed by the ordinary medical practitioners. This itself implies that vedic medicine was becoming magico-religious.

From the point of view of the development of Indian medicine the rational elements contained in the *Atharva-Veda* is significant. In A.V.X.2. is a hymn, in which the several parts of the skeleton are carefully and orderly enumerated. This enumeration formed the basis of the osteology of the Ātreya-Caraka school of classic medicine. In A.V.II.33. almost all the important organs of the body are enumerated. In A.V. 1. 17.5 are mentioned *dhamanīs* and *sirās,* names familiar in classic medicine. The theory of *vāyus,* met with in all lǝter literature, is alluded to the *prāṇa apāna, vyāna* and *samāna vāyus* are mentioned in A.V. 1.2.13. The *ojas,* which occurs in later medical works, is mentioned in A.V.11. 18.

The Brāhmaṇa-Upaniṣad Period (800-600 B.C.)

The *Chāndogya Upaniṣad* (VII.1.2) mentions among the other subjects pursued in this period the *Atharva-Veda,* the *Pitrya* (rules for the sacrifices for the ancestors), the *Daiva* (the science of fortunes) the *Bhūtavridyā* (the science of demons, the *Sarpavidyā* (the science of serpents or poisons). These studies must have comprised the sum total of medical studies at this period. Medicine was stationary and had made no progress beyond Vedic medicine in this period.

Mention is made in classic medical literature of "*āyurveda*" the science of life. Suśruta says it was an *upāṅga* of the *Artharva-Veda.* Vāgbhata I speaks of it as an *upaveda* of the *Atharva-Veda.* But no mention is made of it in Vedic literature. The *Āyurveda* was supposed to have consisted of eight divisions : *Śalya* (surgery), *Śālākya* (minor surgery), *Kāya-Cikitsā* (medicine proper), *Bhūtavidyā* (demonology), *Kaumāra-bhṛtya* (Children's diseases), *Agada-Tantra* (the science of poisons), *Rasāyana-Tantra* (the science of rejuvenation), and *Vājikaraṇa* (the science of acquiring sex-strength). The subject of *Bhūtavidyā* and *Sarpavidyā* were contained in the *Atharva-Veda.* Besides these, we have in the *Atharva-Veda,* hymns dealing with the securing of long life and increasing virility. These were treated in the *Āyurveda* under the names of *rasāyana* and *vājīkaraṇa.* Four new subjects make their appearance in the *Āyurveda viz.*, *Salya, Śālākya, Kāya-cikitsā* and *kaumārabhṛtya.* These must have come into existence between (600-400 B.C.), and allied themselves to the *Atharva-Veda.* The tradition of an *Aṣtaṅga Āyurveda* must also have come into existence during this period (600-400 B.C.); as there is a reference to *Aṣtaṅga Āyurveda* in the *Mahābhārata* whose date is now assigned to 400 B.C.

The Classic Period (600 B.C. to 1200 A.D.)

The sixth century B.C. was an important century in the history of humanity. From Athens to the Pacific the human mind was astir. About the sixty century B.C. there is evidence, in the older civilizations of Egypt. Mesopotamia and China, of a leap forward in speculative thought of a new birth in ethics, of a religion of conscience, threatening to take the place of the religion of custom and magic. In India also, this was a period of great intellectual ferment and spiritual revolt, leading to the establishment of new faiths like Jainism and Buddhism. It was also a period of a quiet philosophic movement which gave rise to the six systems of Indian philosophy. "The earliest beginnings of most systems of Indian thought can be traced to sometime between 600 and 100 B.C. It is extremely difficult to say anything about the relative priority of the systems with any degree of certainity. It is possible that earliest speculations of some form of Sāṃkhya Yoga and Mīmāṃsā were prior to Buddhism. The Vaiśeṣika system is also probably pre- Buddhistic."[7]

The emergence of Indian medicine during this period from its intimate association with religion and magic and its association with philosophy is colsely connected with the rise of these schools of philosophy and its influence on medical thought. Generally speaking medical thinking, in analyzing man and his environment, in diagnosing diseases and prescribing therapies, adopts a scientific, non-theological view of the entities and energies concerned. The doctrine of the human body, as well as the greater part of diagnosis and therapy in classic Indian medicine, are based on the conception of certain constituents or elementary substances (*bhūta, dhātu* and *doṣa*) which pervade the organism and maintaining its functioning. These concepts were taken over from the cosmological speculations of Indian nature philosophers who considered matter as composed of certain elementary bodies called *bhūtaṣ.* Even as early as the *Upaniṣads* this idea is traceable. The *Upaniṣads* speak of five elements (*bhūtas) viz.,* space (*akāśa),* Air (*vāyu),* fire (*agni),* water (*ap)* and earth (*pṛthvī*). The two philosophical systems which have influenced the Indian medical writers are the *Nyāya-Vaiśeṣika* and the *Sāṃkhya.* These two systems accept this classification.

Indian medical tradition traces medicine from a mythical, through a semi-mythical, to an historical beginning. According to this tradition, Indra taught the science of medicine to Ātreya and the science of surgery Dhanvantari. This may be taken to mean that Ātreya, the physician, and Dhanvantari, the surgeon, were understood to have been the founders in their respective departments, of medicine as a science. From this time onwards the systematic development of Indian medicine proceeded, primarily, on two principal lines *viz.,* one that of Ātreya and the other that of Dhanvantarī. Ātreya taught medicine of his six disciples. Similarly Dhanvantari taught surgery to his six disciples. Each of these disciples wrote a treatise on medicine or surgery. Of these, the tantras of Agniveśa, Bhela and Harita, have survived in medicine and that of Suśruta in surgery.

There were two periods in the early medical literature of India, the Tantrakalpa period and the Saṃhitā period. Tantras dealt with separate branches or special subjects and kalpas are monographs on special subjects. The writings of the disciples of Ātreya were called medical tantras and those of Dhanvantari were called surgical tantras. Of the medical tantras we have the tantra of Agniveśa and of the surgical tantras we have the tantra of Suśruta on *śalya.* These tantras and kalpas formed the early medical literature and the basis of teaching in the medical schools. Caraka refers to the existence of various schools of medicine and also to various treatises on medicine before his time. He also mentions that diversity of views with regard to medical theories existed. It was the existence of these diverse treatises, expressing diverse opinions on medicine, that called for the systematization of the then existing medical knowledge. This the saṃhitā attempted to do. Thus following the Tantra-kalpa period, we have, the Saṃhitā period.

The saṃhitā period may be called the creative period of Indian medicine. We have three important saṃhitās viz., Caraka, Suśruta and Bhela saṃhitās. The saṃhitās of Caraka and Suśruta from the classics of Indian medicine. The medical school of Bhela and Caraka conform to the tradition of an astāṅga-āyurveda. Their saṃhitās consist of eight divisions but these differ essentially, from the eight divisions of the Āyurveda, as to their contents. These eight divisions are : Sūtra, Nidāna, Vimāna, Śarīra, Indriya, Cikitsā, Kalpa and Sidda sthānas. In the surgical school this tradition does not seem to have been adhered to. Suśruta's original treatise consisted only of five divisions, *viz.,* Sūtra, Nidāna, Śarira, Cikitsā and Kalpa sthānas. Later Suśruta, the junior added an Uttara-Tantra, consisting of the divisions Śālākya, Bhūta-vidyā, and Kaumāra-bhṛtya. Thus Suśruta's treatise was made to conform to the traditional Āyurveda. Both the Vāgbhatas follows the example of Suśruta Saṃhitā and their works contained six divisions, *viz.,* Sūtra, Nidāna, Śārira, Cikitsā, Kalpa and Uttarastāna and not tantra. The original of Caraka Saṃhitā was the Agniveśa-Tantra. Agniveśa was one of the six disciples of 'Ātreya, who according to the Buddhist Jātaka was the professor of medicine in the Univesity of Taxila, at the time of Buddha. So he must have flourished at some time in the sixth century B.C. Caraka, the redactor of the Agniveśa tantra, was the physician of the Emperor Kaniṣka, who reigned about 125 A.D. Caraka does not seem to have completed his redaction. Seventeen chapters of the Cikitsā sthāna, and the whole of Kalpa and Sidda sthānas were redacted by Dṛiḍhabala, who lived in the ninth century A.D. Suśruta must have lived about the sixth century B.C.

In classic Indian medicine the body was considered as a conglomeration (Samudaya) or the modification of the five elements (*bhūtas), viz.,* water *(ap),* fire (*tejas),* air (*vāyu)* earth (*pṛthvī*) and ether (*ākāsā).* The modifications of these five elements (*bhūtas)* which co-operate together to uphold the body were called *dhātus.* The *dhātus* are formed from the digested food. The food after digestion is converted into a pure portion (*ahara-prasada)* which is fit to be built into the system and a refuse (*kitta or mala)* which is not fit to be built into the system. From the pure portion, or the ahara-prasada, are produced the dhātus proper, *viz*., the food juice (*rasa*), blood (*rakta*), the flesh (*māṃsa*), the fat (*medas*), the bone (*asthi*), the marrow (*majjā*) and the semen (*sukra).* From the refuse or kitta, are produced urine, sweat, *faeces, vāyu, pitta, kapha* etc.

These substances when they are in their proper measure were supposed to uphold the body i.e., they functioned as *dhātus* and were called *mala-dhātus.* Of all the waste products (*malas), vāta* (air), *pitta* (bile) and *kapha* (phelgm) were consisted primarily to be responsible for all the morbidities of the body and therefore were called doṣas or vitiators. When the dhātus, (the *dhātus* proper and the *mala-dhātus*) were in their normal measure they were said to be in equilibrium and this state was called *dhātu-sāmya.* When the normal measure of the *dhātus (dhātus* proper and *mala-dhātus)* was either increased, decreased or displaced, then their equilibrium was upset and this state was called *dhātu-vaiṣamya.* On these concepts were based the famous *tri-dhātu* or *tri-doṣa* theory. The *doṣas* are three : they are *vāyu, pitta* and *kapha.* When they are in their normal measure and state they are beneficial to the body. When, however, they become disordered, verily, they afflict the body with disease of diverse kinds. This is the earliest enuciation of a "humoral theory" in medical history.

The sole aim of Āyurveda is to prescribe diet, medicine and a regimen of life, such that, if they are followed, a normally healthy person may maintain the equilibrium of his *dhātus* (the *dhātus* proper and the *mala-dhātus),* and a person who has lost the equilibrium of the *dhātus* (the *dhātus* proper and *mala-dhātus),* may regain it i.e., to advise a person how to preserve or secure health (*dhātu-sāmya).* In this statement is comprehended their whole therapeusis. This emphasis on medicine as the science of positive health, is well in advance of their times. Great emphasis was laid on the regimen of life to be followed. Elaborate regulations were laid down as to day-to-day duties *(dinacarya)* as to the modification of dietetic regulations according to the change of the seasons (*ṛtucarya),* as to bodily exercise (*vyāyāma)* and as to good conduct (*sad-vṛtta*). Diagnosis was the greatest achievement of ancient Indian medicine. Caraka lays very great emphasis on correct diagnosis as the basis of any rational treatment. Ancient Indian medicine also developed prognosis to a fine art.

"Surgery constituted the summit of the attainment of Indian medicine and although looked upon as *ultimum refugiens,* it yet commanded an elaborate technique and was from its nature removed from the influence of speculation. Surgical treatment was founded upon a rich experience which showed itself in bold interference, accurate diagnosis, and not the least, in thoughtful after treatment. The treatment of fractures, dislocations, tumours, fistula, removal of foreign bodies, the performance of paracentesis in dropsy etc., all rested upon rational considerations and upon a firm foundation of knowledge. The most astonishing performances of Indian surgeons, however, were in the domain of the laporatomy, lithotomy and plastic operations.[8] In Suśruta saṃhitā surgery achieves a leading position, as an indispensable element of general medical training. Suśruta recommends that every student of medicine must be taught both medicine and surgery. So also Caraka recognizes surgical treatment as an integral part of treatment in general. This co-operation and understanding between the Ātreya school of medicine and the Suśruta school of surgery is unique and contributed not a little to the progress of Indian medicine in the classic period.

The creative period of ancient Indian medicine comes to an end with Caraka and Suśruta. Caraka accomplished the final synthesis of Indian medicine and Suśruta that of Indian surgery. Their works have, thereafter, held undisputed authority of Indian medicine, till the rise of the Rasasidda school of the later middle age. Original works on medicine including surgery, practically ceased from the time of the early saṃhitās. The Indian medical writers, after Caraka and Suśruta, were but their imitators and abstractors, and commentators. No real original contribution was accomplished after them.

One of the most important documents in connection with ancient Indian medicine is the Bower Manuscript discovered in 1890. The second part of this manuscript is called the *"Nāvanītaka"* and consists mostly of formulae. The date of the manuscript, which is a copy of the original, is about 350-375 A.D. But the *Nāvanītaka* belongs to an earlier date and Hoernle assigns it to late second century. It is not an original work. It is a compilation of the then existing medical tantras and kalpas. It is of very great importance as a source book for ancient Indian medicine. It confirms the existence of the ancient medical classics of the classic period. It gives an idea of the growth of Indian medical literature. It confirms the existence of the tantra-kalpa period. It offers invaluable help in the fixing of the dates of the various medical classics. From a study of it, we learn, that the six tantras of the pupils of Ātreya are the oldest, next come the Caraka saṃhitā, that portion attributed to Caraka, the *Śalya-tantra* of *Suśruta,* and Uttara-tantra of Suśruta, the junior and last the Bhela saṃhitā.

Caraka, Suśruta and Vāgbhata from the famous "Triad of the ancients". There were two Vāgbhatas, *viz.,* Vāgbhata I and Vāgbhata II. Vāgbhata I is the author of *Aṣṭāṅga Saṃgraha,* which is frequently quoted in commentaries. It contains much independent material and is therefore of the greatest value for verifying as well as supplementing Caraka and Suśruta. Vāgbhata must have probably flourished either late in the sixth century or early seventh century.

A mention may be made to Mādhavachārya, the author of a compendium of pathology or *nidāna* called simply *Nidāna.* A popular stanza assigns to him a rank equal to that of the "Triad of the Ancients". Mādhava is considered the foremost authority on diagnosis. Mādhava may be placed in the eighth century A.D.

Vagbhata II is best known, as the author of *Astāṅga-hṛdaya-saṁhitā.* There is nothing original in this work. As the name implies it is compilation of existing medical works. He may be placed in the eighth century later than Mādhava.

Thus we come to the conclusion that original works on medicine seem to have practically ceased, from the time of the early *saṁhitās* A new start would appear to have been made with commencement of the later middle age, when the treatment with mercury *(rasa)* came into vogue. It remains to point out one important characteristic of the medicine of the early period up to 1200 A.D., which is not sufficiently realized by writers on Indian medicine. These characteristics may be listed: in the field of pharmacy calcination of metals and very little of metals in general is mentioned; mercury and its preparation rerely mentioned and when mentioned for use, only, externally in skin disease; no mention is made of *Nāḍiparīkṣa* in the medical examination; and no mention is made of opium. All these feature make their first appearance in the time of Śāraṅgadhara who belonged to the thirteenth century. The rise of Rasasiddha School and its repudiation of the medical theories of Caraka, Suśruta and ancient medical schools, their universal use of mercury *(rasa)* in treatment, is intimately associated with their rise of Indian alchemy after 1200 A.D. do not belong to this period under consideration.

References

1. Sahani, M.R. (1952). *Man in Evolution*, Orient Longmans Ltd., Chap. VII.

2. Hopkins, E.W. (1895). *Religions in India*. Ginn & Coy, Boston, Chap. xviii.
3. Wheeler, Mortimer, Sir (1953). *The Indus Civilization*, Cambridge Univ. Press, p. 4.
4. Piggott, Stuart (1950). *Prehistoric India*, Penguin Books, pp. 147, 168, 257, 261, 268.
5. Macdonell, A.A. (1925). *A History of Sanskrit Literature*, William Heinemann Ltd., London.
6. Zimmer, H.R. (1948). *Hindu Medicine*, The Johns Hopkins Press, Baltimore, p. 2.
7. Dasgupta, S. (1951). *A History of Indian Philosophy*, Vol. I., Cambridge Univ. Press, p. 5.
8. Neuberger, Max. (1910). *History of Medicine,* Vol. 1, Oxford Univ. Press, Translation by E. Playfair, pp. 57-58.

2

Medical Heritage of Ancient India

"Oh, East is East and West is West, and never the twain shall meet", has been disproved in this astronautical age. The closer we come to each other in the present century, the more we realize our common ancestry, our common heritage, the common fountainhead of our cultures, and the identity of our aims, aspirations and experiences as one man in one world. Shades of Wendell Wilkie? No! It is the spirit of scientific inquiry of this century. We no more live in ivory towers and no more recognize any international boundaries or intellectual barriers.

Medicine is as old as mankind; and the science of medicine, like any other form of knowledge, is better appreciated from the records of its evolution. A student of medicine cannot afford to lose sight of the discoveries of the ancients and their hypotheses that may appear to be erroneous today, were, nevertheless, the foundation of most of the scientific discoveries that we cherish today.

The primitive man, nay even the lower animals, instinctively found treatment for all their ailments and injuries. As the mind of man matured, the archaic medicine became a combination of religious, megical and empirical views and practices. Thus, in the ancient civilizations, extending from the Indus to the Nile, where religion formed an important part of their daily life, disease was considered as a punishment from the heavenly bodies, the spirits, the demons and the witches. This led to the creation of various gods, demigods and mythical heroes, who probably had an earthly existence; and the powers to protect the people against evil and cure their ills were attributed to them.

The antiquity of achievements of the Hindus in analytical and creative thought is universally acknowledged. But skepticism still persists in many a mind with regard to our achievements in the natural sciences in ancient times, even when it is conceded that the genius of any race is indivisible and its accomplishments in any field of human endeavour are closely related to its spirit of analytical thinking and creative activity. This skepticism is partly due to the fact that the sacred lore, which also encompasses the Indian scientific thought, was transmitted from man to man, and finally when it was put down on parchment, the self-renouncing sages dedicated all their works to their ancient predecessors, whether mortal, mythological or immortal. Establishing the chronology of our ancient and medieval texts has been beset with difficulties — at times insurmountable. The only way, therefore, left to us to ascertain the period in which a particular text was originally composed, is the internal evidence available in the text itself and its various commentaries written during later periods. This varies with the different interpretations put on various passages in the text by different scholars. These, at times, have been governed by considerations other than the objective approach based on sound philological principles.

Another factor which has proved to be a stumbling block in our efforts to establish the truth of the statements in biological sciences, made by our ancients, is the total absence of illustrative material in our ancient biological texts. However factual the description mentioned in the text, it is acknowledged on all sides that "one picture is worth a million words". It is more so when one is discussing the biological and medical sciences. Efforts have been made over a period of years to probe into the physical evidences from the past which could throw some light on the science of medicine and the art of surgery, as practised in India in that remote antiquity, and propogated by our ancestors.

There is some evidence available regarding the knowledge of anatomy during the chalcolithic (Copper Age) period, and the health conditions prevalent in prehistoric times, from which one can surmise the kind of medicine practised during that remote period in the history of India.

Many centuries before the advent of the Aryans into the Indus Valley, civilization flourished in this region, as evidenced by the excavations in Mohen-jo-Daro in Sind, Harappa and other minor sites, which was closely related to the civilizations of Elam, Sumer, and Crete. In the absence of any literary records of that period, one can only deduce from the archaeological findings the kind of medicine the Indus Valley people practised in the fourth millennium BC. Like other civilizations of the same period, their medicine must have been a combination of magical, religious and empirical practices. A few substances have been found in the ruins which form a part of the Ayurvedic pharmacopoeia even today and were probably used as drugs during those times. The public health facilities found in the ruins of the Indus Valley cities far surpass those found in the ruins of other ancient civilizations and indicate the high level of their achievement in the field of health and medicine.

When the Aryans entered the Indus Valley, they brought with them their gods and medical knowledge too. But, there is definite evidence to show that many elements of the Indus Valley culture were taken over and assimilated by them. The chief sources of the Aryan culture and medicine are the four *Vedas*. These are said to have been originally revealed by the creator, Brahma to the sages some six thousand years before Christian era, according to Indian traditions. The Western scholars, barring a few, believe that the oldest *Veda,* the *Ṛg Veda,* was compiled during the second millennum B.C. The *Rig Veda* is considered by most of the scholars as the original source of Hindu medicine, and is comprised of hymns and prayers addressed to different deities whose medical and surgical skills are also extolled. The *Sāma Veda* and the *Yajur Veda* are closely related to the *Ṛg Veda* and contain many humns derived from the latter. These consist of collections of sacrificial prayers and ritual texts. But, the *Atharva-Veda* which was composed at a later date, is replete with prayers, incantations, spells and charms to protect people against all kinds of disease and natural disasters. It is to this *Veda* and to the practices provided by another later work of the *Atharva Veda,* the *Kaushika Sūtra,* that we are indebted for our knowledge of medicine during the Vedic period. The texts of the *Vedās* were later organized into encyclopaedic *Saṁhitās,* and commentaries were written and attached to each of these texts. Even in these purely religious texts we find a reflection of anatomical, physiological, pathological, psychological and therapeutic views which are rational even though they may have some symbolic origin. Therein, side by side with the magico-religious formulae, empirical and rational elements are evident, which show that the Vedic people knew the signs and symptoms of the diseases and their treatment with drugs, and performed many a surgical procedure with skill and ingenuity. During the later Vedic and the Puranic periods much of the medical history got involved more and more with the mythological figures. The seers and sages, who might have had an earthly existence and contributed to the advancement of medicine during the early Vedic Period, were raised to the status of divine beings. To sift and sort out the real from the mere creation of the mind of man, is a task that will have to await further historical evidence. Since the extant works available point out the contribution which the mortals as well as the immortals made to the science of medicine, mythology, like that of the ancient Greeks and Romans has become an integral part of ancient Hindu medical history.

The word *Āyurveda* (in Sanskrit *Āyu* means life, and *Veda* means to now) which means the knowledge of life or the knowledge by which the nature of life is understood and thus life prolonged, does not figure in the vedic text. The traditional Vedic medicine, that must have flourished for several centuries, was handed down orally from the master of the pupil, and it is only at a much later stage that the traditional Hindu medicine was named *Āyurveda.* It may be noted that the ancients anticipated our attitude towards the practice of medicine and they did not name it as a science of therapy or cure, but as science which pervades all knowledge of life. The origin of the healing art, as in other ancient civilizations, was traced back to the creator, Brahma who became the fountain of all knowledge contained in the text of *Āyur Veda.* During the period of rational medicine which began around 600 BC, the *Āyur Veda* became intimately associated with the *Atharva Veda,* and later it was raised to the status of the original *Vedās,* thus confirming on it the necessary authority and sanctity.

Brahmā, the first teacher of the universe, according to Hindu mythology, originally composed the Āyurvedic texts in 100,000 hymns divided into one thousand chapters; but, realizing the fact that it would be beyond the comprehension of the mere man. He abridged it and divided it into eight parts with medicine (*Kāyachikitsā),* and surgery (*Shalya Tantra)* as the main subjects. Having propounded the science of healing, Brahmā propagated this knowledge through Daksha Prajāpati, who taught the science to the legendary Ashwinī Kumārās, the celestial physicians to the gods. The Ashwinīs appear in the *Vedās* also under the names of Dasra and Nāsatya. It may be pointed out that these and many other names of the Vedic gods appear in the documents found in the excavations in Boghaz Koyi in Cappadocia, northwest Mesopotamia. It is, therefore, believed that the Mitanian kings used to worship the Vedic gods as early as 1600 B.C. The Ashwinīs imparted the science of the medicine to Indra, considered chief of the gods in heaven, who, in turn is said to be the first god to hand over this knowledge to his mortal protagonists. According to the popular school of medicine represented by Charaka, the first mortal who received this science from god Indra was Bhardwāja. He then imparted it to Ātreya and other great sages of whom Agnivesha seems to have been the first to compose the text of *Āyurveda.* Charaka in his text claims to have reproduced the actual words of his master, Ātreya.

However, according to the old Dhanvantari School of Surgery, represented by the celebrated surgeon Śushruta, Indra favoured Dhanvantari with the entire knowledge of *Āyurveda.* Dhanvantari, who warded off death, disease and decay from the celestials, appeared in the form of Divodāsa, the king of Kāshī (modern Benares or Vārānasī). On being approached by a group of sages who were moved by the human suffering, Dhanvantari agreed to admit them to his hermitage and delivered to them the science of healing. The sages selected Sushruta to be their spokesman, who it is believed recorded the very words of Dhanvantari himself. But, the South of India, like the

South anywhere, has its own traditions; and, it credits the sage Agastya with the dissemination of the knowledge of *Āyurveda* during ancient times. It is unfortunate that the *Āyur Veda* is no more available in its original form but most of its contents are revealed to us by the *Samhitās* or the encyclopaedic works of Charaka and Sushruta. These texts were originally written about 1000 BC, and are considered the most authentic and renowned representatives of the original *Āyur Veda*. They contain all the information regarding the status of medicine in the ancient times. They, on the whole, have similar contents, analogous divisions, and corresponding theoretical and practical data; except for the fact that the *Sushruta Saṁhitā* is richer in the field of surgery. These *Samhitās* contain an abundance of material in an extremely condensed form, and have a rational approach. The exception being the use of magic and the *mantrās* (the holy incantations) in cases of delirium, in demoniac possessions, in some diseases of children, and in the ceremonies connected with birth. The state of health and of disease is explained on the basis of interplay of the constituent elements of the body, the general and alimentary regimen, and the influences of time and season.

Charaka, in his writings, has a combined role of a moralist, philosopher, and above all a physician; whereas, Sushruta has tried to cast off whatever shackles of priestly domination remained at his time, and created an atmosphere of independent thinking and investigation, which later characterized and the Greek medicine.

The *Sushruta Samhitā* is acknowledged as one of the greatest of its kind Sanskrit literature; and, is especially important from the surgical point of view (Sarton). The glory of first changing the art of surgery into a practical science, during the remote antiquity, must go to Sushruta, the author of the original *Sushruta Samhitā*. In its revised and redacted version this original *Samhitā* has been passed on to posterity by Nāgārjuna (second century B.C.) in the form of the present *Sushruta Samhitā*.

The science of medicine received the greatest support and stimulus in India during the Buddhist period. The Buddha (563-477 B.C.), himself, was a votary of medicine and regularly attended on the sick disciples in his camp. When the Buddha declared that this is the noble truth of suffering that "to be born is to suffer, to die is to suffer, and to fall sick is to suffer", his followers considered tending to the sick to be one of their religious obligations. The practice of surgery received the greatest setback in the later Buddhist period and surgery completely recorded into the background, since Buddhism put a stop to animal sacrifices and prohibited dissection. Yet Jīvaka (sixth century B.C.), the personal physician to the Buddha, practised surgery with success, and is known to have performed cranial surgery on many occasions. I-tsing, a Chinese traveller to India in the seventh century, quotes from a *Sūtra* (text on medicine, which, according to him, was preached by the Buddha himself.[1]

The old Buddhist text of *Mahāvagga,* belonging to the *Mahāyāna* sect of fourth century B.C., deals with the practice of medicine as prevalent in those days. It is in no way different from the Āyurvedic medicine of the period, and speaks of *Tridosha* (three humours or elements), various drugs of the Āyurvedic *materia medica,* inclusive of nasal remedies, eye ointments, and asafoetida, fomentations, and even laparotomy. Charaka is believed by some scholars to have been the court-physician of a Buddhist King, Kanishka (first century), whose wife he attended on as obsterician during her difficult delivery. Nāgārjuna (second century B.C.), the famous physician and alchemist, who revised the *Sushruta Samhitā* was also a Buddhist, and the *Samhitās* of the Vāgbhattās show traces of Buddhist influence in them. The famous Bower Manuscript found in a Buddhist stupa in Kashgar, and written in Indian Gupta script, probably by a travelling Hindu scholar-physician about 450, has several references to the Buddha as *Bhāgava* and *Tathāgata.* The later *Mahāyāna* Buddhists even raised on of the *Boddhisattva Mahāsattvās* to the status of a god of medicine, the *Bhaishajyaguru,* who in China and Tibet is known as "Bhu-guru" and in Japan even today is worshipped as *Yakusha Niyorai.* The ancient *Āyurveda* which travelled with the Buddhism everywhere, thus, flourished in the Buddhist *vihārās* (monasteries), and they became the hub of medical education also. Hiuen Tsang (Yuan Chwang) and I-tsing, two ancient travellers from China, who stayed for years in India to study religion, philosophy and medicine during the seventh century, give an excellent account of these monasteries[2].

After the death of the Buddha, his son Rāhul, and later his famous disciple Emperor Ashok (died 232 BC), established charitable hospitals for animals and men. In the fourth century another Buddhist king, Buddhadāssa of Ceylon (Shri Lankā), himself a physician, wrote a medical text *Sarattha samgaha,* and maintained physicians for both his troups as well as elephants and horses, and erected hospitals throughout his country (*Mahāvamso).*

With the spread of Buddhism to the Asian countries, the science of *Āyurveda* also travelled far and wide, and found a congenial soil in these countries. Even to this day, the ancient *Āyurveda,* in the garb of indigenous medicine, is being taught and practised in their native schools of medicine. More than 2,000 years ago, the Hindu culture and civilization reached Indonesia, and *Āyurveda* became the medicine of the Islands. Bali has preserved the rich Āyurvedic theory and practice. More than 250 medical texts in palm-leaf (*lontār,* in indonesian) manuscripts are known to exist in the land including *Ushada* (in Sanskrit, *Aushadha* means medicine) and *trinādī* (in Sanskrit, three channels). The medicine of Tibet, Untouched by wars until the Chinese occupation of this land, is based on *Āyurveda*. Several Sanskrit texts that were translated into Tibetan, including the *Rgyud Bzhi* (Four *Tantrās)*, whose original Sanskrit text is now lost, have preserved the rich heritage of the Indian medicine in Tibet. The Chakpori Medical College at Lhasa was one of the oldest institutions of its kind. From Tibet, *Āyurveda* travelled to Mongolia and distant Northeast Siberia; and all the Buddhist monasteries in these areas became great centres of medical learning. The medical college of the Kumbum monastery in Sinkiang attained special renown, as it was the birthplace of Tson-Khā-Pā, the founder of the Yellow Sect. It has in its possession a vast array of charts illustrating ancient Hindu medical texts. Another famous Mongolian medical college was at the Young Ho-Kung monastery, a monument to a great era in Peking, where once the Mongol students from Urga, Kiakhta and Kobdo, the Buryats from the Baikal Lake, the Kalmuks from the Volga, the Manchus from Tsi-tsi-Khar, the Tanguts from Koko-nor, and the Tibetans from Lhasa, repaired from medical training. One of the most famous physicians from these Mongolian medical schools, known for his Āyurvedic practice and success in this therapy during the recent times in Leningrad, was a Siberian, N.N. Badmaev. He counted among his patients, some of the prominent Communist leaders, Bukharian and Rykov, the famous writer Alexei Tolstoy, and even Joseph Stalin[3]. With the gradual revival of the Brahminism during the later Buddhist period the Elder Vāgbhatta of Sind (second century B.C.) attempted to bring about reconciliation between the texts of Charaka and Sushruta in his text called the *Ashtānga Samgraha.* Later on, one of his descendents the Younger Vāgbhatta (Eight century) wrote the *Ashtāngahridaya Samhitā,* a lucid and versified presentation of the whole *Āyurveda,* with special reference to surgery as dealt with in the *Sushruta Samhitā,* from which he had borrowed extensively. The works of Sushruta, Charaka and the Elder Vāgbhatta later came to be recognized as authoritative texts on *Āyurveda,* and the three texts were reverently called *Vriddha Trayī* , the "Triad of Ancients".

The medical literature during the early medieval period (500-1200) become entirely receptive and passive. One work that deserves mention is that of Mādhavāchārya (eight century) whose *Nidāna,* literally meaning pathology, occupied such an undisputed position of authority in *Āyurveda* for many centuries — to come, that it was later ranked equal with the above "Triad of Ancients". As a matter of fact, there is a popular Sanskrit quote among the practitioners of *Āyurveda,* which states, "Mādhava is unrivalled in pathology, Vāgbhatta in principles, Sushruta in surgery, and Charaka in therapy". This Mādhava or Mādhavkara, son of Indukara, made further advance in the enumeration and description of diseases, and listed them in 79 chapters (*Nidānās)* under their causes, symptoms and complications. He devoted a special chapter to smallpox (*Masūrikā)* which was classified as only a minor disease by the earlier writers.

The *Nidāna* of Mādhava remained as standard textbook for a long time to come, and is quoted profusely by the sixteenth century author Bhāva Mishra in his *Bhāva Prakāsha,* which was later translated into Arabic under various titles of *Nidān, Badan* and *Yedan.* The style of presentation in *Nidāna,* which was a great improvement on the text of Charaka and Sushruta, shows that it must have been composed for the guidance of students and practitioners of medicine; and that during the Purānic period, before the Arabs conquered Sind and the northern India, the training of physicians must have been very systematic and thorough.

The last revival of the orthodox school of *Āyurveda* in the sixteenth century, was mainly due to the eminent physicians like Bhāva Mishra who practised and taught medicine in Kāshī (modern Benares, Vārānasī) and is considered by the later authors as "a jewel of a physician and the master of the Text". Bhāva Mishra summarized the theory and practice of medicine as enunciated by all the well-known previous medical writers, in his universally acclaimed text *Bhāva Prakāsha* (1558-59). This text is the first to mention syphilis (*Firanga roga,* literaly meaning the Portuguese disease, since the Portuguese first introduced it into India) and discusses in detail its various stages and treatment.

The Arabs had contacts with India much before the birth of Islam, since the Indian products trekked along the trade routes passing through the Arabian countries. During the spread of Buddhism into Northwestern Asia, the Indian scholars travelled through Persia and Arab countries which brought them still closer to Indian culture. Many words of Indian origin like *kāfoor (karapūra* in Sanskrit; camphor) and *Zanjabīl (Shringavera* in Sanskrit; ginger) appear in the Koran. There is a tradition current among the Muslims in India that Adam descended from Paradise onto the Indian soil and received his first revelation in India. Some Indian scholars are believed to have been in the company of the Prophet Mohammed himself, and it is reported that during the Prophet's time a famous medical school flourished in Senna, in Southern Arabia, whose Principal Harith bin Kaladah had acquired his knowledge in India.[4]

It is recorded that many Hindus were settled in Mesopotamia during the early part of the *Umayyad* regime, and when Sind was conquered by the Arabs in 636-37, and annexed to the *Umayyad* Empire many Arabs also settled there. The superiority of the Hindu civilization astonished the Arabs, and the sublimity of the Hindu philosophy and the richness and versatility of their intellect were a strange revelation to them. Thus started a great influx of Indian men, materials and manuscripts in science and medicine into West Asia. The court at Baghdad extended its patronage to the Hindu scholars, and the second *Abbāsid Khalīfa* al-Mansoor (753-774) received emissaries from Sind, including Hindu pandits who presented him with two Indian books on astronomy. These were later translated into Arabic by al-Fazari, and also by Yāqūb ifn Tāriq. Another influex of the Hindu learning into Arabia took place during the reign of *Khalīfa* Hārūn al-Rashīd (786-814), under the influence of the Barmecides who had attained the highest position in the *Abbāsid* court. These Barmecides were the descendants of the high priests (*Pramukh,* Arabicised into *Barmak)* of the Buddhist temple at Balkh and had, therefore, a special interest in Indian sciences. They encouraged the translation of Indian texts into Arabic, and appointed many Indians to run the Royal Barmecides Hospital in Baghdād. One of the first Indian physicians appointed was Manka (Mānikya), a successful physician and a philosopher of saintly character, who had a profound knowledge of Persian and Sanskrit languages. The other was Ibn Dhan (a descendant of Dhana, Dhanvantari or Dhanapati), who was appointed the Director of the Royal Hospital by Yahya, the Barmecid. Both these scholars translated several Indian medical texts into Persian or Arabic. Another famous Hindu practitioner in Baghdad during the reign of Hārūn was Sāleh bin Bhela (Shāli, son of Bhela), who seems to have cured Ibrāhīm, a cousin of the *Khalīfa,* after Hārūn's personal physician Gabriel, an expert in Greek medicine, had declared Ibrāhīm dead!

Among the various Sanskrit texts that were rendered into Arabic during the *Abbāsid* period, the following medical works in Arabic were commonly used by the Arabs until the end of the ninth century; the *Charaka Samhitā* known as *Sharak* in Arabic; the *Sushruta Samhitā* as *Sasrad* and *Susrud;* the *Ashtāngahridaya,* rendered into Arabic by Ibn Dhan as *Astānkar, Astagar* and *Asankar;* and the *Nidāna* of *Mādhava* as *Nidān, Badan* and *Yedan.* The *Siddhayoga* also translated by Ibn Dhan, was known as *Sindhastaq* or *Sindhshān;* and there was a treatise on women's diseases written in the eight century by an Indian women whose name appears as Rusa in Arabic texts.

With the coming of the Muslim conquerors to India, from the tenth century onwards, corruption gradually began to creep into the latter of the ancient Hindu texts. The glories of *Āyurveda* were on a rapid decline and the Hindu medicine slipped down many grades for want of patronage from the rules. Due to the peculiar aversion of the Brāhmins to contact with blood, pus and the corpse, during the post-Buddhist and Muslim period, surgery was allowed to pass into the hands of lower classes, until bleeding was left to the barbers, bone-setting to the herdsmen and the application of blisters to anyone!

The medicine in India during the later medieval period was thus dominated by the Persian and Arabic influences, which produced an amalgam of the Greek or *Unānī* medicine, as it passed through the hands of the Persians and *Āyurveda* of the Hindus. The pattern of medical practice changed throughout the country from the days of Muslim dominance until the arrival of the Europeans on this subcontinent.

Although there was an attempt at the revival of the ancient systems of medicine in India during Emperor Akbar's time (1555-1605), and the *Unānī* and Āyurvedic systems were being amalgamated, no real advance was made in the field of medicine similar to what was happening then in the West. The only significant achievement of this period of Indian medicine was the translation of most of the medical texts written in Arabic into Persian since Persian happened to be the court language of the period. By the time of Emperor Ālamgīr's rule (1658-1707), all the Arabic texts that were being used by the *Unānī* school of medicine were available in Persian also. During the later part of the nineteenth century most of these texts were again translated into *Urdū,* the language of the Muslim population in particular, in Northern India.

The so-called modern medicine was introduced into India by the Portuguese in the sixteenth century when Albuquerque (died 1515) conquered Goa in 1510, and founded the Royal Hospital, which was later handed over by the Portuguese to the Jesuits in 1591. The Jesuits managed this institution remarkably well and in 1703 introduced a rudimentary form of medical training at the hospital with Capriano Valadares as its Master. In 1842 this was converted into School of Medicine and Surgery. Although the Portuguese first brought the modern medicine to India, it was the French and the British who later established and consolidated the modern medical system in India.

This succinct summary shows the hoary, glorious past of *Āyurveda* its achievements and contribution to the civilizations of the world, the inroads that other systems of medicine made into the body of *Āyurveda* its progressive decline, its efforts at survival, and its ambitions today to contribute again to the restoration of health, rehabilitation of patients, prevention of disease and promotion of health. *Āyurveda* is still today a living science, since millions of people in India are being treated according to this system. A system that has survived through the centuries, cannot be lightly dismissed as being unscientific. Therefore, let us go back and take a look at the salient features of the ancient Āyurvedic system and study the content of its curriculum prescribed for a student of medicine in ancient times.

The curriculum for the training of a physician was comprehensive. The entire subject of medicine was divided into eight main fields, and the science of *Āyurveda* was, therefore, known as the "eight-limbed" (*Ashtānga Āyurveda).* The eight branches were (1) *Kāyachikitsā* or internal medicine, which included principles of Physiology and pathology; (2) *Shalyachikitsā* or surgery, including anatomy; (3) *Shālākyachikitsā* or eye, ear, nose and throat diseases; (4) *Kaumārabhritya* or pediatrics, including obstetrics and embryology; (5) *Bhūtavidyā* or demonology, which included psychotherapy and analysis of dreams, etc; (6) *Agada Tantra* or toxicology; (7) *Rasāyana* or rejuvenation with reference to geriatrics; and (8) *Vājīkarna* or virilification and use of aphrodisiacs. Apart from these fields of medical science, the medical student was expected to know ten arts that were considered indispensable in the preparation and application of his curative measures, and in his undertaking of the clinical and experimental work. These ten arts were : distillation, operative skills, cooking, horticulture, metallurgy, sugar manufacture, pharmacy, analysis and separation of minerals, compounding of metals, and preparation of alkalis. The curriculum, in general, had a clinical bias, and the basic medical sciences were not taught as distinct disciplines, as is being done in the modern schools of medicine. Proper emphasis on teaching of anatomy, physiology, pathology, microbiology and pharmacology was, however, laid during the teaching of relevant clinical subjects. For example, anatomy was included in the teaching of surgery; embryology formed a part of training in pediatrics and obstetrics; and the knowledge of physiology and pathology was interwoven in the teaching of all the clinical disciplines, particularly the internal medicine.

Sushruta laid great stress on direct and personal observation of anatomy of the body by a surgeon and gave details of dissection (*Avagharshana).* He directs that

"Any one desirous of acquiring a thorought knowledge of anatomy should prepare a dead body and carefully observe (by dissecting it) and examine its different parts. For, a thorough knowledge can only be acquired by comparing the account given in various texts with personal observation" The dead body selected for dissection, he advised, should not be of a person who had lived up to 100 years, that is, not too old, nor of one who had died of any protracted disease or of poisoning. The excrements were first removed from the intestines, the body was covered entirely with a sheath of grass, hemp or rope, then securely placed in a cage so that it was not a prey to the animals or fish, and finally left to decompose in the still waters of a solitary pool. After seven days, when the body was thoroughly decomposed, the student was instructed to scrape off the decomposed skin, etc., with a whisk made out of grass roots, hair, or strips of split bamboo, and carefully observe with his own eyes all the different organs, external and internal, beginning with the skin. Charaka also emphasized that a physician who knows the anatomical enumeration of the body, together with the description of all its members, is never a victim of ignorance. It appears from the methods employed for dissection, during the ancient times, that the details and the minutae of most of the organs were not known, nor were they needed then. However the topographic description of the various organs, bones, joints, muscles, ligaments and nerves has been given with a fair amount of accuracy. As the method of dissection was not perfect enough to provide a precise knowledge of the regional anatomy, the medical scholars surmounted this difficulty by designating vital points, called the *marmās,* on the surface of the body; and warned the physician to approach these points with extreme caution and care. During the later times, the discontinuation of dissection due to the prevalence of stricter notions of purity, when touching a corpse became a taboo, proved fatal to the progress of surgery. Even the profession of physician which during the early period of Hindu history was defined, began to be held in low esteem, and the doctor was considered as a defiler of the company as the dinner table ! (*Manu Smriti*).

The detailed description of the *marmās* and the effects of injury at these vital points, as observed by the ancient Hindus, right from the Rig Vedic times, give a good insight into their ideas regarding the functions of various neurovascular elements and other important structures that lie close or deep to these *marmās*. The heart and the pelvic regions have been considered as among the most vital places of the body; and the "life-breaths" and all the special senses are said to depend on the head. The *marmās* are the sites where important vessels, nerves, tendons, muscles, joints, bony points and organs are situated at varying depth. A superficial or deep injury at these points on the body, gives rise to certain symptomatology; and as a corollary to these symptoms and signs the ancients hypothetised the functions of the structures lying in close proximity to these points.

There are 107 such points marked on the body, 11 in each excremity 12 in the thorax and abdomen, 14 in the back, and 37 in the head race and neck region. The *marmās* are classified according to the damage caused by the injury. The injury to some of these *marmās* is fatal immediately. These are called *sadyah-prānahara marmās.* Injury to others results in death after some time. These are designated *kālāntara-prānahara marmās.* The injury with foreign bodies lodged at some of the *marmās* does not cause much damage, until attempts are made to dislodge the foreign body, which may then result is severe haemorrhage and consequent death. These *marmās* are called *vishal yaghana.* The *marmās* where injury causes permanent loss of a limb or its activity are called *vaikalyakara* (deforming or maiming) *marmās*. The remaining *marmās,* when injured, cause intense pain and are called *rujākara marmās.*

It may not be out of place to illustrate some of the *marmās* and the effects of injury to them to grasp the idea how the ancients inferred the function of various structures and organs from the study of the *marmās.* It is recorded that the bilateral injury to the *vitapa marma,* which lies between the scrotum and the groin on each side, results in loss of sexual activity in the male. By inference, therefore, the ancients knew the function of the vas deferens which is situated at this point. The injury to *hridaya marma,* it is stated in the medical *Samhitās,* causes death immediately, since this is the point just above the pit of the stomach between the two breasts where the heart lies. The injury to *stanamūla marma* which is situated immediately below each breast, it is emphasized, fills the thoracic cavity, with the deranged *kapha* (phlegm) and gives rise to cough, difficulty in breathing, and death. In the neck region the change in the voice to hoarseness and dumbness, sometimes accompanied by the loss of taste, was observed to occur if the injury was inflicted on *nīla* or *manyā marmās,* which are situated respectively anterior and posterior to the larynx (*kanthanādī).* In the head, an injury to the *sīmanta marmās,* which are situated at the junctions of the sutures of the calvaria, results in mental excitement, fear, loss of intellect and ultimate death.

The Indian medical scholars considered the human body as a conglomeration of the modified five elements (*pañchamahābhūta),* which are *prithvī* (earth), *ap* (water), *tejas* (light, fire or heat), *vāyu* (air or motive force), and *ākāsha* (space, vacuum or ether). The five elements in various proportions combine to form seven basis tissues (*dhātūs)* which uphold the body. These tissues are *rasa* (plasma), *rakta* (blood), *māmsa* (flesh), *medas* (fat), *asthi* (bone), *majjā* (marrow), and *Shukra* (semen). The decrease and increase in the basic tissues *(dhātūs)* in the body causes deteriorating changes in it. *Rasa,* for example, if decreased causes heart disease, trembling, a feeling of emptiness and thirst; and its increase causes nausea and salivation. The quintessence of all these elements is called the *ojas* (vitality) or *bala* (power), which governs the functions of all the external and internal organs of the body. *Ojas* is described as an oily, white, cold, soft fluid that permeates the whole body. It is demolished by injury, grief, exhaustion, hunger etc., and its derangement is manifested in three stages, the worst of them leading to death. From all the attributes characteristic of *ojas* it appears this term was applied to the tissue fluid in the body.

The Ayurvedic theory of *tridosha* or *tridhātu* meaning three elements or humors, namely *vāyu* or *vāta* (air), *pitta* (bile), and *kapha* (phelgm), on which the whole of physiology and pathology of the ancient Hindus was based, has been misunderstood by many scholars to mean *literally* the elements of air, bile and phlegm. The ancients used these terms in a very broad sense, with variable meanings depending on the conext in which they were used. The term *vāyu* or *vāta,* for example, comprehends all phenomenon of motion that come under the function of life, the cell development in general, and the functions of the central nervous system in particular. *Pitta* does not essentially mean bile alone, but signifies the functions of metabolism and thermogenesis, including digestion and the formation of blood, various secretions and excretions *(mala),* which are either the means or the end-product of tissue combustion. The term *kapha* does not mean mere phlegm. but is used primarily to imply functions of cooling, presevation and thermotaxis or heat regulation; and secondarily to denote the process of production of protective fluids like mucus, synovial fluid, etc. The imbalance of these elements (*dhātūs)* beyond normal variations was considered to cause bodily disfunction and disturbance.

The personality of an individual would depend on the predominance of the above three humors. For example, those with predominant *vāta* are usually alert, voracious, atheist, lovers of music, witty, and enjoy sports, and are, in general, extroverts. They can also be unstable, disaffectionate, thin, tall, weak, miserable creatures with trembling voice. The persons with predominance of *pitta* on the other hand are cultured, clean, intelligent, prudent but coward individuals. They do not easily fall in love with nature or with opposite sex. These individuals perspire much, have brown hair on the head, very little hair on the body and become permaturely grey, etc. The *kapha* type of individuals are intelligent, trustworthy, faithful, truthful, patient and grateful. They are very fertile, with high forehead and thick dark hair, etc.

The functions of vital organs like the liver (*yakrit),* spleen (*plīhā),* heart (*hridaya),* and brain (*mastishka)* were explained on the basis of the flow and exchange of the tissue elements in the body. The heart was considered as the chief receptacle of the three most important fluids of the body, *rasa* (plasma), *rakta* (blood), and *ojas* (tissue fluid). The plasma which is considered as the end-product of digestion of food, is according to them, converted into blood in the liver and spleen, from where it goes as arterial blood to the heart. The heart, in turn, gives rise to many vessels and ducts, which carry the blood, the lymph, as well as the nervous impulses. The various terms for the blood and lymphatic vessels and ducts arising from the heart were used indiscriminately, although some of the authorities feel that the terms *vāta-vaha, pitta-vaha, kapha-vaha* and *rakta-vaha srotas* should be identified with the nervous cords, venous, lymphatic and arterial channels respectively. The Āyurvedic scholars did not distinctly delineate venous from arterial system, nor was pulmonary system well understood by them, although they did speak of two kinds of blood, the red and the blue. Charaka, some authors claims, has clearly described the systemic circulation, in his statement that "from the great centre (the heart) emanate vessels which carry blood into all parts of the body — an element that nourishes life of all animals, and without which life would be extinct. It is that element which goes to nourish the fetus in the uterus, and which flowing into its body returns to the mother's heart"[5].

The ancient medical texts describe many ducts or canals (*srotas)*. Āmong them they assign two each for breathing, for ingestion of food, and for drinking water; and two each for carrying each of the various materials like chyle, blood, flesh, fat, urine, feces, sperms and ova[6].

Although right (? *kloma)* and left (*phupphusa)* lungs have been mentioned in various texts in different contexts, their function as respiratory organ has not been clearly stated. The word 'Chest' (*uras)* has been used instead, whenever the respiratory movements are described. The trachea, along with its ducts, has been clearly mentioned as one of the ducts (*srotas)* close to the heart, which forms with it the root of all the ducts that carry the "life-breaths" (*prānavaha)*.

The nutrititive power of various foods, the ancients believed, depends on various qualities (*gunās)* of food substances; and the taste (*rasa)* was considered the most important of these qualities. The different varieties of taste, according to them, are sweet, sour, salient, pungent, bitter and astringent. This quality of food depends upon the preponderance of different basic elements (*bhūtās)* which go to form each article of food, and each modality of taste is responsible for producing different physiological effects. The other qualities of the food are heavy or light, cold or hot, wet or dry, mild or sharp, solid or fluid, soft or hard, smooth or rough, etc. The digestion of food is done by "digestive fire" (*pāchakagni*). The food is brought through the agency of one of the "life-breaths" or motive forces (*vāyu*) called *prāna* to the stomach (*āmāshaya*), where it is churned into liquid form. Another motive force called *samāna*, stirs another "fire" and digests the food, converting it into chyle (*rasa*) and excretions (*mala*). When the food is half-digested, it passes out into the beginning of the small intestine where it meets with the biliary secretions (*pitta*). Finally, the food comes down towards the last part of the intestines where it is dried up by another "fire" and converted into a compact mass, which is voided as feces.

The digested food material, in turn, is converted into several tissues (*dhātūs*) by process of "cooking" (*pāka*) through the agencies of five different types of "elemental fires" (*bhūtāgnīs*) and seven "tissue fires" (*dhātvagnīs*) which respectively act on the constituent elements (*bhūtās*) of the food, or on the various tissues (*dhātūs*) like the plasma, blood, flesh, fat, bone-marrow and semen.

The products of metabolism are of two varieties. The part of the food substances (*prasāda*) which nourishes and sustains the body, and the remaining portion that is converted into various excretions (*malās*), which also include some secretions. The waste products among the excretions (*malās*), when present in the body in normal quantity, do not damage; but if they increase or decrease in quantity they cause derangement in the body and can ultimately destroy it. The by-products or the waste materials (*malās*) of the digested food are the feces and urine; of plasma is the mucus; of blood is the bile; of flesh are the excretions of eye, ear, nose, skin-pores and genitals; of fat is the sweat; of bones are the nails and the hair; and of marrow are the oily secretions of eyes and skin.

"*Vāyu* is the support for the function of the body. It has five forms: *prāna, udāna, samāna, vyāna and apāna.* It stimulates all the senses, and carries all the sense impressions to the mind. It holds together the various elements of the body in proper proportion; and maintains the cohesive unity of the body as a whole. It is the promoter of speech; basis of sound and touch; it is the origin of joy and enthusiasm; the kindler of fire (*agni);* the drier of the elements which cause derangement (*doshās);* and expulser of the waste products. It divides the microscopic (*sūkshama)* and the macroscopic (*sthūla)* channels of the body. It is the maker of the embryonic form, and stands as an evidence of existence of life when not excited". (*Charaka Samhitā,* 1.12.7)

Vāyu or *Vāta,* as Charaka has explained above, was the term applied to the motive forces in the body, particularly the nervous impulses. Functionally these motive forces are classified as:

1. *Udāna* which acts in the region of the throat, causes vocalisation and is responsible for speech, music, etc. The derangement of this "life-breath" is responsible for the disorders which occur in the region of the neck and head (*shālākya).*
2. *Prāna,* located in the region of the heart, propels the food and mouth into the gastrointestinal tract. The derangement of *prāna* is responsible for asthma, hiccup and similar disorders.
3. *Samāna,* which resides in the gastrointestinal tract, carries out the digestive functions and converts the food substances into various elements. If *samāna* is deranged, there is poor digestion, diarrhoea and edema of the body.
4. *Apāna* situated in the pelvic region, is the driving force for defecation, micturition, ejaculation, menstruation and parturition. The disturbance of

this "life-breath" gives rise to dangerous disorders of the rectum, urinary bladder, reproductive system, and surprisingly to diabetes!

5. *Vyāna,* which pervades the whole body, causes the flow of the tissue fluids, lymph and blood, the secretion of sweat, and the various movements of the eyes. The later authors consider all motility in the various organs within the body under the overall control of *vyāna,* and therefore its derangement afflicts the whole body. With the simultaneous derangement of all the above five "life-breaths" (*vāyūs)* the man ceases to exist (*Bhīva Prakāsha).*

The brain (*mastishka)* as different from the head (*shiras*) has been mentioned even in the *Atharva Veda* (X.26.8.26). The heart, is the early texts, was the centre of *manasa* (mind); but Bhela, who is as old as Charaka, considered the brain to be the centre of mind, which he said is "the highest of all senses and has its seat between the head and the palate. The brain knows all the sense objects and all the tastes which come near it". The *Biela Samhitā* distinguishes between *manasa* (mind) which is recorded as the cause of all cognition, with its seat in the brain; the *chitta* (consciousness) as the cause of all activities, feelings and judgment, with its seat in the heart; and *buddhi* (intellect) which is considered as a special function of the *chitta* (consciousness).

Sushruta, even though he does not attach significance to the brain, however, considers head as the centre of all special senses and describes certain cranial nerves connected with specific sensory functions. He describes two nerves lower down the back of the ears (*vidhura),* which, if cut, produce deafness; a pair of nerves (*phana)* situated inside the two nostrils, which if cut, cause anosmia; a pair of nerves below the outer ends of the eyebrow, near the external corner of the eyeball (*apānga)* which, if cut, cause total blindness.

The five special senses, and sense perception have been well described in the medical *Samhitās.* The five special senses mentioned are vision, hearing, smell, taste and touch. The five elements (*bhūtās)* pervade all these senses, but one of these elements predominates in each of the senses. For example, earth predominates in the sense of smell, water in taste, light or fire in vision, air in touch and ether in hearing. The *Sushruta Samhitā* states : "Ten nerves maintain the functions of the body by carrying impulses of sound, touch, vision, taste, smell, respiration, sighing, yawning, hunger, laughing, speech and crying. A pair of nerves each responds to sound, touch, vision, taste, and smell. Yet with other two man speaks, with two makes sound, with two he goes asleep and with two he wakes up. Stimulation of two of them causes lacrimation, of other two causes lactation in the female and ejaculation in the male (?)." (3.9.4).

Charaka states that : "The memory is caused by the following eight : impressions, their similarities and dissimilarities, co-ordination of the mind, practice, consciousness, concentration, repetition of sight, hearing or perception (as tasting and smelling) (4.1.117-118). . . The man sleeps when sense organs cease to operate, being tired by the fatigue of the mind". (1.21.35).

The later Tāntric School considered cerebrum as the seat of soul, and the spinal cord as the centre for vital functions of the body. The whole of the nervous system, according to this School, is divided into various plexuses (*Chakrās),* which extend from the root of the vertebral column upwards into the cranial cavity. These centres (*Chakrās)* are inter-connected by and give rise to numerous nerves which are approximately 72,000 in number. These centres control the physical and mental activity of the body; and are located at the points on the body deep to which, according to modern concepts of neurology, different autonomic ganglia and plexuses are situated. The functional significance of these plexuses also corresponds, to some extent, with our modern concepts. The Indian scholars have tried to correlate the natural phenomenon with the powers attributed to various gods in the Hindu pantheon, who in turn, have been associated with various centres (*Chakrās)* within the nervous system. The centres have symbolic names, and from sacral region cranialward, they are (1) the *mūlādhāra chakra,* corresponding to the sacral plexus, which is associated with the autonomic functions of the pelvic organs including genitals. (2) The *Svādhisthāna chakra,* corresponds to the hypogastric plexus, (3) the *manipūra chakra* to the epigastric plexus, (4) the *anāhata chakra* to the cardiac and pulmonary plexuses and (5) the *vishuddha chakra* to the various nerve plexuses in the neck. (6) The *ājnā chakra* which corresponds to the hypothalamo-hypophyseal axis in its action is sitauted between the eyebrows. (7) The highest *sahasrāra padma chakra* (thousand-petalled lotus) is situated inside the cranial cavity, and is concerned with the special senses of hearing, touch, sight, smell and taste, and sleep, or the absence of all these. It is also concerned with all the higher functions, and with emotions, memory, etc.

The practice of *Kundalinī yoga,* a special technique of breathing and physical exercises, which goes back to primitive pre-Aryan antiquity, is aimed at establishing these centres within consciousness and thus bringing them into active play.

The science of embryology was a matter of considerable speculation and controversy in the various schools of philosophy and medicine. One entire *Upanishad* has been devoted to the speculations with regard to the formation and development of the human embryo[7,8]. This *Garbha*

Upanishad, literally a brief treatise on embryo, is considered to be of greater antiquity than the rest of the *Upanishads* of the class to which *Garbhopanishad* belongs. There are ample references to the development of the human embryo in the *Vedās* themselves. It is surprising to read in them and the various medical texts, the ideas of the ancient Hindus regarding the biological evolution, reproduction, generation, preformation and spontaneous regeneration, which at a first glance appear to be borrowed from a modern text on embryology!

The derangement of three humors *(tridosha)* was the basis of pathogenesis of all the disease. On this basis, Sushrùta divided all the diseases into 1120 types, whereas Charaka considered them to be innumerable. The disease so caused is called a *nija* disease, as compared to the conditions caused by external factors, called *āgantuka,* which include mental afflictions. Another classification, based on the etiological factors, divided the diseases into seven categories : (1) the hereditary conditions caused by the diseased germ cells *(ādibalapravratta);* (2) the congenital disease *(janmabalapravratta);* (3) diseases due to the disturbance of humors *(doshabalapravratta);* (4) injuries and wounds *(sanghātabalapravratta);* (5) seasonal diseases caused by change in weather *(kālabalapravratta);* (6) diseases due to the divine will *(daivabalapravratta);* and (7) the natural conditions, like hunger *(svabhāvabalapravratta).*

In the field of *materia medica* the properties of drugs and foods were investigated. The drugs were described by a terminology, which when transliterated, does not fail, in many instances, to give correct insight into their therapeutic uses. The drugs of the Hindu *materia medica,* have found a prominent place in the Hippocratic and Arab medicine. The Āyurvedic works of the later period have incorporated, in their own *materia medica,* some of the foreign drugs which were found by them to have valuable therapeutic properties, like rhubarb, opium, jamaica, sarsa, etc. (*Bhāva Prakāsha*).

The diagnosis, it was enjoined, was to be made by the five senses supplemented by interrogation. The basis of diagnosis was built on (1) cause (*nidāna*), (2) permonitary indications (*pūrvarūpa*), (3) symptoms (*rūpa*), (4) therapeutic tests (*upashaya*), and (5) natural history of the development of the disease (*samprāpti*). Sushruta declares that "The physician (*bhishak*), the drug (*dravya*), the attendant or the nursing personnel (*upasthātā*), and the patient (*rogī*) are the four pillars on which rests the success of the treatment". And the physician, with a profound understanding of the science of medicine, was considered the first and the strongest pillar of therapy. The different methods of treatment, based on the diagnosis of the case, were outlined, and the drugs were classified into seventy-five (75) types according to their therapeutic effects. The whole doctrine of medical care was considered to consist of the following factors, which are to be kept in mind in achieving successful results : (1) the organism (*sharira*), (2) its maintenance (*vritti*), (3) cause of disease (*hetu*), (4) nature of disease (*vyādhi*), (5) action or treatment (*karma*), (6) effect or result (*kārya*), (7) time (*kāla*), (8) agent or the physician (*kartā*), (9) the means and instruments (*karana*), and (10) the final decision on the line of treatment (*vidhi vinishchaya*).

The microbial origin of the disease, and the infective nature of some, such as eruptive fevers, leprosy, smallpox, tuberculosis, etc., have been clearly indicated. Sushruta states that "All forms of leprosy and some other skin conditions are not only due to the derangement of *vāyu*, *pitta* and *kapha*, but are also of parasitic origin. Various skin diseases, leprosy, tuberculosis, fever, ophthalmic and epidemic diseases borne by the air and water, are usually capable of transmission from one man to another". He further states in *Uttara Tantra* that "There are various fine organisms which circulate in the blood and are invisible to the naked eye; usually these look like round bodies of copper colour and are without legs. They give rise to various forms of skin diseases, etc."[5]

In surgery the progress made by the ancient Hindus was phenomenal indeed, and justifies the remark by Sir William Hunter (1718-1783) that "Hindu medicine was an independent development. Arab medicine was founded on translation from Sanskrit treatises, and in turn, European medicine down to the seventh century, was based upon the Latin version of the Arabian translation"[9]. The training of a surgeon was thorough and methodical. The principles of surgery were based on well-established foundations. The student was demonstrated and instructed to practise surgery on various subjects, such as cucumber, gourd, melon, all types of phantoms, and stretched skins of animals with hair intact. The students practised puncturing on distended bags, probing on openings in worm-eaten wood or lotus root, extracting teeth on dead animals, suturing on thick cloth or soft leather, and bandaging on the limbs of manikins.

The surgical operations were classified by Sushruta into eight categories : excision (*bhedana),* incision (*chhedana),* scarification (*lekhana),* puncturing (*vedhana),* probing (*eshana),* extraction (*āharana),* evacuation and drainage (*visrāvana),* and suturing (*sīvana).* A variety of instruments and appliances is included in the armamentarium of a surgeon. Sushruta grouped these under two types : *yantra* or blunt instruments numbering 101, and *shastra* or sharp instruments numbering 20. It was impressed upon the physician that he must consider his hand as the first, the best and the most important instrument of all, as it is with its assistance that all surgical operations are performed. It is enjoined that the instruments should be made of the best steel, and should be well-shaped, with sharp flawless edges, and should be kept in a handsome portable case with a separate compartment for each instrument. Fourteen types of bandages (*bandha or patta)* with their specific uses are described. The surgical operations on all parts of the body have been given in detail, such as laparotomy, craniotomy, caesarian section, forceps application, plastic repair on the torn ear lobule, cheiloplasty, rhinoplasty, excision of cataract, tonsillectomy, excision of laryngeal polyps, excision of anal fistulae, repair of hernias and prolapse of rectum, lithotomy, amputation of bones, reduction of dislocations, and many neurosurgical procedures. Pre-operative preparation of skin with some medicaments and dressing of wounds with medicated oil was routinely done. Haemostasis was achieved by the use of ice, caustics or actual cautery. Venesection and cupping were in general use, and the poultices and fomentations formed a routine part of the treatment. The anaesthetics were not unknown either. Medicated wines were liberally used pre and post-operatively to assuage pain. Sushruta distinctly laid down that the wine should be used before operation to produce insensibility to pain. Charaka advised the use of wine to alleviate the pain of operations. A drug called *Sammohinī* (producer of unconsciousness) was administered before major operations, and another drug, *Sanjīvanī* (the restorer of life) was employed to resuscitate the unconscious after operation or shock[10,11,12].

The science of obstetrics and gynaecology had progressed well inspite of the fact that it was not considered as a distinct division of the original eight limbed *Āyurveda.* The menstrual disturbances, the diseases of the female genital tract and their treatment have been classified. The clinical course and the various stages of labour, the management of peurperium, the miscarriage (*makkalla)* and abortion of various types, and the difficult labour (*mūdhagarbha)* have been discussed in detail. The different malpositions of the fetus at birth were well understood, and the different methods of treatment by version, embryotomy, caesarian section, etc., are described[13].

The general care of the infant, the diseases peculiar to children including nine types of conditions causing convulsions in them, are described. Since the suddenness with which a serious illness appears and disappears in children cannot be explained easily, and the innocent children are most vulnerable to the evil influences of the demons, the children's diseases are particularly attributed to the demoniac influences. *Jumbha* and *Naigamesha* are two such demons, described in the *Atharva Veda,* who make children sick. Sushruta named nine evil spirits (*grahās)* which torment the children. The voluntary offences of the mother or wet-nurse are blamed for the attack by these *grahās* which can be driven out by medicine, baths, fumigation and special sacrifices to propitiate the individual demon.

The diseases of the head (*shiroroga),* nervous diseases (*vātavyādhi),* and other mental afflictions are well classified and their treatment is given in detail. The various nervous disorders mentioned are convulsions (*ākshepaka),* apoplectic fits (*apatantraka),* hysteric fits (*dāruna apatānaka),* stick-like stiffness of the body (*dandāpatānaka),* bow-like body or tetanus (*dhanuhstambha),* dorsal bending (*bahirāyāma),* ventral bow -like bending of the body (*ābhyantarāyāma),* hemiplegia (*pakshavadha),* total paralysis of the body (*sarvāngaroga),* facial paralysis (*ardita),* lockjaw (*hanugraha),* stiff neck (*manyāstambha),* paralysis of the tongue (*jihvāstambha),* sciatica (*gridhrasi),* St. Vitus' Dance (*kalāyakhanja),* paralysis agitans (*vepathu),* etc. Fainting (*mūrchhā),* giddiness (*bhramaroga),* and apoplexy (*sanyāsa)* were treated with cooling agents and stimulants. Four kinds of epilepsy (*apasmāra)* were distinguished and the treatment outlined. It is enjoined that once the attack is over one should not rebuke the patient, but should attempt to cheer his soul. Six kinds of madness (*unmāda)* were differentiated. The worst forms were attributed to the demoniac influences and called *bhūtonamāda* (possession). Along with the violent remedies suggested it was also recommended, as in case of epileptics, that the possessed one should be cheered with friendly talk. Sushruta devoted one complete chapter to the analysis of dreams, and he believed that a favourable or an unfavourable termination of a disease could be predicted from the messengers, omens and dreams.

Dietetics and hygiene formed as much a part of the religious ritual as of medical practice of the ancient Hindus. Therefore, the dietetic regimen and the hygienic principles were almost mandatory. A sensible physician is advised to take into consideratiion first the regulation of diet of the patient in all diseases, and then turn to the treatment of the disease with drugs.

Could ancient Hindu medicine be called scientific? The answer is certainly yes, for the time in which these Āyurvedic texts were originally written. Science is not born only within the four walls of a laboratory with bubbling vats, eight-channel recorders and computers working round the clock, as is the notion of our modern times. The Greeks are given their unique place is history by the West, as originators of all the arts and science cherished by the modern civilization, because they evinced a spirit of scientific inquiry and astute observation. Considering the knowledge of the ancient Hindu in medical sciences, as detailed in the above summary, one cannot help but conclude that they had a similar spirit of inquiry, acuity of observation and sense of clinical acumen. It has been an unfortunate custom of the Western historians, until recent times, to look for an answer to the origin of any scientific thought among the Greeks. That there might have been some others before them who lit the torch of science and handed it over to the Greeks to keep it aglow, very few of us are disposed to enquiry. There is no denying to the fact today that the torch of learning was handed down to the Greeks by early Babylonians, Egyptians, Persians, and most certainly, by the Hindus, as acknowledged even by the ancient historians and philosophers like Solon (638-558 B.C.), Pythagorus (580-498 B.C.), Herodotus (484-425 B.C.), Plato (428-348 B.C) and Philostratus (third century B.C.)[14] (Bjornstjerna). It is surprising, therefore, to find many historians in the West particularly perturbed by the "lack of definite chronology in the study of ancient Indian science" and the difficulties to solving the question of priorities. Captain Johnston-Saint (1929)[15], who felt strongly about Asia and India being totally ignored by the Western historians of science, in his address to the Royal Society of Arts in London declared that "Asia can benevolently give but it does not need to borrow. Its ideas and fantasies are as exuberant as its vegetation. . . . If we were to speak the truth we must call Greece not the parent of our modern medicine, but only its nurse". Julius Jolly, an authority on Indian culture, during the early part of this century commented, "Medicine can now be regarded as the oldest of Indian sciences and has been proved to be the science in which the Indian specialized first".

Bibliography

Ashtāngahrdaya Samhitā Vāgbhatta: A compendium of the Hindu System of Medicine, Composed by Vāgbhatta, with the commentary of Arundatta. Revised and collated by Anna M. Kunte, 2 vols., Bombay. 1880.

Aṣṭāṅgahrdayasamhitā, Vāgbhata's: ein altindisches Lehrbuch der Heilkunde, aus dem Sanskrit ins Deutsche ubertragen, mit

Einleitung, Anmerkungen und Indices von Luise Hilgenberg und Willibald Kirfel, Leiden. 1937-1940.

Ashtānga Sangraha of Vāgbhatta: (Sanskrit), with the commentary by Indu, edited by T. Rudraparasava, 3 vols. Trichur, 1913-24.

Atharva Veda : Translated in English by Ralph T.H.Griffith, 3 vols. E.J. Lazarus and Co., Benares, 1916.

Beal, Samuel : Chinese Accounts of India, Translated from the Chinese of Hiuen Tsiang, 4 vols., Susil Gupta, Calcutta, 1957-58.

Bhāva Prakāsha of Sri Bhāva Mishra : (In Hindi), Edited by Bhishagratna Pandit Shree Brahma Shankara Mishra, Chowkhamba Sanskrit Series Office, Varanasi, 1961.

Bhela Samhitā : (In Sanskrit), Edited by Ashutosh Mookerjee, Calcutta University, *Jour. of Dept. of Letters*, Calcutta, vol. 6, 1921.

Bjornstjerna, Count M.: The Theogony of the Hindoos. London, John Murray, 1844.

Bower Manuscript, The: Facsimile leaves, Nagari Transcript, Romansad Transliteration and English Translation with Notes, Edited by A.F.R. Hoernle, Part 1, 2, Archaeological Survey of India, New Imperial Series. Vol. 22, Calcutta, 1893-1912.

Charaka Samhitā, The : Edited and published by Shree Gulābkunveebā Āyurvedic Society, 6 Vols., with translations in Hindi, Gujarātī and English Jāmnagar, 1949.

Gordon, B.L.: *Medicine Throughout Antiquity*. Philadelphia, F.A. Davis and Co., 1949.

Johnston- Saint, P.: Quoted by the *Pioneer*, Allahabad (India), May 31 and June 1, 1929.

Jolly, J.: *Indian Medicine*, C.G. Kashikar, Poona, 1951.

Kaushika Sūtra: The Kaushika Sūtra of the Atharva Veda, Edited by Maurice Bloomfield, *Journal of the American Oriental Society*, Vol. XIV. New Haven, 1890.

Keswani, N.H.: "Anaesthesia and Analgesia among the Ancients. Part I". *Indian Journal of Anaesthesia*, Vol. 9, No. 4, pp. 321-342, Nov. 1951.

Keswani, N.H. : "Evolution of Surgery", *The Medicine and Surgery*, Vol. I. No. 8-9, pp. 9-20, Nov. - Dec. 1961.

Keswani, N.H. : "Anaesthesia and Analgesia among the Ancients. Part II (The Egyptians and Mesopotamians)", *Indian Journal of Anaesthesia,* Vol. 10, No. 1, pp. 51-58, Feb. 1962.

References

1. Takakusu, I.T.: I-tsing: *A Record of the Buddhist Religion* as Practised in India and Malay Archipelago (671-695 A.D.). English Translation, Clarendon Press, Oxford, 1896.
2. Beal, Samuel: *Chinese Accounts of India*, Translated from the Chinese of Hiuen Tsaing, 4 Vols., Sushil Gupta, Calcutta, 1957-58.
3. Lokeṣh Chandra: *Personal Communication.*
4. Lassen Ch.: Indische Alter thumskunde, 4 Vols., Leipzig, 1843-72.
5. Sen, G.N., *Hindu Medicine — An Address on Ayurveda* delivered at the foundation ceremony of Benares Hindu Univ. in 1916.
6. Jolly, J: *Indian Medicine*, C.G. Kashikar, Poona, 1951.
7. Keswani, N.H.: Anaesthesia and Analgesia among the Ancient Part: II (The Egyptian and Mesopotamians)" *Indian Journal of Anaesthesia*, Vol. 10, No. 1, pp. 51-58, Feb. 1962.
8. Keswani, N.H. and N.K. Blide: "Garbha Upanishad, A Brief Sanskrit Treatise on Ancient Indian Embryology, Clio Medica; London, Vol. 1, pp. 65-74, July 1965.
9. Gordon, B.L. Medicine Throughout Antiquity. Philadelphia, F.A. Davis & Co. 1949.
10. Keshwani, N.H. : "Anaesthesia and Analgesia among the Ancients, Part I," *Indian Journal of Anaesthesia*, Vol. 9, No. 4, pp. 231-42, Nov. 1961.
11. Keshwani, N.H.: "Ancient Hindu Orthopaedic Surgery", *Indian Journal of Orthopaedico*, Vol. 1, No. 1, pp. 76-94, June 1967.
12. Keshwani, N.H.: "Physical Medicine and Rehabilitions in Ancient India. Proceedings of the First Industrial

Assembly — Asian Pacific League of Physical Medicine & Rehabilitation," Colombo, Ceylon, pp. 79-84, Nov. 1971.

13. Keshwani, N.H.: & D.C. Sharma : "The Vedas and the Obstetrician," Souvenir, in XVI All Indian Obstetric and Gynaecological, Congress, New Delhi, pp. 50-52, March 1972.
14. Bjornstjerna, Count M: *The Theology of the Hindus*. London, John Murray, 1844.
15. Johnston — Saint, P.: Quoted by the *Pioneer*, Allahabad (India) May 31 and June 1, 1929.

3

Glimpses of Sciences in the Vedas

Vedic texts, particularly the text of the *Atharvaveda* and the *Ṛgveda,* mention various human ailments and describe their treatment. Medicine was practised by priests as well as others conversant with it. Diseases were considered as a punishment against various human sins, inflicted by gods directly or through various demons or through the witchcraft of the enemies. The appropriate treatment was placating the irate gods, fighting and driving out the demons or the magical means such as wearing of different amulets. This was coupled with empirical knowledge of a variety of vegetable drugs. Some of the gods and demons were said to cause only particular diseases, for example, Varuna caused dropsy, Rudra caused acute pains with his sharp arrows and the demon of fire and Yakshma caused fever. Symptoms as such were considered as diseases. The frequently-mentioned symptoms were fever, cough, consumption, diarrhoea, jaundice, dropsy, abscesses, tumors, retention of urine, paralysis etc. Some of the structures of the human body as well as of the horses, that were frequetly sacrificed, are well described. The *Yajurveda* says that *pitta* (bile) acts on the human body as fire acts on water, *i.e.,* it supplies heat. The most important and vital element, as also the prime mover of life is *prana* which governs not only respiration but other physiological processes also.

The astronomical observations that are recorded in the Vedas are mainly in connection with the performance of religious sacrifices. The *Rigveda* describes a year as having 12 months and 360 days. The *Atharvaveda* mentions an intercalary thirteenth month of 30 days in a cycle *(yuga)* of five years, the total number of days in one cycle being 1830. It mentions eclipses of the sun and the moon whose cause is said to be devouring of the sun or the moon by the demon Rahu, the restorers being the gods Soma and Rudra. Garga is known to be the first person to have enumerated various constellatins (*nakshatras*) along the heavenly path of the sun and moon. The *Atharvaveda* mentions only a list of 28 constellations, the *Yajurveda* mention only 27. Lagadha, around 900 B.C., systematized and arranged in the form of a formal treatise called *Jyotiṣa Vedāṅ*ga, the astronomical observations made during the Vedic period.

Ṛgvedic people were familiar with extraction of metals such as gold, silver, copper and making of bronze. They knew of the tanning of leather, could dye woollen textiles and made fermented (soma) and alcoholic (sura) drinks. Yajurvedic people, in addition, knew of iron, lead and tin also.

Vedic language shows that large numerals were in common use, Medhatithi, to whom hundreds of verses in the *Ṛvgeda,* the *Yajurveda* and the *Atharvaveda* are ascribed, enumerated numerals upto 10. We do not know whether these numerals were written also as they were spoken. There is very good evidence contained in various sulba sutras to show that vedic Indians were familiar with geometrical principles which they utilized in the construction of various sacrificial altars. Baudhayana's sulba sutra is the oldest and belongs to a period 500 to 300 B.C.

Rigvedic Philosophy

The beginning of science life (*ayurveda)* is traceable to the beginning of life itself. The science of life is viewed as eternal, with no boundaries and ever developing and has been perceived as of Divine origin. The earliest image of "the Divine" Lord of the universe and of all knowledge including that of *Ayurveda, Siddha* and *Yoga* is seen on the seal found in Mohenjodaro — the image of Siva Pashupati.

The earliest knowledge related to human anatomy, physiology, pathology, health, diseases and their treatment (both medical and surgical), medicinal herbs (*bheṣajas)* and causes of diseases, is found in Vedas particularly in *Ṛgveda* and *Atharva-Veda.*

The *Rigveda* is the basic book. *Sāmveda* appears to have emerged from it. The two *Samhitās* of the *Yajurveda* (the Black and White) followed the *Ṛg* and *Sām Vedas* with additional matter. The fourth veda is Athurvaveda.

The Vedas, have *Upveda* like *Ayurveda.* The later *Vedic Samhitās* are *Brāhmanas, Aranyakas* and *Upaniṣads.* They are associated with Vedas. For example *Aitarey Brahmana,* with *Rigveda, Panchavimsa* with *Sāmveda,* and *Satpata Brahmana,* with *White Yajurveda; Gopata Brahmana* with the *Athurvaveda.*

The *Aranyakas* are a transitional stage to *Upanishads. Aranayaka* means forest. The *Aranayaka* appear to have been prepared in the solitude of the forest.

The *Rigveda* has basically two parts, viz., philosophical (*janankand)* and ritualistic (*karamkand).* Both are reflected in varying degrees in later vedic literature. A continuous search for truth and reality is seen. The climax is observed in emergence of *vedant* expounded by sages is *Upanishads.* "Up" and "ni" both mean nearness, "sh" means final emancipation, and "da" means giving. "ni" also means continuance. The word *Upnishad* thus means continuation of knowledge giving final emancipation. *Upnishads* or *vedant* is the climax of such knowledge. We find that the ritualistic ceremonies are rejected in *Upnishads.* The focus of knowledge and use of that knowledge are directed towards unity of self with all pervading Supreme Spirit (*Brahman),* righteousness and liberation. There are a number of *Upaniṣads.* The *Chandogya* and *Brihdaranyaka* are stated to be oldest. Among the youngest is perhaps *Garbhaupnishada.* The most venerated is *Bhagvad Gitā Upanishad.* The vedic and later vedic literature have profoundly influenced post vedic science of health in ancient India.

The exploration of the health science in Vedic period is beset with difficulties. There is wealth of poetry, prayer, rituals and secular and non-secular thoughts. In them are scattered statements full of words of wisdom. In many cases the knowledge reflected in them is astounding. From the mix of secular and non-secular thoughts, scattered in Vedic and later Vedic Samhitas, some perceptions and practices related to health held at that time, can be identified. The searth for further details is disheartening. No details are found, e.g., artificial limb of iron is mentioned, but no further details of surgical operation. There must have been details in some other documents, either they are lost or have yet to be discovered.

Social Structure

Ṛgvedic society was well organised and highly developed. The family unit was patriarchal, and monogamic. Child marriages were unknown. Economic life centred round agriculture and the cattle. The people were politically organised. They gradually developed into five formations in the following ascending order : the family (*kulapa),* the village (Grama), the Canton (Vis), the people (*Jana)* and the country (Rashtra). The authority of the king was limited by the peoples bodies — the *Sabha* (Council of elders) and peoples representatives (*Samiti).* "The concord between the king and the *Samiti* was essential for the prosperity of the realm". Within this setting the physician had an important place. It is stated that during the wars, the physician's camp was next to the King. There are references in ancient texts of distinguished physicians to the king. They can be considered as important official of the king. Reference to sages like Asvins reflects their influence on and veneration by people. This views must have influenced the members of the *Sabha* and *Samitis.*

Food

Food consisted of cereals, pulses, fats, vegetables and fruits. Milk was given most important place along with its products — butter, clarified butter *ghee* and curds. The cereals, cultivated in Vedic period, included yava, *vrihi, upavaka, anu, godhuma, nivara, priyangu, syamaka;* pulses included *mudga, masa* and *masura;* oils *tila* and vegetables and fruits were plenty such as *urvara, urvaruka* (Rv. III, 45, Av. 127.4).

There seems to be no doubt that there was knowledge in vedic period of the food that should be eaten for good health, and accordingly the selection of cereals, pulses, oil producing plants and rearing cattle for milk and its products were developed.

Education

The educational forums were: residential school, wandering scholars (*Charakas),* group discussions with or without experts, academies for advanced studies, (*parishads),* dialogues between seekers of knowledge and learned sages and learned conferences. The ultimate objective was to attain the highest knowledge, the knowledge, of the *Atman (parva-Vidya).* A notable feature of these intellectual pursuits was active participation of women. Gargi and Matreyi are well known examples. There were other notable women such as Visvavra, Ghosha, Apala.

We get some idea of the subjects of study from the statement of Narada in *Chandogya Upnishad,* when he was seeking knowledge of *Para-Vidya.* Narada said that he had the knowledge of the following subjects : *Rigveda, Yajurveda, Samveda,* and *Atharvaveda;* the fifth veda the history and Puranas; the Veda of Vedas *Vyakarana* (grammar); *Shradha- kalpa* (rituals related to the dead); *Ganit* (mathematics); *Utpatpatgyan* (knowledge of unusual phenomena); *Nidhi* (minerology); *Tarksastra* (logic); *Nitishastra* (ethics); *Deva-Vidya* (knowledge of God or worship of gods); *Brahmavidya* (the knowledge of the Supreme Brahman); *Bhutvidya* (psychiatry or demonology); *Kshatra-vidya* (science of war); *Nakshatra-Vidya* (astronomy); *Sarpa-Vidya / Garuda-Vidya* (toxicology including treatment of snake bite) and *Deva-jana-vidya.*

The *Deva-Jana-Vidyā* may be read as *Deva-Vidya* and *Jana-Vidya* or *Ayurveda.* They may include a number of other subjects. The sage Santkumar while telling Narada that all these were names, repeated the names of subjects as stated by Narada. He also mentioned art, music and sculpture. (*Chandogya Upaniṣad,* VII.I).

The earliest work of Indo-Aryans in *Ṛgveda Samhitā.* It continues to be venerated by a large number of people in India. One of its *mantras* — the *Gayatrimantram* is recited daily by millions of persons and reflect one of the most (if not most) important element of *Ṛgvedic* philosophy.

Gayatri Mantra

Aum bhu bhuva sva tatsvitur varynyam bhrgo devasy dhemhi dhiyu yuna prachodyat. (Ṛgveda, 3.62.10)

The first word *Aum* has a very special place in Vedic literature. *Aums* described as *Pranavrupa* (Supreme Being). *Aum* is also called the bow, *Atma* being the arrow and *Brahma* the aim, *i.e., Atma* aims to reach realisation *Atma* and gets absorbed in Atma (*Dhyanbindu upnishad*) *Aum* is also stated to be *Agnimandal* (A); *Vayumandal* (U); and *Suryamandal* (M) (*Nadibindu Upaniṣad).*

Aum is identified with *Bhulok* (BHU) *Antriksh* (GE) and *Swarglok* (UT) *Utgebhu,* also past, present and future; *Akar* is identified with universe viratswaroop and fire, *Ukar* with *Hirnygarbha Vayu and Tejas; Makar* with *Ishwara, i.e.,* universe (*Chandogya Upnishad).*

Besides the three words *Aum* a fourth *matra* is also mentioned. This is stated in one place as *ardha mantra* and in another place without *matra, (Viram).* This signifies *Satchit Anand Shudda Chetnatatav.* (*Mundukuy Upnishad).*

The meaning of the other words of mantra are as follows:

Bhu the *Brahma* the *Iswara* giver of life to all in Universe and this earth; *bhuva* the *Brahma,* the *Iswara* the regulator, the master the ruler of intermediate region *sva* the *Brahma* the *Iswara* pervading the Universe the ruler of cosmos the heaven. We meditate (*dhemhi*) on that (*tat*) Sun (*Svitu),* giver of the light of *gyan* (*devasya*), the one fit for worship (*varyanam)* and pure *bhrga.* May He (Sun) (*ya),* give light (*Prachodyat)* to our (*Na*) buddhi (*dhiya).*

Briefly it means: "Supreme being pervades the universe. I meditate on the brilliant and full of excellence, the Sun, with all my intellectual faculties. May He inspire me".

The hymns of the *Rigveda* are in praise, adoration and worship of the Supreme Being who has brought order in the universe and also gods. The gods represent : (*a)* the principal phenomena of nature, *viz.*, sky (*dyaus)*; earth (*Prithvi*); the sky god proper (*Varuna*) also as cosmic and moral order (*Rita)* and thunder-storm causing rain (*Indra),* Sun (*Surya),* also called *Savitra, Mitra; Pushan* representing its various qualities; Vishnu, Storm (*Rudra),* storm gods attendig on Rudra (*Maruts),* wind, (*Vata),* rain, waters and river (*Parjanya),* the dawn (*Usha)* and morning and evening stars (*Asvins); (b)* domestic gods (the sun in the heavens, the lightening and the terrestrial fire (*agni),* draught of immortality (*Soma*); and (*c*) abstract dieties, viz., faith *(Sraddha)* and wrath (*Manyu)* and other minor deities such as serial eves (the *Ribhus),* water nymphs (the *Apsaras)* and aerial spirits (*Gandharvas).* Another classification of gods is : (*a*) terrestrial (*prithvisthana)* such as Prithvi, Agni, Soma, Brihspati and rivers; (*b*) aerial (*antarikshasthana),* like Indra, Rudra, Vayu-vats, Apammapat, Parjanya, Apah and Matarisvan; and (*c*) celestial (*dyusthana)* like Dyus, Varuna, Mitra, Surya, Savitur, Pushan, Vishnu, the Adityas, Usha and the Asvins. (Rv. I.39). Overtime Vishnu is recognised as separate god, Rudra is also called Siva, and the concept of cosmic trinity is observed Brahma the creater, Vishnu the preserver and Shiva the destroyer. The three facets of the Supreme Brahman.

Vedic Rishis

There seems to be four stages of Vedic learning, over a span of centuries : (*a*) the growth of earliest hymns, (*b*) multiplication of hymns at different centres or schools and the different priestly families, (*c)* selection of hymns in the *Rigveda Samhita,* and (*d*) growth of the other three *Vedic Samhitas* out of the original material presented in the *Rigveda samhita.* The selection and arrangement of hymns were made in *Rigveda Samhita* very methodically. First, six of the Rigvedic *Rishis* (sages) were chosen as the most representative ones whose work was worthy of conservation. These were Gritsamada, Visvamitra, Vamdeva, Atri, Bhardvaja, and Vasistha.

These sages were associated with the science of life (*Ayurveda).* Bharadvaja was the great physician who taught Atreya Punervasu. Visvamitra as medical author is quoted in *Nivandha Samagrah.* Atri (father of Atreya was a great saint *Mahrishi* and a physician. A formula of a pill for the cure of *Prameh* is attributed to Vameda. Vasistha was author of a law book (*Vasistha Dharmsatra)* and a treatise on medicine (*Vasistha Samhita).* The formula of *Haritkari Avaleha* is also attributed to him.

Supreme Being Originator of Science of life

We have noted that Pasupati (Siva) in the Indus Civilization is the Supreme Lord and propounder of science of health several gods mentioned in *Rigveda* are stated to be repository of science of life. In *Ayurvedic Samhitas* we find Brahma is originator of science of life from whom the knowledge of this science was learnt by Prajapati Daksha, who in his turn taught Asvins and Asvins taught Indra; and Indra taught Bharadvaja and Dhanvantri, and Kasyapa, Vasist, Atri and Brigu. *Brahma Samhita* is stated to have been written by Brahma himself. Sixteen medicinal formulas are attributed to Brahma. Ten medical formulas are attributed to Vishnu and Sixty-two to Siva. Brahma, in the *Yajurveda,* is referred as the first physician (*prathmo devya bhisaj).* Siva (called Rudra). In *Rigveda,* is addressed as the lord of all medicines (Rv. V. 42.11) and the best physician and in Puranas as the first propounder of the science of medicine. Vishnu has thousand names including "the knower of all knowledge" (*vidya),* "the personification of all medicines" (*Osadhis)* and "medicinal herbs" (*bhesajas),* and propounder of knowledge/philosophy (*Terathkar). (Vishnusahastranam,* the 164th, 287th, 578th and 691st names).

It may be noted that specific medicinal formulas are attributed to Brahma, Vishnu and Siva separately. In due course they were considered as one. This is very forcefully underlined in *Brhanndraiya* in the verse that reads : Vishnu is Siva and Siva is Vishnu and whosoever thinks differently goes to hell (*Harirupo Mahadevah, Lingrupi Janardanah isad apy antaram nasti bhedakrn narakam vrajet*). The unity of the three is obvious in the word *Aum* which proclaims and symbolises one God. "A" for Vishnu, "U" for Siva and "M" for Brahma. (*Akaro Vishnurususdidsht, Ukarastu Maheshwara, Makrastu rmuno Brahma pranyastu triyatmaks (Vayu Puran)*. *Atharvaveda* explicitly states that there are a number of splendours (magnificient) forms of one light (*ekam jotir bahuda vibhuti*). (A.V.XIII.3.17). The idea conveyed by cosmic trinity is that "the divine pattern and the potential matter, both these are derived from God, who is the beginning, the middle and the end-Brahma, Vishnu and Siva. God with his creative ideas is Brahma, God who pours out by his love and works with a patience, which is matched with His live is Vishnu (who is all prevading and protecting all, Vis means pervades); who is perpetually at work saving the world. When the conceptual becomes cosmic when heaven is established in the world, we have the fulfilment represented by Siva (*Things in their natural course dissolve or perish or destroyed and Siva is associated with it*). God is at the same time wisdom, love and perfection. The three functions cannot be torn apart. Brahma, Vishnu and Siva are fundamentally one though conceived in three fold manner".

It may be assumed that the medical formulas attributed separately to Brahma, Vishnu and Siva were written by sages over the years. They felt that all their efforts were due to devine grace and inspiration and attributed them to one of the three forms of God. The association of medical formulations with one of the trinity could have been for gaining faith of the people in their efficacy. This however appears to be rather a distorted view, as sages were highly respected and venerated and given in many cases the title of *Bhagwan* an epithet applied to gods, semigods and other holy or respectable personages.

Among the gods mentioned in *Ṛgveda,* Asvins are remarkable skilful physicians and surgeons. These twin divine physicians appear very human, with astounding medical skill. Perhaps they were the first two physicians in human history whose achievement are well documented. There is also mention of Saraswati and Sinivali. Some details, as recorded in *Rig Veda,* about them, may be given.

The Asvins

Considering the number of hymns addressed to the Asvins in *Rig Veda,* their position among gods appears to be very high. "In some Samhita and Brahmana texts of *Yajurveda,* however the Asvins are looked down upon because as physicians they have to mix too freely with men. *Taittiriya Samhita, Satapatha Brahmana and Aitareya Brahmana* further record that "one time, surgeons were looked upon as unclean and unfit to mix in respectable society; but the success gained by the Asvins in the case of Yajna at once raised them in the estimation of all".

It is notable that they are also described as *Nara* (men) with human qualities and human characteristics rather than legendary gods.

The Asvins are described as handsome, with garlands of lotus flowers round their neck, long armed, swift handed, young and ageless, powerful, deliverers, rescuers and wonder workers. They are fond of honey and *Soma,* and their approach is heralded by sound of conchshell. Rbhus made for them a golden car, triangular in shape with three wheels, and three columns. This car is drawn by horses

(*Hari)* or by asses, or even without any steed. Their golden car usually runs along terrific paths, and is capable of going anywhere. In addition to the car they have a ship with one hundred oars. Their transport thus provided speed and mobility. The power with which the car without steed was driven can be conjectured.

The cures performed by the Asvins include rejuvenation of Cyavana, Kali, Vandana, Kaksivan, Atri and Ghosa, curing Vadhrimati of sterility, delivering Hiranyahasta and Vamdeva from their mothers womb with case; restoring eyesight of Rjrasva and Kanva, hearing to son of Nrsnganda, eyesight and hearing of Kaksivat, power of limbs of Paravrja, curing Ghosa of leprosy (or leucoderma), Srona of weak knees, resuscitating Ṛsi Reva who was drowned in a well, and successfully treating Syava whose body had been in three pieces. An interesting incident recorded is about aid given to Vaspala:

"When in the time of night, in Khelas battle a leg was severed like a wild birds pinion, straight he gave Vispala a leg of iron that he might move what time the conflict opened." (ṚV. I. 116.15).

The is the earliest record of providing an artificial limb.

Other incidents associated with the Asvins are equally interesting. They made cow of Sayu, who had left off bearing, to yield milk, gave rain water to Manu and Dirghasrava, produced fire by friction of wood, and rescued Bhujya in their ship when he was left in mid-ocean. There are numerous other legends in which they helped human beings and animals including saving of a quail from the jaws of a wolf. (Ṛv. i, vi, vii, viii, x).

Caraka Samhita and Susruta Samhita further also mention three incidents namely curing some of serious lung disease and restoring handsome features to Candra and joining the severed head of Yajna and successfully treating Pusan for loosened teeth, and Indra for still arm.

The Asvins are credited with authorship of *Cikitsasara Tantra* (abstract of treatment), *Haritaki Kalpa* (chebulic myrobolana), *Asvin Samhita* (treatise on medicine), *Dhaturatnamala* (metallic and mineral powders) and *Nadi Naidana* (the science of feeling pulse). About forty formulae including enemas, gruels, powders, medicated oil and formula for treatment of haemorrhage, etc., are attributed to the Asvins.

In addition to the aspect of the Asvins as healers, there are a cosmical legend also associated with them. They have been identified as moisture and light, heaven and earth, day and night, Sun and Moon.

Their resemblance with the two Lattic gods the twin Horsemen of Greek mythology, the sons of Zeus, the Greek Dioskouri, the Chiron the centaur who taught medicine to Aesculepius, and Castor and Pollux the twin constellation of the Gemini is very striking. It is also interesting to observe the name of the Asvins (Nasatyas) in the cuneiform inscription excavated at Boghaz Keui in Cappadocia in North-Western Mesopotamia : *I lani Milt-tra-as-si-il-ilani. U-ru-w-na-as-si-i-il-ilu In-da-ra-ilani Na-sa-at-ti-ia-an-na.* It seems that the Asvins along with Mitra, Varuna and Indra were worshipped by the Kings of Mitani in the Euphrates Valley about 1400 B.C.

The personality of these twin great Indo-Aryan figures appears to be very human and humane. In the history of medicine in India the Asvins (after Brahma and Daksa) appear to be the earliest practitioners of medicine and surgery. They were perhaps outstanding horsemen, heroes and leaders of their time with wonderful deeds to their credit. The legends created round them raised them to the status of gods possessing medical skill and cosmical attributed. This is not surprising. Their influence and reputation was great and is well illustrated in the following hymn of the *Ṛv Veda*.

"Bearing rich treasures in your car O'Asvins come. The mortals who present oblations, Keep at a distance penury and sickness, Lovers of Sweetness, day and night preserve us" (Ṛv. VII. 71.2).

Saraswati First Female Physician

There are two very notable goddesses mentioned in the *Rig Veda, viz.,* Saraswati and Sinivali.

Saraswati is variously described, such as benevolent mighty river bestowing wealth and fertility (RV. VII. 95); the beautiful goddess purifier and of wonderous gait with two prolific breasts — sources of all prosperity, riches and happiness (RV. I. 164.49. RV. VI. 49.7.); (in later period Goddess of learning, speech and eloquence). Saraswati belongs to the group of gods and goddesses associated with procreation (*garbh dhhi Saraswati).* Saraswati is the first female physician in the history of ancient medicine in India. She worked with the celebrated physicians the Asvins (RV. X. 131.5). She is considered to bestow offsprings and wealth (RV. VII. 95.2) (RV. II. 41.17). She is stated to be the propounder of a formula of an oleogenous medicine (*Sarswati Ghrta)* for cure of sterlity in women and seminal insufficiency in men.

Saraswati was revered by the physicians. In the *Kasyapa Samhita,* during the initiation of the medical students, the libation to Saraswati follows offerings to Dhanvantri. Such mention of the name of Saraswati alongwith names of other propounders of *Ayurveda* further supports the assumption that she was considered as a distinguished physician and composer of medical precepts and aphorisms (*sutrakar).*

Sinivali First Birth Attendant

Sinvali is stated to have beautiful arms, nice figure, many children and reputed to have delivered many women easily (RV. II. 32. 6). She seems to be able to prevent miscarriage. A hymn reads : "Sinivali. O' Saraswati hold the embryo" (RV. X. 184. 2). Sinivali was either an obstetrician or a birth attendant, who worked with or side by side with Saraswati. In later Ayurvedic literature we find the qualities of Sinivali included in the qualities of the birth attendant. Raka, Gungu and Anumati are other medical goddesses.

Both Saraswati and Sinivali like Asvins appear very human, busy medical practitioners and were given divine status because of their exceptional skills. (ṚV. 32-4-8).

Herbs and Witchcrafts

During the Rigvedic period there was wide use of herbs. But at the sametime faith in supernatural powers continued, and fear of witchcraft lingered.

The first statement on plants as medicine, in the medical history, is in *Ṛg Veda.* Plants are classified in three categories *viz.,* trees (*Vraksh),* herbs with medicinal properties (*Osadhis)* and other herbs (*Virudhis). Ṛg Veda* mentions 107 *Osadhis,* (ṚV. 1.9. 64, 67, 20, 22. X.97).

The physicians must have contributed to and assisted in the development of biology, botany, pharmacology and other sciences. Their involvement in botany is obvious from statements in *Caraka Samhita,* (A much later compilation than Vedas). A physician was required, to know the herbs botanically and pharmocologically, and to administer drugs with due reference to climate and season and only after examining each and every patient individually.

The Ṛgveda describes the morphology, physiology, internal structure and classification of plants and presence of plants before animals on this earth especially before human beings (ṚV 1.3.5; 1.6; VI 3.4; 1. 64. X.97). Great stress was laid on trees *(Vraksh)* construction of gardens and parks for health and recreation. Gardens were formally consecrated for public use (RV. III. 8 II). This is the earliest reference to arbori-horticulture in human history.

There is also an indication in the hymns of *Rigveda* that the Vedic Indians had some knowledge of the manufacture of food, the action of light on the processing and storage of energy, in the body of the plant.

The place given to plants was high. "Plans, I hail thee' "Divine Mother of Mankind" said the Vedic sage (RV. X. 97.4).

Air, Water, Sun, Heat

Almost similar adoration is seen for water, air, sun, heat *(agni),* and malevolent forces as illustrated from following verses :

"*amrit* (nectar) is in the waters, in waters there is healing balm".

"Within the waters . . . dwell all balms that heal".

"Waters teem with medicine to keep my body safe from harm" (Rv. XXIII. 19-21). "Hither O wind, blow healing balm, blow all the diseases away. For thou who hast all medicines comest as an envoy of the Gods".

"May *Savetur* (The Sun), maker of fair things, be gracious and lengthen out the days of your existence. (Rv. 10. XVIII. 6). "*Agni,* he who blesseth all". (Rv 10. IX. 6).

Rigveda is by no means simple reading to assess the knowledge of that period. F.Maxmuller observes : "What can be more tedious than the *Vedas* and yet what can be more interesting, if once we know that it is first word spoken by the Aryan man. . . .The veda have two fold interest. It belongs to history of the world and to the history of India. As long as man continues to take interest in the history of his race, and as long as we collect libraries and museums the relics of the former age, the first place in that row of books which contains records of Aryan branch of mankind will belong to *Rig Veda.*

Atharvavedic Philosophy

Atharvaveda, has a high place among Vedas. The three Vedas have been equated with a bird with one wing; and *Atharvaveda* with a bird having two wings. (*Gopatha Brahmana* 3.2)

Mundak Upnishad throws some light on authorship of Vedas including *Atharvaveda.* The verses of this *Upnishad* indicate that Brahma imparted *Brahmvedya* to his eldest son Athurv, who passed it on to Angir, and Angir further passed on the knowledge to Satyavaha, a descendent of Bharadwaj gotra. There was a great sage Shauank, the chanceller *(adhishtata)* of a university with 28000 scholars. He asked Angira the meaning of *Brahmvedya.* Angira replied that knowledge is of two types. *viz.,* one *para* and another *apara.* The *Apara* includes *Rigveda, Yajurveda, Samveda* and *Atharvaveda,* in these are given instructions, time or period, details of results from study, all subjects and articles mathematics, astrology, etc. The knowledge of realisation of the real *Parambrhma Parmeshwara is Para. Mundak Upnishad* along with other *Upnishads,* is remarkable treatise which explains further the relationships between *para* and *apara, para* pervading everything still away from everything, visible and at the sametime invisible; the simple words "*AUM*" is a symbol of *para;* gives primacy to truth which is other name for *para* explains relationship between the soul and the senses.

Atharvaveda is an integral part, of *Brahmvedya,* embodying closely inter-related all aspects of the *Brahmvedya. Atharvaveda has* 731 hymns, with about 600 verses, almost 2/3rd are repetitions from *Rigveda.* About 114 hymns relate to health, diseases and plants for cure of diseases. Physical diseases and disorders along with their cure include injury, poisonous arrows headache, blindness, earache, dumbness, abdomenal problems, anaemia, jaundice, leprosy (may be leucoderma), abortion, urinary disorders, fever and others. The plants are classified and praised for medicinal properties. The medicine and plants identified includes reeds, *Haridra, Kustha, Chitraparni, Masaparni, Loksmana, Putrajani, Putrakanda,* and *Putrada.* etc. (AV. I.3; II, 5; V, 4; VII, 7 XIX, 3). The plants for the cure of wounds include *Arundhati* (silaci), *Plaksa Khadira, Dhava, Nyagrodha, Parna and Pippali* (AV. IX. 12, V, 5; VI 109) Management of bleeding daring pregnancy, prevention of abortion, and infertility, method for conception of male child (AV. III 3) are mentioned.

Medico Religious Approach

Alongwith scientific-secular approach, maladies due to supernatural agencies are listed, *e.g.,* demons, ghosts, *Yoksmas,* curse of gods. It is noticed alongwith incantations, or invocations, or exorcism in several cases, drugs are used simultaneously such as *Druva, Apamarga, Asvatha, Banyan, Ajasrngi, Avaka, Varna, Sahdevi Sadampuspa, Jangida, Satavara, Guggula.* Amulets were also prescribed for prevention of injuries and prologation of life, etc.

There are hymns on harmony, love marriage and long life. Ideal life span at that time seems to be 100 years as seen from the verse : "May we see 100 autumns (A.V. 67) Plants for virility and success in love making are mentioned. Amongst the latter a large number of plants are mentioned like *Madhuka, Yastimadhu, Patha, Vanaparni, Kapitthaka, Arka, Canda, Sankhpushpika.* (AV. I. 34, III 18; IV4, VI72, 107, 138, 139, VII, 38). A list of plants for personal beauty, improvement of appearance (VI 30, 136, 137) and growth of healthy hair and prevention of baldness are given.

Heart

Vedic physician are stated to be familar with circulation of blood. No hymn however, gives details of the knowledge of blood circulation as is known at present. There is mention of heart as core of vital activities. (AV. 113, VII, X, 4) and *Madhuka* and *Madhuga* plants are mentioned for heart disorders. It can be surmised that the Vedic physician heard the beating of the heart by direct application or ear to the chest. He also noticed that when heart-beats stopped the person died.

Bleeding

The relationship of bleeding from wounds and blood vessels and procedure to stop bleeding through manual pressure is suggested in the hymn 1.17 of the *Atharvaveda*. The hymn reads :

"Stop lower one ! Stop upper one ! Do thou stop midmost one !

If the smallest stops, shall stop forsooth the great one *(dhamni)*

Of the hundred tubes, of the thousand veins, have stopped.

Have stopped forsooth these midmost ones, the ends have rested together".

Stopping Bleeding with Drug

The bleeding appears to have been prevented by the sap of the Creeper *Arundhati* called *Laksha* (V.12;V.5).

The trees associated with the creeper *Arundhati* are: *Plaksa, Asvattha Khadira, Dhava, Parana and Nyagordha (banyan).*

Healing of Bones

The creeper *Arundhati* seems to have anti-inflamatory and great healing qualities. The hymn in its praise reads:

"Grower art thou, grower or several bones, make this grow O' Arundhati

What of thee is torn, what of thee is inflamed, crushed
May creeper excellently put that together again
Let marrow be put together with marrow
Let skin grow with skin
Let thy blood, bone grow
Let flesh grow with flesh
Fit thou together hair with hair
Fit together skin with skin
Let thy blood bone grow
Put together what is served O'Herb" (A.V.IV.12).

Retention of Urine

One of the most notable hymns relates to retention of urine. Use of a reed is mentioned to relieve the distressing condition. Whether this reed was a probe or a metal catheter (*nadyantrani)* is a matter of conjecture. It appears to be some instrument, may be hollow reed. There is no doubt that this instrument was passed into urinary bladder through urethra. Reference is made to bladder and urethra thus : I split up thy urinator, like the weir of the tank, so be thy urine released out of thee, with a splash; all of it. (A.V.I.3, 6-8).

Mosquito And Malaria

Fever appears to have been major cause of illness in ancient times. The story of flying insect is of special interest as the knowledge existing in Vedic period was rediscovered after centuries in 1898 A.D.

Some of the earliest references to this fever occur in the *Atharvaveda* believed to have been composed about 1500 B.C. It was classified even in *Atharvaveda* according to the periodicity of attack of fever, *i.e.,* quotidian (*sadandim),* tertian (*tritiyakam)* and quartan (*vitrtiyam).* It was also classified according to the season in which the fever made its appearance, *viz.,* winter (*sitam),* summer (*graismam)* and rainy season (*varsikam).* It was common especially where there was excessive rain (*mahavrsah)* or too much grass (*mujavanta).* It also leads to the assumption that such fevers were common in *Gandhara (*Peshwar District and Hoti Mardan), *Anga,* (country about Bhagalpur) and *Magadha* (Bihar State).

"trtiyakam vitrtiyam sadandimuta saradam

takmanam sitam ruram graismam nasaya varasikam".

(A.V.V. 22. 13).

"oko asya mujavanta oko asya mahavr sah

yavajjatastakmamstavanasi bahlikesu nyocarah".

(A.V.V. 22.5)

From the numerous references to it and analysis of its characteristics it would appear that malaria was the commonest type of fever. Its association with mosquito may be surmised by the descriptions which give nearly all the charcteristics and habits of mosquito, especially needle-like proboscis (*kusula)* bloody mouth (*lohitasyan)* and the habit of visiting the dwellings after sunset (*salah parinrtyanti sayam).* There is also reference to the use of odourous or fumigating medications used to destroy them.

In ka 5 sukta 22, reference is made to *takman.* Caraka and Susruta use the word *jvara* for fever in general. It continues to be the group name of all diseases with fever as the main and dominating sign. The authors of the Ayurvedic period classify fever into five types instead of four of *Atharva veda, viz.,* continuous (*Samtatah)* remittent (*Satatah),* quotidian (*Anyedyuskah),* tertian (*Trtiyakah),* and quartan (*Caturthaka).*

"ye salah parinrtyanti sayam gardabhanadinah

kusula ye ca kuksilah kukubhah karubah srimah

tanosadhe tvam gandhena visucinan vinasaya".

(A.V. VIII. 6. 10).

"ye kukundhah kukurabhah krittirdursani bibhrati

kliba iva pranrtiyanto vane ye kurvate ghosam tanito nasayamasi".

(AV. VIII. 6.11)

"ye suryam na titiksanta atapantamamum divah

arayan bastivasino durgandhimllohitasyan makkan nasayanasi".

(A.V. VIII 6.12)

"ye suryat parisarpanti snuseva svasuradadhim

bajasca tesam pingasca hrdaye dhinividhyatam".

(A.V.VIII. 6.24)

"Punah pancavidho drsto dosakalabalabalat

samtatah satato nyedyustrtiyakacaturthakah".

(Ca. Ci. 3.34)

"Anyedyuskah pratidinam dinam hitva trtiyakah

Dinadvayam yo visramya pratyeti sa caturthakah".

(Ca. Ci. 3. 67)

"Saptaham va dasaham va dvadasahamathapi va

Santatya yovisargi syat santatah sa nigadyate

Ahoratre satatako dvau kalavanuvartate

Anyedyuskastvahoratradekakslam pravartate

Trtiyakas rtiye'hni caturthe'hni caturthakah".

(Su. U. 39. 69. 70. 71)

The similes given by these two authors to explain the advent and periodicity of this kind of fever are very significant. Caraka, for instance, compares the phenomena to the seed sown in the ground which takes one day to grow in case of quotidian, two days in case of tertian and three days in case of quartan; when they grow up they invade the whole body and not being counteracted by antibodies (*pratyanika)* they cause the fever. When the force of these invading elements is exhausted, they return to their original habitat and again begin to grow up. Susruta compares the advent of fever to the tide and ebb of the ocean. Caraka's account of the life history of malarial parasite is of special interest. Both the authors also state that this kind of fever is common in low land or land at the foot of the mountain. Besides these indirect references to malaria, we find in the *Susruta-Samhita* a direct reference to five species of mosquitoes, viz., sea-born, globular in shape, the huge type, black in colour and the mountainous. The bite of the mountainous species (*parvatiya)* is stated to bear the same characteristics as that of deadly insects (*Pranahara Kita Damsana).* Later references to malarial mosquitoes or malarial fever in *Vagbhata, Madhava* and *Bhavamisra,* are simply repetitions of the statements made by these two authors. Presumably the use of mosquito-nets (*masakahari)* was also prevalent in India as would be evident from Marco Polo's account as early as the 13th A.D.

"Adhisete yatha bhumim bijam kale ca rahati
Adhisete tatha adhutum dosah kale ca kupyati
Sa vrdhim balakalam ca prapya dosastrtiyakam
Caturthakam ca kurute pratyanikabalaksyat
Kṛtva vegam gatabalah sve sve sthane vyavasthilah
Punarvivrdhah sve kale jvarayanti naram malah".

(Ca. Ci. 3. 68. 69.70)

"Yatha vegagame velam chadayitva mahodadheh
Vegahanau tadevambhastatraivantarnitiyate
Dosavegodaye tadvadudiryeta jvaro'sya vai
Vegahanau prasamyeta yatha'mbhah sagare tatha".

(Su. U. 39. 73. 74)

"Masakah — samudrah, parimandalo, hastimaskah, krsnah, parvatiya iti panca; tairdastasya tivra kandur damsasophasaca, parvatiyastu kitaih prancharaistulyalaksanah".

(Su. Ka. 3. 36)

It will be obvious, therefore, that malaria as a disease and its association with the mosquito was known as early as the Vedic period in ancient India. The word for mosquito in the *Atharvaveda* is *makka* which is the same as '*masaka*' in classical Sanskrit.

Soil Fertility

Increasing fertility of soil by various ways, such as crop rotation, cowdung manure, was well developed in Rigvedic period. Further developments must have taken place in Atharvavedic period. We come across tributes to rain in *Atharvaveda* : . . let the juices of the waters attach themselves to the herbs; let gushes of rain gladden the earth, let herbs of all forms be born here and there, let the herbs become full delight with the coming of the rainy season" (AV. IV. 15). The favour of God of plenty was invoked for abundance of grain for food.

Environment

A remarkable hymn is on cutting or digging out trees. "What of thee I dig out, let that quickly grow over, Let me not hit thy vitals or thy heart". There is clear exhortation in the hymn to plant a tree in place of the one removed. We will find in Post Vedic period a continuation of the above precept on conservation of forest in Asoka' Pillar Edict; which reads : "Forest are not to be burnt, either uselessly or for killing animals".

Marital Relations

Great emphasis is laid on love between husband and wife and harmony within one's-self and society.

The hymn on husband wife reads :

"The eyes of the two be of honey aspect;

Our face (be) ointment put thou me within thy heart;

May our minds be verily together". (AVV. VII. 36).

Harmony

Special emphasis is laid on harmony. It is underlined that there should be harmony between body and mind, harmony between kind and knowledge, harmony between the members of the family, harmony in the neighbourhood and with every other person (strangers). (AV. VII. 52).

Upanishadic period

The Aryans of the Vedic period were essentially religious-minded people who made sacrifices to their gods and goddesses, many of whom represented observable natural phenomena. After the eighth century B.C., the outlook of some of the intellectul Brahmins was observed to be changing. The philosophical dialogues of the Upanishads of this period indicate a shift in the attitude of thinkers from the outer tangible world and its phenomena to the inner intangible. Self (*atman*). Brahma was being considered as the source of all the forces of nature and man's individual self (*atman*) as a part of that. The Upanishadic sages were striving to attain and hold themselves in a state of unmitigated self (*atman*) awareness through sheer thinking, systematic self-analysis, breath control and other stern physchological disciplines of Yoga.

The outcome was the formulation of various systems of Hindu philosophy. Kanada, who composed *Vaiseshika Sutras,* in which he described pramanus as the ultimate basic constituents of everything in the universe, was the first atomist philosopher scientist of this period. Aksapada Gotama, who formulated *Nyaya Sutras* and described the four methods, namely, perception, inference, comparison and testimony, of establishing the true identity of a phenomenon or an object was the originator of the ancient

Indian scientific methodology. Kapila propounded his theory of the creation of the universe. Patanjali set our Yoga doctrines.

Glorious Period

The period from the fourth century B.C. to the sixth or seventh century A.D. — of about a thousand years — covering the Maurya, Shaka, Kushana, and the Gupta empires, was one of exchange of ideas with the outer world and of general prosperity, social, cultural and scientific development inside India. Medicine astronomy and mathematics made remarkable progress.

During this period there were great centres of learning in India where large number of students resided and obtained knowledge in various subjects. Of the later part of this period, Chinese pilgrims, Hsuan Tsang (A.D. 629-649) and I Tsing (A.D. 675-685), who resided as students at Nalanda, have given a description of this centre of learning.

Nalanda was a residential university with a population of 8,599 students and 1510 teachers and other staff. It provided food, clothing, bedding, tuition and even medicine, free to the residents. It was supported by liberal grants for this purpose by royal and private philanthropy. Hundreds of villages were attached to it and managed by it and this provided many of the necessities of life. To be a student of Nalanda was the highest academic distinction in itself and 'Nalanda brother' was treated with respect wherever he went.

For centuries, the students of Nalanda went out in unending streams to work in foreign countries like Nepal, Tibet and China, to introduce to them the wisdom of India and the texts in which it was embedded. Foreign students from Korea, Mongolia, Tokhara, Japan, China and Tibet came here to put an end to their doubts. I Tsing counted 56 foreign students at the time at Nalanda.

Medical Sciences. During the sixth century B.C., and even much later, there was a great centre of medical teaching at Taxila (near Rawalpindi) where students were taught by "world-renowned" teachers. The famous Jivika, physician to the Buddha and the emperors Bimbisara and Ajatasatru, had his training at this centre. There were also large establishments in the big cities maintained by the kings where food and medicine was given free. Special mention bas been made of such places by Fa-Hien, a Chinese pilgrim, who visited India in the fifth century A.D., at the time of Chandragupta, the Gupta emperor. The king's household kept stocks of medicines and the state maintained special botanical gardens for cultivation of medicinal plants.

To this period belong the famous physicians, Atreya and Charaka, and the surgeon Susruta, and their texts *Charaka Samhita and Susruta Samhita. Charaka Samhita* describes human embryology, anatomy, physiology, various diseases and their treatment as well as measures to prolong life. *Susruta Samhita,* essentially a surgical work, describes many difficult and intricate surgical operations such as of making a nose where the original has been cut off, removal of the stone from the urinary bladder and delivering the foetus through on operation on the abdomen. Such operation, in later times, was given the name of Caeserean section.

Vagbhata, the third of the great authorities on medicine, belonged to the sixth or seventh century A.D. Another great physician of this period was Shalihotra, who specialized in the treatment of horses and is considered to be the father of ancient veterinary sciences in India.

Similarities between *Charaka Samhita* and *Susruta Samhitas* on the one hand and Hippocratic and other medical works from Greece on the other, confirm the exchange of many ideas between the two civilizations.

Astronomy. Beginning with the first few centuries of the Christian era, there was a great spurt and upsurge in the Indian astronomical literature which is more clearly seen from 400 A.D. This happened because of the contacts with the more developed Greek astronomy whose influence is clearly seen in various Indian astronomical siddhantas treatises such as of *Surya, Romaka,* and *Paulisa.* Many of the Greek astronomical methods were modified to suit the Indian requirements of calculations and part of the Greek terminology was also adopted. Greek astronomy and astronomers were spoken of in praiseworthy terms in Indian literature of this period.

Of the fifth century A.D., Aryabhata was the greatest Indian astronomer. He contradicted the orthodox views and stated that the earth was a sphere which rotated on its axis, the eclipses were not caused by Rahu (demon), the moon was essentially dark and was illuminated by the sun.

Varahamihira the author of *Pancha Siddhanta* and Brahmagupta of *Brahmasphuta Siddhanta,* who flourished between the sixth and seventh centuries were eminent, in their fields, yet they denied that the earth rotated.

Much of the algebraic knowledge which the Indians possessed in abundance, they utilized in the solution of various astronomical problems so that even though they borrowed some of the knowledge from Greek sources, they independently developed it further as well.

Mathematics. Development of the place-value system of numerical notation and the concept of zero and very significant Indian contributions of this period. Considerable skill is also shown in handling problems leading to equations of more than one unknown and the study of indeterminate equations in which they went so far ahead that they anticipated some of the discoveries of the modern algebra. Aryabhata devoted considerable attention to trigonometry and his introduction of the sines and versed sines was notable achievement.

Propagation to Other Lands. Indian science and thought during ancient times ran parallel to the Greek in its mode of spread in foreign lands. Visit of the Indian scholars to foreign countries and of foreign students to India led to propagation of Indian sciences in Indo-China, China, Japan, Indonesia, Tibet and Mongolia. In Tibet, Indian sciences continued to have a particularly great influence even in later times.

Indian science were transmitted to the Arabian countries through translations of the Sanskrit literature into Arabic, or indirectly from Sanskrit to Persian and then Arabic. It is said that during the eighth century, when Sindh was under the actual control of the Calipah Mansur (753-774 A.D.), scholars from the part of India went to Baghdad and they took with them works of Brahmagupta. These works were translated by Arabian scholars with the help of Sanskrit pundits. It is through them that the Arabians first became acquainted with Indian Mathematics and astronomy.

Another proliferation of Hindu learning took place under Harun-al Rashid (786-908 A.D.). The ministerial family of Barmak engaged Hindu scholars to come to Baghdad, made them chief-physicians in their hospitals and asked them to translate from Sanskrit into Arabic, books on medicine, pharmacology, toxicology, snakes, veterinary sciences, etc. A favourite subject with the Arabians was Indian mathematics. Soon afterwards, when Sindh was no longer politically dependent on Baghdad, this activity ceased and the Arabic world sought other channels of learning and their attention was mainly directed to the Greek sources.

Indian sciences, alongwith Indian culture, suffered decadence mostly because of foreign invasions and subjugation. People forgot about their brilliant past in the midst of their deprivations.

Discovery of the Past Glory.

Little was known of the ancient Indian history or sciences before the eighteenth century. English historians were of the view that Hindus had ever been in the same abject condition in which the English found them. It may be of interest to know that Indians themselves at that time did not know better of their past except in the vaguest possible terms. The works of early oriental scholars like William Jones, Pricep, Bohtlingk, Max Mueller, Wilson, Fergusson, Rajendra Lal Mitra and the archaeological explorations started in 1861, brought home to the educated Indians a vivid picture of the past glory and greatness of ancient India.

History of Āyurveda

Āyurveda, *i.e.,* the Old Indian Medicine, is the oldest medical science of the world, and history has distinctly shown that the Western Medicine is the offspring of Āyurveda. The references to this effect are amply found in the works of Weber and Buck who are none too partial towards India's claim to precedence in the matter of medicine. Criticising Stenzler's suggestion of the likelihood of Suśruta having borrowed from Greek Medicine, for there is a considerable similarity in both, even Weber in his book *History of Indian Literature* has to say that "no internal grounds whatever appear to exist; on the contrary, there is much that seems to tell against the idea of any such Greek influence. Amongst the individuals enumerated as contemporaries of Suśruta there is not one whose name has a foreign sound. Besides, Suśruta and other writers expressly assign the cultivation of medicine to Kāśī (Benares) and other eastern provinces which never came in contact with the Greeks." Buck, in his book *the Growth of Medicine from the earliest time to* 1800 at one time seems to belittle the influence of the Old Indian Medicine on the Old Greek Medicine, the progenitor of the present Western Medicine. But probing the history further he has to modify that opinion and say "that it is reasonable to suppose, although directly confirmatory evidence has not yet been discovered, that through the channels of trade between the two countries, some knowledge of the doings of the physicians of India must have reached the ears of their Greek brethren. On the other hand at a later period of history (after the invasion of Alexander, the Great) the relations between the two countries became quite close and were kept up without a break for several hundred years. During the earlier part of this period, as appears from the writings of Hyppocrates, Diosorides and Galen, various drugs and methods of treatment employed by the physicians of Indian were adopted by the practitioners of Greece." This seems a half-hearted admission of the influence of Indian Medicine on the Greek Medical System. In making such halting admission he only considers the direct contact between Greece and India; but he seems to forget India's indirect influence on Greek Medicine exerted through Egypt, Persia, and Arabia. Egypt (the old Misra or Misar) was the first country to be profited by Eastern learning including medicine, for it seems it was once colonised by ancient Ārayans. Sir William Jones in the report of the Royal Asiatic Society is also led to believe it. Major Wilfred considers the "Misra sthāna" of Puranas to be no other than "Misra" the old name of Egypt. Perhaps it may be argued tht during the close contact of the two countries Egypt may have given its medical system to India. But then there is nothing in its system that is not found in the Indian system, while there is much in the Indian system that is nowhere to be found in the Egyptian system of Medicine. Besides this India influenced the Greek

Medicine through Arabia. Famous Arabian physicians Serapion, Avicenna and Rhazes, whose works are translated into European languages, have been known to quote freely Caraka, Suśruta, and Indian writers with great respect. That Indian Medicine was a very efficient science and that Indian had some very skilful doctors is evident from the fact, that amongst the presents offered to Alexander, the Great by the defeated Hindu king was a physician of such skill "that he could even revive the dead." Arrian, the Greek historian, writing about the invasion of Alexander on India (BC 400), says "the Grecian physicians found no remedy against the bites of snakes; but the Indians cured those who happened to fall under that misfortune." Alexander issued the order that those afflicted by it should come to the camp to be treated by the Indian Physicians of his court. Nearchus also supports the above statement (Wise P. VII.). Alaxander not only took with him the medical science, but actually took some Indian physicians with him. Then later on at the Muhammadan invasions in the 10th century, the invaders took this system of medicine with them to their countries. Thus not only did the system go there, but it was later on followed by the Hindu doctors who were invited to translate and teach their system and also serve in the courts of these Muhammadan rulers as physicians. It seems that Indian Medical system was known to Arabians before this period, for Prof. Wilson says "that the Arabian of the 8th century cultivated the Hindu works on Medicine before those of the Greeks, and the Caraka, the Suśruta and the treatises called Nidana were translated and studied by the Arabians in the days of Harun and Mansur (773 A.D.) either from the originals or more probably from the translations made at a still earlier period into the language of Persia." The Arabic version of Suśruta is called Kelale-Shawshūre al-Hind. From Arabic they were translated into Latin. From Arabia this system went to Egypt, and the Egyptians in their turn taught it to the family of Hyppocrates and Pythagoras who are reputed to have originated the system of Western Medicine. Referring to this Dr. Wise says "all these medical systems have a common source; being originally derived from the family of Hyppocrates. Those distinguished benefactors of mankind first explained the nature and treatment of disease, and reduced to theory the various phenomena of human body. The Greecian philosophers were assisted by Egyptian sages who appear to have obtained much of their knowledge from some mysterious nation from the east. Egypt, after having had her institutions destroyed by the sword of the conqueror, became the seat of the Greecian learning; which was afterwards transferred to the East, where under the fostering care of the Calyphs of Bagdad medicine was cultivated with deligence and success. it received still further additions from the east, and thus improved, it was conveyed by Muhammedan conquerors into Spain. From thence it was communicated to the other parts of Europe; where it has exercised the genius of many great men, with so much advantage of suffering humanity." That Western Medicine as originated by Greece was based on the Old Indian Medicine is evident from the facts : (1) that therein appear the names of drugs which are essentially Indian drugs; (2) that there are certain decriptions in the western medicine that bear great resemblance to the writings in the Old Indian Medical books that are older than any of the earliest Greek Medical books.

From the Arabian writers like Serapion (Ibn Serabi), Rhazes (Al-Razi) and Avicenna (who is better known as Aflatūn in India), it is absolutely clear that Arabia borrowed its medical system from the Hindu doctors. The royal courts of the old Muhammedan countries were also reputed to be medical schools. Not only did the Hindu doctors served in the Persian and Arabian courts as physicians but also taught their system of medicine and helped in translating their works into the Arabic language. That Western medicine and especially its surgery (or at least some part of it) originated in India is clear by the inclusion of the operation of Lithotomy, which could only have come from India, for Persia and Arabia not only did not practise this operation, but considered it disreputable even to witness it.

So far we saw the origin antiquity, and history of the Āyurveda or the Old Indian Medicine. Now let us examine the charge of quackery which is in season and out of season levelled against this system. To do this we have to see what constituted the old Indian Dentistry and medicine.

Āyurvedic or Old Indian Dentistry

Dentistry in all its branches was well known to and practised by the old Hindu doctors. Searching into Āyurveda one finds that there is a whole chapter devoted to the mouth-cavity, wherein are described all the operations such as (1) extractions by forceps, (2) extractions by elevators, (3) lancing of the gums, (4) removal of the Tartar, (5) fitting of the artificial dentures that are known to the present day Western dentistry. That dentistry must have existed then is certain, for even to-day we come across cases in which front teeth are decorated with gold or jewel studs by Indian jewellers. Even a dental surgeon also finds difficulty of drilling a through and through hole which is required for such decorations, without killing the nerve in these teeth; and yet thousands of teeth are with impunity perforated for this docoration. The work is so well done that any modern dentist can be proud of it. In Āyurveda one also finds a whole chapter on mouth-hygiene. Therein instructions are given for use of a tooth-brush (which in those days, as now among Hindus, mainly consisted of Baphal and Lim or Nim twigs) and tooth-powders and tooth-pastes. The drugs recommended for those powders were tobacco, salt, burnt beetlenuts. In the chapter on Diatetics some very useful instructions are given as to the order of dishes that would be conducive to the health of the mouth-cavity and the general body. These instructions are "take soft viands first, hard and buteraccons food in the middle and liquids at the end of the meals. Similarly the sweets must be taken first, then the acid things and the bitter and pungent things the last of all." Why even to-day there is a custom in some parts of India, for example Broach, where the people start their meal with sweets. Bohras also do the same. In that chapter there is also enjoined that there should be no hurry over the meals, and the food must be well chewed and that the mouth must be cleaned from inside and out after each meal : and the food-particles must be picked out from between the teeth by tooth-picks. These instructions compare very favourably with those given by present day mouth hygiene. Question may arise that could a medical system that had for its dental branch such dentistry possessing all the operations known to the present day dentistry be called quickery? That far from being a quackery, the Indian Medicine was a perfect science, will be clean to every body when they are gradually taken through all the branches of medicine that were known to that system of Āyurveda. This Āyurveda consisted of almost all the branches known to the present day Western medical system. As the Western medicine, Āyurveda had its Medicine, Surgery, Midwifery, Hygiene, Backteriology, Chemistry, Materia Medica, Physiology Anatomy and so on.

No doubt there are all the proofs of the existence of all these branches in the old Indian system of medicine. But to convince someone that the Indian Medical System was a perfect science, one has to give some proofs in connection with some of them. We shall examine them in the order given above.

Midicine

Medicine, *i.e.,* the branch that deals with diseases curable by medical treatment. This is one of the two (other being Surgery) branches that made the Indian Medical System famous. We will examine some of its features. The Indian Medical System has based all the diseases of the body on the three humours of the body *viz.,* Wind (vāta), Bile (pitta), and Phlegm (kapha). That Pythagoras (430 B.C.) Plato, and Hyppocrates (460 B.C.) also believed in humoural theory of diseases, is clear from their writings. This theory they must have borrowed from the Indian Medical System for these humours of the body are mentioned in the Rig Veda (i.34.6) which was written long before Pythagoras and Hyppocrates flourished. Enfield in his *History of Philosophy* says that Pythagoras learnt his Philosophy from Oriental philosophers, meaning the Hindus. If he borrowed his philosophy from India, and since his medical theories bear such resemblance to the theories of Old Indian Medicine it is easily conceivable that he must have learnt his Medicine from India also. This humoural pathology has existed for ages, and it is round this pathology that this wonderful system of medicine (Āyurveda) is evolved. There are some exponents of Western Medicine who deride this pathology as ridiculous and not worthy of their notice. They do so because they do not appreciate that real meaning of the words vāta, pitta and kapha which they literally translate as wind, bile, and phlegm, while they really mean much more than these English words seem to signify. Vāta or vāyu means the nerve force; pitta or pittam means the process of metabolism; and kapha means the unutilised product of the system, *i.e.,* the process of excretions. When they will realise the real meaning of these words they will appreciate this humoural pathology round which this system is evolved. Diagnosis of the diseases and the prognosis of the cases from the pulse was and still is the special feature of the Indian medical system. The knowledge of the old Hindu doctors of the variation of the pulse in various diseases was so perfect that they could easily diagnose the disease by it. There are some medical men who ridicule the idea of diagnosing the diseases by pulse. Sir John Woodroffe, the late Chief Justice of Bengal, in his book called Bharat Shakti, writing about Āyurveda says : "One of the things I most regret is the neglect of the Āyurvedic teaching the loss of valuable remedies, and of the great experience and knowledge of the pulse of the best old time Kaviraj." So efficient was the old system of medicine that even treatment like Mesmerism, Hydropathy, and Massage which are only recently introduced in Western Medicine, were well understood and practised by the old Hindu doctors of thousands of years ago. Why the annual Jātrās of Hoonai near Billimora, and Vajrabai near Kalyan (the places noted for their hot water springs) are the proofs of the existence of the treatment of Hydropathy in ancient India. That Indian Medicine did appreciate the good effects of Massage on the body is clear from the fact that Massage, in its crude form, is practised by the Hindus even unto this day. A Hindu wife massaging the tired limbs of her husband in the evenings is a familiar sight in a Hindu household. And that is the vestige of the past treatment of Massage of the old Hindu doctors. Why even the most recent additions to the Western Medical Science, *i.e.,* the question of Immunity and Postural treatment, were not unknown to them. The familiar sight in small villages of the snake charmers curing the cases of snake-poisoning by sucking the wounds and the existence of inoculation (perhaps in a crude form) for small-pox, are the proofs positive of their knowledge of Immunity which in Āyurveda is called "Vaishnavi-Shakti", *i.e.,* disease-resisting power of the body. One Dr. Huillet of Pondicherry says "Vaccination was known to a physician Dhanvantri who flourished before Hyppocrates." Having examined their Medicine let us now look into their surgery.

Surgery

The old Indian Surgery contained practically all the operations that are known to the present day Western Surgery. Old Hindu Surgeons performed even such tricky operations like Rhinoplasty, Lithotomy, Abdominal Surgery, Caeserian Section, removal of the cataract in capsule and even brain surgery (which is supposed to be the greatest achievement of the Western medicine). That Western medicine owes its surgery to India is clear from the facts that countries from which Western medicine has taken its inspiration were never good at surgery; and that some present day operations like Rhinoplasty and Lithotomy, are essentially Indian operations originated and practised in India centuries before Western Medicine even existed in name. Weber in his *History of Indian Literature* says "In surgery Indians seem to have attained a special proficiency and in this department European Surgeons might even perhaps even at present day still learn something from them, as indeed they have already borrowed from them the operation of Rhinoplasty." Standard surgical works make no secret of their having borrowed them from Indian medicine. Sir Frederic Treeves actually offered his thanks to Prof. Shah of Kathiawad for demonstrating the operation of Rhinoplasty to Western Medicine. Writing about this operation Dr. Hirschberg of Berlin says : "The whole plastic surgery in Europe had taken its new flight when these cunning devices of Indian workmen became known to us". The transplating of sensible skin flaps is also an entirely Indian method. He also gives credit to the Indians for discovering the art of "cataract-couching" which was entirely unknown to Greeks, Egyptians, or any other nation. That surgery existed then is evident from the varieties of surgical instruments that are known to have existed and their classifications mentioned in the old surgical works of which the Suśruta

Saṁhitā is the best example. That old Indian Surgery appreciated the value of and actually practised Asepsis and Antisepsis is clear from the instructions about burning some incense in the operation room before and during the operation, boiling the instruments and dressings used in operations, and cleaning the parts to be operated just before the operation. It also appreciated the value of anaesthesia during operations, for they were done under both general and local anaesthesia. They used a drug called "sammohinī" in place of chloroform. After the operation they used a drug called "sanjivinī" to bring the patient back to consciousness. The like of this drug does not exist in the Western Medicine.

Midwifery

India that abounds with Dāīs, the present corrupted remains of the once perfect sect of midwives, could not be destitute of the science of midwifery. Old Indian midwifery knew all that present day Western midwifery does. Even operative interference was freely resorted to in cases of difficult and complicated labour. Indian midwifery contains some useful instructions to be observed by women during pregnancy and confinement. There are also some fine observations on infant-feeding. The present day Western midwifery has no better instructions to give than those given by the old Indian midwifery. The Postural treatment, which is only recently introduced in gynaecology and surgery, was long known to and practised by the old Hindu doctors. Postural treatment as a means of easy impregnation, as a means of facilitating easy labour and as a factor in curing some internal disorders was the speciality of one Hindu doctor called Koka. His famous book *de rebus reneris* or Koksāstra as it is commonly called in Gujarati, though held in doubtful repute, because of the extreme delicacy of the subject treated in it, is translated into several languages. India can easily claim the credit of having first propounded this theory.

Bacteriology

It is often argued that the fact of germs causing the diseases, and the science (bacteriology) and the instrument (microscope) dealing with these germs could not have been known to the old Indian medicine. That system must have had its microscope or some magnifying device, for without such device they could not have talked of germs (meaning blood-corpuscles) floating in the blood; and malaria and other fevers being caused by germs conveyed by flea-bites, Āyurveda, talking as it does of diseases by contagion, sexual intercourse, evacuation of towns during epidemics, isolation of the people of the house where there is a death from some infectious disease, cleaning and sterilising the instruments used for an operation, could not have been destitute of Bacteriology. That Āyurveda had its bacteriology is certain from the fact that inoculation for small-pox was known to it hundreds of year before Jenner taught it to Western Medicine.

Materia Medica

It is but natural that India, a fertile country having all the periodical seasons of the years, should abound in vegetable drugs. It is not possible that the country with such wealth of vegetable drugs should not make use of them for the welfare of humanity. Thanks to the ancient Aryans who took the trouble to study and examine all these herbs, the old Indian Medicine possessed such Materia Medica that is the marvel to the modern investigator. And yet we often hear of some medical men versed in Western Medicine, making researches in these drugs, and declaring that the results are no better than with the allopathic drugs. The reason perhaps is that they forget that these drugs to be effective should be collected in particular seasons and in particular periods of their growth, and not indiscriminately as perhaps it is done now; and that when used in differrent ways they have different effects. Some wonderful properties of some rare drugs were taught to Indian medicine by the old ascetics, who used these drugs only, to keep their bodies and soul together. Though some of this knowledge became public property, and got incorporated in the old Indian medicine, most of this knowledge was handed down from teacher to pupil, or from father to son, and forms the bulk of the unwritten and traditional lore on the nature and properties of the Indian curative agents. Not only was Indian Materia Medica acquainted with the vegetable drugs only, but its knowledge of animal and mineral drugs was also very considerable. Writing about Materia Medica Weber says : "Information regarding the medicinal properties of minerals (especially precious stones and metals), of plants, and animal substances, and the chemical analysis and decomposition of these, covers certainly much that is valuable. Indeed the branch of Materia Medica generally appears to be handled with great predilection and thus makes up to us in some measure at least for the absence of investigations in the field of naural science." That Indian medicine made considerable use of minerals, is clear from the fact of pearl, gold, siver, mercury, diamonds, etc., being prescribed by the Āyurvedists and Yunani Hakims of even present day. These drugs, before they could be given internally, had to pass through some chemical processes which, it seems are now unfortunately lost; and which loss is deplored by Sir John Woodroffe in one of his books. The use of gold, in certain forms, only recently made by the Western medicine, was well known to the old Hindu doctors. That Western Materia Medica has borrowed, and borrowed freely from the Indian Materia Medica, is clear from the mention of some essentially Indian drugs (such as Tila, Jatamansi, Shringavera, and Marchi or Black Pepper) in the medical works of Hyppocrates, Dioscorides, and Claudius Galen. Galen, to whom Western medical Scienc is considerably indebted, describes some medicine as hot or cold. This idea he seems to have borrowed from India where it prevails unto this day. Not merely are these drugs mentioned by them only, but they are actually classified by them in the way done in Āyurveda. Materia Medica was taught to the old Hindu doctors in a much better way than it is done now in the Western Medical Schools. In those old days Medical students were taken by the teachers in the jungles, and were taught on the spot to recognise these drugs in their natural state their season of flowering, period of growth when they possess their peculiar properties, localities from which they should be gathered, the manner of treating and extracting their active principles and preserving them.

Physiology and Anatomy

That the old Indian medicine well understood physiology, *i.e.,* the normal working of the body, it clear from some fine descriptions of some physiological processes like the circulation of blood, and the digestion of human food. Dr. William Harvey is credited with the discovery of the circulation of blood in 1628. It seems that he must have had his inspiration from earlier Hindu writers, for they have given similar descriptions of the circulation of blood in books written centuries before Harvey was born. That description is as follows : "That Rasa (Rakta) is propelled from the heart by the Vyāna Vāyu to circulate through the arteries and veins, and that it nourishes the body as water converged through the canals irrigates the fields." Hārīta, another famous old physician, in his work Hārīta Saṁhitā, also refers to circulation when dealing with the disease Paṇḍuroga, *i.e.,* Anaemia. However we must give Dr. Harvey the credit of greater precision in the matter. Perhaps some people may argue that the description mentioned in the old Indian physiology is of the circulation of a substance called Rasa and not of blood (Rakta). But there is no difference in these two fluids except in colour and specific gravity. According to the old

Hindu doctors, Rasa is the most essential fluid that supports the body. It takes up the colour on its passage through the spleen and lever.

As for the anatomy it may be said that it was understood even better than physiology. It has so precisely mentioned the number of bones, muscles nerves, arteries, etc., in the body. Its anatomy, far from being based on mere guess work was based on the sure foundation of the dissection of the body. Dr. Wise (to whom we owe much of our present knowledge of the old Indian medicine) talking on its anatomy says : "The Hindu philosophers undoubtedly deserve the credit of having though opposed by strong prejudice entertained sound and philosophical views respecting the uses of the dead to the living; and were the first and scientific and successful cultivators of the most important and essential of all the departments of medical knowledge — practical anatomy." That the old Hindu doctors attached a great importance to the department of anatomy in general, and dissection in particular is evident from the writings of Caraka and Suśruta. Caraka has said "that a practitioner should know all parts of the body, both external and internal, and their relative positions against each other. Without such a knowledge he cannot be a proper practitioner." Suśruta has said "that a Yogī (a holy man) should dissect in order that he may know the different parts of the human body; and a surgeon and a physician should not only know the external appearances but the internal structures of the body; in order to possess an intimate knowledge of the diseases to which it is liable, and to perform surgical operations so as to avoid the vital parts. It is by combining a knowledge of books with practical dissection that the practitioner will alone attain an intimate knowledge of the subject in his profession". Besides human anatomy they knew also the anatomy of goat, sheep, horse, etc. Writing of strong prejudice Dr. Wise, refers to the agitation of Gautama Buddha against the dissection of the human body. His agitation knocked the Old Indian Medicine on the head, by knocking on the head of dissection, for since then (543 B.C.) it is supposed, the Indian Surgery began to decline.

Such, was the Āyurveda, *i.e,* Indian medicine that is called a quackery by some people. If quackery is of this sort, then give me that quackery back. Indian medicine was at its zenith at the time of the Muhammedan invasions in the 10th century when it received its first rude shock. Since that date Āyurveda, *i.e.,* the pure Indian medicine got mixed with the Yunānī, *i.e.,* the Arabic medicine brought by Muhammedan doctors (Hakims) accompanying the invading army. The reason of its decline is obvious, for nothing can flourish without the support of the state. It was during the time of the Muhammedan rule (1001-1707) it seems that Indian first came in contact with the European nations. That first contact seems to be signalised by the introduction of that dire diseases — syphilis — in India. A Hindu doctor named Bhava Miśra, who flourished in about 1550 A.D. for the first time calls that disease Firangī Roga. *i.e.,* the disease of the Firangese, *i.e,* Portuguese. After the Muhammedan rule the Peshwas came in power (1715-1818 A.D.), and under them the old Indian medicine struggled to revive, and some important medical works were written during this period. After the Peshwas came the English and their advent in the 18th century brought about the death of that once famous and perfect medical science, because the English came with the preconceived notion that the Indian medicine was a quackery and the Hindu works on a subject, a repository of sheer nonsense. Not only did this notion prevail amongst the English people, but also amongst some Indians with a mentality that thinks that everything European is good, and everything Indian is bad; and who, because of such mentality have lost their confidence and national pride in the Indian medicine. It is something to be thankful for that there were and still are a few Englishmen with reasoned and well balanced judgment, and Indians with national pride who hold a different opinion of Indian medicine. As an example of what some Indians think of it let us quote from the report of the Committee appointed by the Madras Government to report on this indigenous medical system. They reported that "the indigenous system of medicine is perfect, logical, and scientific from the stand-point of science and art, and that it is quite self-sufficient and economical; and that they are of opinion that only through the promotion of the Indian system that the Government can help to achieve the idea of bringing medical relief in the reach of all people." A better refutation of the charge that Indian medicine is a quackery, one could not wish for. But if one must have it, it lies in the existence of an actual college in Delhi for teaching this system; and in the opinion of Sir John Woodroffe, the late Chief Justice of Bengal. He says, "The country abounds in valuable herbal and other remedies. Āyurvedic remedies are effective, as I personally know in respect to those which I have tried. They do not harm as some allopathic drugs do for nothing is a medicine in Āyurveda which in any case is harmful. Like all Indian things they are gentle and natural in action; they are cheap, easily available, to be had almost for the cost of gathering them." But no, all that will not do. "Give me English Medicine," as a sick servant of mine said, for faith in his own had gone. And so the dispensaries distribute, and private persons purchase Western allopathic medicine brought from thousands of miles away at a cost which, compared with the local remedies, is great. One of the things we most regret is the neglect of Āyurvedic teaching, the loss of valuable remedies, and the great experience and knowledge of the pulse of the best old time Kaviraj. We hear now of factories of Indian drugs. The Western idea again ! But no factory can equal the hand preparation of Indian remedies extending over great lengths of time. The charitable dispensary with its imported medicine, is but only one out of many instances of that lack of faith in one's own, which is one of the most obvious causes of the inert and dependent condition of this country. A man or people who have no faith in themselves will not and do not deserve to succeed. For he who has no faith must lean on another. A man who says he is not fit to do a thing cannot do it. Meanwhile if people prefer imported medicines, and being opened out with great skill by Western Surgeons and their Indian disciples, that is their affair. It may be that surgical operations are in some cases and in the last resort necessary. But the country can get along without foreign drugs. Perhaps some European with his enterprise and ability will take in hand the indigenous drugs. He will probably then find the usual imitators. Some time back an Indian friend told me that a German traveller had taken away from the Kangra Valley a number of rare Rasāyana Tantras. Why, asked my friend sarcastically, was he troubling his head over things which had been "exploded by science", for to many science is always "exploding" something or other. His reply was instructive : "We will perhaps recast what is there and send it back to your country." Those who now reject will certainly receive anything Indian, if it is presented with western impremature. Even the Upanishads had need of such a "chit". Though its adherents do not recognise it, this chit-system is symbolic of a wide spread evil — the dependence on what others and nor we ourselves approve. Such, was the indigenous system of medicine, which some persons dare to call a quackery. There are now no two opinions on the glorious civilisation that India enjoyed when Europe was in a barbarous state. Talking of it to the Englishmen coming out to India Sir Monier Monier-Williams had said that "India has a polished language, a cultured literature, an abstruse system of philosophy centuries before English existed even in name." It is hard, nay it is absolutely impossible, to believe that India possessing as it deed such language literature, and philosophy, could for its medical system encourage quackery.

It is often argued by medical and other people that when we have a good system in Western medicine, why try and put life in the petrified bones of the old Indian medicine which is a dead science. But Indian medicine is not dead. It is yet alive, though not fully awake to-day. It is precisely because it is a living force that it provokes antagonism from those who dislike, or fear its culture. Does any one now fume against or ridicule the medical systems of Greece, Egypt, Persia or Arbia? They are left, as things which are dead and gone, to the scientific dissection of the cool historian. But while touching Indian medicine even the scholars could not be impartial. Why? Because Indian medicine is not the mere subject of academic talk, but is a living force. Indian medicine is still feared where she is not loved. Why again? Precisely because she lives, because she is still potentially powerful to impose her ideas upon the world. She is still an antagonist to be reckoned within the conflict of medical cultures. Why has she with her pathology, so unique and so different from any other of the West been preserved? Indian medicine lives because of the world purpose which she has to fulfil : because the world be enriched by what she can give to the other medical system." It deserves to be preserved and investigated in the right spirit of seekers after Truth. When that is done it will be seen that the Western medicine has yet more to learn from the old Aryan Medical Science.

Ayurvedic Literature

Charaka Samhita. Charaka Samhita is a huge treatise on ancient Indian medicine. It contains eight divisions (ashtanga sthanas) *viz.,* sutra, nidana, vimana, sharira, indriya, chikitsa, kalpa and siddha sthanas. Each division is further divided into numerous chapters. It describes not only the existing knowledge about medicine in all aspects but also the logic and philosophy behind the medical system.

The present manuscript of *Charaka Samhita* has a long history behind it. It was originally composed by Agnivesha, one of the six students of Atreya, and it embodied the teachings of the latter. Agnivesha's treatise appears to have been available till the eleventh century, as Chakrapanidatta, its commentator, quotes from it.

With the passage of time, as new knowledge accumulated, it looks, it was felt necessary that *Agnivesha tantra* should be revised. This was done by Charaka and the revised edition of *Agnivesha tantra* came to be called *Charaka Samhita.*

During the ninth century, *Charaka Samhita* was again edited and reconstructed by a Kashmiri Pandit named Dridhabala, son of Kapilabala, a resident of Panchanadapura, now known as Panjor sitauted seven miles north of Srinagar. The present form which *Charaka Samhita* has, was given to it by Dridhabala. He not only added the missing chapters but also edited the whole samhita.

Charaka Samhita deals elaborately with subjects such as foetal generation and development, anatomy of the human body, function and malfunction of the body depending upon the equilibrium or otherwise of the three humours of the body, *viz.,* of *vayu, pitta* and *kapha.* It describes etiology, classification, pathology, diagnosis, treatment of various diseases and the science of rejuvenation of the body. It discusses elaborately the etiology of diseases on the basis of the *tridosa theory.* It gives a detailed description of the various diseases including those of the eyes, the female genital organs, normal and abnormal deliveries and diseases of the children. Charaka's materia medica consists chiefly of vegetable products though animal and earthy products are also included in it. All these drugs are classified into 50 groups on the basis of their action on the body.

This vast treatise also gives an idea of the various categories of the practitioners of the healing art, specialization in different medical subjects, physicians and their fees, nursing care, centres of medical learning, schools of philosophy such as Nyaya and Vaiseshika which formed the fundamental basis of medical theories, medical botany and classification of the animal kingdom, particularly in regard to properties of their flesh etc. It also describes various customs, tradition, legends, routine of daily life, habits of smoking and drinking, dress and clothing of the people of that era.

Commentary on *Charaka Samhita* by Chakrapanidatta, called *Charaka Tatparya-Tika* or *Ayurveda Dipika,* done in the eleventh century (1066 A.D.), is very famous.

Charaka Samhita was translated from Sanskrit into Arabic in the beginning of the eighth century and its name *Sharaka Indianus* occurs in the Latin translation of Avicenna, Razes, and *Serapion,* Translation of the Karka from Sanskrit into Persian and from Persian into Arabic is mentioned in the Fihrst (finished in 987 A.D.). It is likewise mentioned by Alberuni. *Charaka Samhita* was first translated into English by A.C. Kaviratna in 1897.

Who Was Charaka ?

The life and times of Charaka are not known with certainty. Some Indian scholars have stated that Charaka of *Charaka Samhita* existed before Panini, the grammarian, who is said to have lived before the sixth century B.C. This, they say, on the basis that Panini mentioned the name Charka in some of the sutras which he wrote. But Panini is known to have mentioned it in connection with the followers of a branch of Vedas and not about the medical man Charaka.

By another theory, it is postulated that Charaka of *Charaka Samhita* is identical with Patanjali. This theory is based, it seems, on confusion in interpretation. Patanjali, who is also said to have expounded the science of Yoga, was said to be the incarnation of Sesha, the cosmic serpent. As Charaka was also considered an incarnation of Sesha, both have been amalgamated into one identity, by some people.

Another school argues that Patanjali wrote a commentary on the medical work of Charaka, which is corroborated by his commentator, Chakrapanidatta. They say that if Patanjali lived around 175 B.C., Charaka must have lived some time before him. But in this argument as well, as confusion prevails. The name Patanjali comes in connection with three things : commentary on *Charaka Samhita,* a grammar and *Yoga Sutra.* The author of all three works is regarded by some as one person; others regard the grammarian also the author of *Yoga Sutras;* still others regard the medical writer as the author of *Yoga Sutras.* Till such time as we can sort out the true identity of Patanjali, who commented upon *Charaka Samhita,* it is difficult to fix the date of Charaka from this reference.

Another source about the identity of Charaka and his times is provided by the French orientalist Sylvan Levi. He discovered in the Chinese translation of the Buddhist *Tripitaka,* a person name Charaka who was a court physician to the Indo-Scythian king Kanishka, who in all probability reigned in the second century A.D. On the basis of finding this name there, Levi concluded that he was the man whose name is associated with *Charaka Samhita.* Some doubts have also been raised by scholars about this hypothesis. First there is no evidence to identify him with the author of the samhita or with anywork, at all. Secondly, if he were the author of this samhita, he would in all probability, have mentioned the name of the king in his book in an appropriate manner, as being a royal physician he depended on the king for the honour provided to him and for other things. Thirdly, as Buddhist influence predominated in Kanishka's court, there would have been some evidence of it in the Samhita also, which is not so.

From the above discussion, it would seem that Charaka may have lived between the second century B.C. and the second century A.D. Till such time as further and more conclusive evidence is available, to narrow down this period would not be justifiable.

Susruta Samhita

This treatise is the main source of knowledge about surgery in ancient India. *Susruta Samhita,* as we know it now, is not in the original form which Susruta gave it and which he called *Shalya Tantra;* Susruta's *Shalya Tantra* was later revised and supplemented as well.

Susruta's *Shalya Tantra* consisted of only five divisions, *viz., sutra, nidana, sharira, chikitsa, and kalpa.* Later addition of *uttara-tantra* consisting of three divisions called *shalakya, bhuta-vidya* and *kalamara-bhrtya,* makes eight divisions in the present *Susruta Samhita.*

Of the commentaries on *Susruta Samhita,* the most renowned is that of Dalhana called *Nibandha Samgraha* written in the twelfth century. Another commentry is by Chakrapanidatta written in the eleventh century. It is called *Bhanumati* and only a portion of it is available now.

Susruta Samhita was translated into Arabic before the end of the eighth century A.D. It was called *Kitabshaw-shoon-a Hindi* or *Kitabi-i-Susrud.* Rhazes, the famous Arab physician, often quoted from it and mentioned Sarad as an authority on surgery. It was translated in Latin by Hassler and in German by Ullers.

It was translated into English, in part only, by U.C.Datta (1883), A. Chattopadhyaya (1891) and Hoernle (1897). K.L.Bhisagaratna translated it in full between the years 1908 and 1917 and it is this translation which is available now.

Who was Susruta, the composer of *Shalya Tantra* and when did he live, is not known with any certainty, but for a hint here and there. In connection with the bones of the human body, Susruta in *Susruta Samhita* introduces his own exposition with a remark pointing to the difference between the Atreya system and his own in respect of the total number of bones. This proves that Susruta could not have lived before Atreya. Another hint is provided by *Shatapatha Brahmana* which seems to be acquainted with Susruta's enumeration of bones. The exact date of *Shatapatha Brahmana* is not known, but it is said to belong to the sixth century B.C. If that is so, Susruta may have lived around the time when Agnivesha composed his tantra under the direction of Atreya.

Susruta of *Shalaya Tantra* was a great surgeon, teacher of repute and an admirable author. He made great improvements in the general techniques of surgery and performed many new and major operations. He also described a variety of surgical instruments.

He taught his students the surgical techniques first on the dummies and later on the dead bodies. His techniques of dissection of the human body are unique, practical and revealing of the structure of the body. His operations of making a new nose or ear-lobe, of lithotomy, of taking out the dead foetus, and abdominal operations, are classical marvels.

Before Susruta's time, knowledge and practice of surgery in India was more or less of the same standard as in other contemporary civilizations like Egypt, Mesopotamia and Greece. In India, the profession of healing was practised by surgeons *(shalya vaidas),* physicians *(bhesajas)* priest doctors *(bhisaj atharvana),* poison-curers *(vishaharas)* and demon doctors *(krtyaharas).* To practise their art, these professionals had to go out into the open streets, calling out for patients. They lived in houses surrounded by gardens of medicinal herbs. Surgery was not considered a respectable profession before Susruta's time.

Bhela Samhita

Bhela was one of the six students of Atreya, alongwith Agnivesha. He is said to have composed a treatise called *Bhela Samhita.* This was not traceable for many centuries, but in the year 1880, a palm leaf manuscript of it, composed in Sanskrit but written in the Telugu script was found in the Palace Library at Tanjore. This manuscript, written about 1650, abounds in mistakes and some of it has been disfigured beyond recognition. But whatever has survived gives evidence of the same ancient tradition as *Charaka Samhita* does. It has also eight divisions like the *Charaka*, and each section ends with : "Thus spake Atreya" as it is in *Charaka Samhita.*

Bhela Samhita essentially corroborates what *Charaka Samhita* says. Occasionally, it differs from it in some details.

The practice of Ayurvedic medicine entered a new phase when instead of the samhitas on medicine and surgery, compendia of prescriptions for various diseases began to appear. The first of such treatises which we have with us now is *Nava Nitaka.*

Nava Nitaka or Bower Manuscript

This manuscript was discovered by a man of Kuchar, an oasis of Eastern Turkestan in Central Asia on the caravan route to China. This route was used by the Buddhist monks of India travelling to far off places. This man dug in the hope of getting some treasure in an area supposed to contain an underground city. He did not find any wealth but discovered a manuscript which was bought for a small sum by L.H. Bower, who had gone there on a private mission from the Government of India. The manuscript was forwarded to J.Waterhouse, the then president of the Asiatic Society. It was deciphered and published by A.F. Hoernle, who spent 21 years on its study. Afterwards, the manuscript was sold to the Bodlein Library in Oxford. This manuscript, collectively called *Nava Nitaka,* came to be known as the *Bower Manuscript.*

Nava Nitaka manuscript by its name or by its contents has been mentioned by different authors between the tenth and the sixteenth century. After that, this manuscript has not been mentioned by any one until it was re-discovered. The present manuscript is composed in very defective Sanskrit mixed with Prakrit. It was written in the Gupta script of the fourth or fifth century. The material on which it is written is birch bark, cut into longish folios like the palm leaves of southern and western India. The contents suggest Buddhistic influence in its composition.

According to Hoernle, the whole manuscript consists of not less than five distinct parts. The author quotes from *Charaka* and *Susruta* and *Bhela Samhita.*

The title 'Nava-Nitaka', meaning butter, is indicative of the manner of its composition; just as a small amount of butter is extracted out of milk, so does this work contain the essential formulae extracted from other larger works. According to one scholar, the author of *Nava-Nitaka* was Navanita.

Nava-Nitatka for the first time gives details about the use of garlic in various diseases such as consumption (*rajya yakshma)* and scrofulous glands in the neck. Tied with a thread, it was also hung on the door; this was supposed to check the spread of infectious disceases like small-pox. Garlic was recommended to be used in winter and spring.

Vagbhata

Vagbhata, according to ancient Indian medical tradition, is one of the three medical authorities (Vridha Trayi or old Triad), the other two being Atreya and Susruta.

While in ancient times, the two medical treatises namely *Ashtanga Samgraha* and *Ashtanga Hridya Samhita* were said to have been composed by Vagbhata, since the beginning of the present century, some scholars have stated that there were two Vagbhatas, each author of one of the two above treatises. A passage in *Ashtanga Hridya* gives that impression, but closer examination reveals the contrary evidence. Though the time of Vagbhata cannot be stated with certainty, the consensus of opinion is to place him and his two treatises in the seventh century. Tibetan, Chinese and Arabian sources also lend support to this view.

Ashtanga Samgraha

It is still studied all over India, more so in the south. It is composed in a combination of verse and prose form. It is predominantly based on the teachings of *Charaka* and *Susruta Samhitas* though it also gives its own views on different topics. Commentaries on *Ashtanga Samgraha* were written by Arunadatta about 1220 A.D. and by Hemadari a few decades later.

Ashtanga Hridya Samhita

Like *Ashtanga Samgraha,* it is divided into *Sutra, nidana, sharira, chikitsa, kalpa,* and *uttara sthana,* following the tradition of Susruta, and not of Charaka. It contains 120 chapters and the author quotes Charaka, Susruta, Bhela, Nimi, Kasyapa, Dhanvantari and other earlier authors and their works; the chief source, however, is *Ashtanga Samgraha.* It gives a complete but concise description of Ayurvedic medicine. Particular stress is laid upon surgery. It does not mention the use of opium in the treatment of diseases and feeling of the pulse for diagnosis. Use of 'killed' (oxidized) metals is also not given in it.

Sutra-Sthana of *Ashtanga Hridya* is especially famous and popular. A popular later couplet says : "The best authorities in medicine are Madhava for nidana (diagnosis), Vagbhata for sutra sthana (theoretical basis or general principles), Susruta for sharira (structure of the body) and Charaka for chikitsa (treatment)."

Ashtanga Hridya has all along been a very popular treatise. Commentaries on it have been written from time to time by as many as 35 important Ayurvedic physicians, each one interpreting it to the best of his knowledge and experience.

Ashtanga Hridya was translated from Sanskrit into Persian in 1473 A.D. by Hakim Ali Mohammed Bin Ali Ismaili Asavali Aseeli, and dedicated to Mahmood Shah I, the ruler of Gujarat.

Ashtanga Samgraha and *Ashtanga Hridya,* particularly the latter, indicates an advancement in knowledge over the two samhitas of Charaka and Susruta. This is particularly noticeable in the new drugs and some of the new surgical procedures that have been introduced. These treatises of Vagbhata were extensively used and, in fact, they overshadowed the earlier samhitas to the extent that some portions of them were lost never to be recovered. Later writers like Sharangadhara, Chakrapanidatta and Bhava Misra quoted these treatises repeatedly in their works.

Madhavakara

The time of Madhavakara, son of Indrakara, cannot be stated with certainty. Vagbhata mentions Charaka and

Susruta but not Madhava. Madhava, on the other hand, does not mention anything about Dridhabala's edition of *Charaka Samhita.* So Madhava came after Vagbhata but before Dridhabala. Furthermore, Vrinda knew about Madhava. These indirect sources indicate that Madhava may have existed in the ninth or tenth century A.D.

Rug Vinishchaya, Madhavakara's famous treatise, is written in simple language and style. It is easily understandable by ordinary physicians and became very popular and came to be known as *Madhava nidana* or simply *Nidana.* It specializes in the diagnosis of the diseases. The order in which it describes the causes, symptoms and complications of the important diseases sets an example for the future authors such as Vrinda, Vangasena and Chakrapanidatta. Its description of diseases shows a significant advancement compared with that of *Charaka* and *Susruta Samhita.*

A special chapter is devoted to small-pox, which previously was described only in a minor way. It, however, literally quotes, many a time, Charaka and Susruta, which shows the borrowing it made from these sources.

In later times, numerous commentaries were written on Madhava's *Nidana,* which indicate the fame and popularity of this work. The most famous of these commentaries was *Madhukosh* by Vijayaraksita and his pupil Srikanthadatta in the fourteenth century. The other commentary *Antak-darpan* by Vachaspati also belongs to the later half of the fourteenth century.

Dalhana

Dalhana, commentator of *Susruta, Samhita* probably lived in the tenth century A.D. He belonged to Mathura. He is said to be the son of Bharatpala. His commentary *Nibandha Samgraha* is still considered as an important work. Chakrapanidatta refutes some of the theories that were put forward by Dalhana, but he does not mention the name of Dalhana.

Vrinda

Vrinda composed a treatise called *Siddha Yoga* probably around 1000 A.D. This treatise is a medico-chemical work which incorporates some of the material from Charaka, Susruta, Vagbhata, Madhavakara and Nagarjuna. This became very popular. A commentary called *Kusumavali* was written on it by Sri Kanthadatta around fourteenth century A.D. The commentator states that *Sidha Yoga* makes a particular mention of the diseases prevalent in western India; may be Vrinda belonged to that region. *Siddha Yoga* is in the nature of a samgraha and follows the methods of Vagbhata and others and gives a survey of the classical method of treatment. This is the first large treatise dealing with the prescriptions; in it Vrinda prescribes mercury for internal use.

Siddha Yoga of Vrinda was considered to be very important treatise. It was among the books translated into Arabic.

Chakrapanidatta

Around the middle of the eleventh century (1066) flourished an Ayurvedic physician Chakrapanidatta who composed a large number of treatises on different aspects of Ayurveda. Chakrapanidatta has given an account of himself in his book called *Chikitsa-sara-samgraha* : "The author of this work is Chakrapani who belongs to the family of Lodhravati, and who is the youngest brother of Banu and the son of Narayana, the superintendent of the kitchen of Nayapala, the king of Gour". His teacher was Naradatta.

Influence of Tantric Cult

With the decline of Buddhism in India, there appeared a popular philosophical and religious movement called tantrism. Though it originated earlier, it flourished between the eighth and the fourteenth centuries. It was a pan-

Indian movement through which the devotees sought deliverance with the help of *mantra, samadhi* and other practices.

With tantrism, developed the art the science of the use of metallic compounds, particularly of mercury and sulphur. This was with the intention of making the human body undecayable and ever-young. The adepts in tantrism were said to possess miraculous powers and were called siddhas. There were many such siddhas, but the one most renowned among them was Nagarjuna.

Nagarjuna

Nagarjuna is said to be the author of *Rasaratnakara.* From the internal evidence of this book, it appears, it is a work composed after the time of Vagbhata, *i.e.,* in the eighth century. Alberuni mentions of a Nagarjuna, resident of the fort Daibhak near Somnath, who composed a book *Rasayana.* According to him, this Nagarjuna lived about a hundred years before his times. It appears, Nagarjuna lived sometimes between the eighth and ninth century A.D.

Nagarjuna composed some other works also, which include *Kakshaputa Tantra* and *Arogya Manjari.* According to Dalhana, a commentator of Susruta, Nagarjuna reconstructed *Susruta Samhita* and added Uttara tantra to it.

Rasaratnakara deals with the preparation and use of metallic compounds, more particularly of mercury (*rasa*). It describes certain recipes in which vegetable or animal products are used to transform other metals into compounds which look like gold and could be passed off as gold. These compounds, particularly of mercury, were prepared and used in order to make the body undecayable and strong.

Nagarjuna was quoted as an authority on rasayana by later authors such as Vrinda and Chakrapani.

Uptil the seventh and eighth century, Ayurvedic drugs consisted mainly of vegetable products. Metals, such as iron, silver, tin and lead, were very sparingly used for medical purposes. Use of metallic compounds particularly began with Nagarjuna and it increased progressively.

Sharangadhara and Nadi-Pariksha (Pulse Examination)

The earliest Indian medical treatise to mention of nadi-pariksha is of the twelfth century. *Sharangadhara Samhita* compsoed by sharangadhara some time between the thirteenth and fifteenth centuries describes different types of pulse in different disease conditions. This treatise is important also for several other reasons.

Sharangadhar. The published manuscript mentions Sharangadhar as the son of Damodhar. But the manuscript itself does not reveal the name of the author. Another treatise called *Sharangadhara padati* mentions the author's ancestral background. In the territory of Shakambari was a king named Hamir. He had in his court one Raghavdev who had three sons named Topal, Damodar and Devdas. Damodar again had three sons named Sharangadhar, Laxmidhar and Krishan. Sharangadhar was the author of *Sharangadhar Paddhati.*

Sharangadhara Samhita is not a tantric treatise though the author devotes the "Madhya khanda" to a detailed description of metals and their purification, mercury and the methods of 'swooning', 'killing' and fixing of mercury. It follows the orthodox system of therapeutics of the ancient classical authorities, but admits into the indian pharmacopoeia, important drugs like mercury and opium, and utilizes them in therapy.

It also marks certain important advances in the physiology of respiration, in medical diagnosis and therapeutics. *Sharangadhara Samhita* was translated into Hindi, Gujrati, Bengali and Marathi; this shows that it was very popular.

Two commentaries on *Sharangadhara Samhita* were written : one by Adhamalla called *Dipika* in the thirteenth century, the second by Kashiram called *Gurartha Dipika* in the sixteenth century.

Bhava Misra

To the middle of the sixteenth century belongs Bhava Misra whose treatise *Bhavaprakasha* is an important medical work. Bhava Misra is the last of the great men of Indian Medicine. He was the son of Lataka Misra and lived at Varanasi in the year 1550 A.D. He was considered as "a jewel among the physicians" and the best of the scholars of his time. He is said to have taught and trained at least 400 students in medicine.

In his important and voluminous treatise called *Bhavaprakasha* he describes the best of the available material of the previous authors and sets forth his own views and experiences. It is also divided into three khandas (parts) : purva, madhya and uttara. In it the author systematically deals with the origin of Indian medicine, cosmology, human anatomy, embryology, physiology, pathology, medicine, diseases of the children, surgery, Materia Medica, therapeutics, dietetics, rejuvenants and elixirs to prolong life. His clear style and excellent arrangement of the subject matter has thrown a flood of light on many obscure and disputed views of the ancient writers. He describes *nadi-pariksha* (examination of the pulse) and also the use of mercury and opium.

By the time of Bhava Misra, foreigners from European countries, particularly Portuguese, had started pouring into Indian to enrich themselves by commercial pursuits. Many of them, however, were suffering from syphilis and so passed on the disease to the Indian population also. Indian physicians were quite unfamiliar with this scourge and all their previous medical treatises were silent on this subject, even though they did describe other diseases of the genital organs. A new name was needed for this malady and as this disease was brought into the country by the Portuguese, it was called *Phiranga roga.* Mercury in the form of calomel, catechu, Spilanthese oleracea and honey in certain proportions are the recommended medicines. Certain other recipes are also mentioned.

Bhava Misra's *Bhavaprakasha* is still popular and is consulted by Ayurvedic physicians in India. He composed another small pharmacological work called *Gunaratnamala.* It mentions China root called Tobchini in the vernacular, as a remedy of "phiranga roga." He was the first to mention certain drugs of foreign countries as badhkashani naspasi, khorabani and parasika vacha (Acorus calamus), sulemani kharjura (date fruit of Suleman) and opium. Surgery is mentioned only in brief.

A copy of *Bhavaprakasha* dated 1558, according to Jolly, was available in Tubingen.

Ayurveda in Buddhist Literature

Buddhist religious books such as *Vinaya Pitaka, Deepavamsa, Mahavamsa* and others provide glimpses of the practice of medicine among the Buddhist monks during the life time of the Buddhist and afterwards.

Mahavagga also gives an account of the physician Jivaka. It decribes his birth, childhood, medical training and treatment of the Buddha and the monks by him.

Jivaka

He was a famous physician of India in the sixth and fifth century B.C. He was said to be the son of Salavati, a courtesan of Rajagriha (near modern Patna) which was the capital of Magadha empire in the reign of Bimbisara. After his birth, Jivaka was thrown on a dust heap where people noticed that he was still alive (*jivati*). The matter was reported to the prince Abhaye, son of Bimbisara. The prince gave him the name of Jivaka, and had him brought up under his own care. That is why Jivaka is also described as Jivaka Kumarabhacca, meaning 'the one brought up by the Prince.'

When he grew up, Jivaka learnt of his antecedents and without informing the prince left for Taxila, the famous Indian centre of learning at that time, situated near Rawalpindi (now in Pakistan). There he studied medicine for seven years under 'a world renowned physician'. At the end of that period, he underwent a sort of practical examination. His teacher asked him to take a spade and go round Taxila for one *yojana* on every side and seek and bring to him any plant which did not possess medical properties. Even after a good deal of investigation, Jivaka could discover no such plant and reported the matter to his teacher.

His teacher was satisfied and gave him the licence to practice medicine and also a little money which could only meet part of his expenses for the journey to his home town. This money sufficed to bring Jivika upto Saket (near Faizabad district in the U.P.) and there he was forced to earn for himself.

One the way, Jivaka treated at Saket, a merchant's wife who had headache for the past several years and got a handsome reward, which, on reaching home, he presented to his patron prince. He cured Emperor Bimbisara of his piles and Chandapajjota, the emperor of Avanti kingdom of his jaundice. He is said to have performed surgical operations on the head and abdomen as well. He treated the Buddha for his wound on the foot as well as of an abdominal disease. He treated Buddhist monks as well.

Other Buddhist scriptures that mention about the practice of medicine are the *avadanas.* They form part of the religious literature of the Mahayana Sect of Buddhism. One such avadana called *kunalavadana* describes a discase that emperor Ashoka suffered from and how its remedy was discovered. Once the emperor became seriously ill. Faecal matter started coming out from his mouth and his whole body smelled of putrid matter. Thinking that he would die of this disease, he wanted to send for his son Kunala from Taxila. Queen Tishyarakshita got terrified as she knew that if Kunala came, he would kill her. She told the emperor that he should not worry much and she would get him well. He should, however, stop seeing his physicians and depend upon her for treating him. The emperor agreed.

Queen Tishyarakshita asked physicians to bring a patient to her who had complaints similar to those of the emperor. When they brought such a patient, she had him killed and then examined his whole body carefully. In his intestines, she saw a large worm which would occasionally obstruct the passage and thus cause faecal matter to be thrown out by mouth. She poured over the worm peppers, *pipali* and then *sondh,* but it would not die. At last when she poured crushed onion over it, it died. Now the queen requested the emperor to take onion as a remedy for his disease. Initially he resisted, saying that as a Kshtriya he could not take onion but ultimately, he took it, and got rid of the disease.

Medical Education

In ancient India, one could become a physician by following any one of the following procedures : he could learn the art and science of it from a teacher by living and working with him in his house; he could go to a *gurukula* where the students lived together with the teachers in the schools situated in the forests away from human habitation; he could join one of the medical centres located in the large cities such as Taxila, Kasi (Varanasi) and Nalanda.

Taxila situated about 20 miles west of Rawalpindi (now in Pakistan) was the most important seat of learning in ancient India dating from the sixth century B.C. It attracted students from all corners of India, *viz.,* from Rajagriha, Mithila, Kashi, Ujjain, Kuru, Koshala etc. Its fame had spread far and wide in foreign countries; students from there were said to come here to learn. The medical school there enjoyed a special reputation, but all arts and sciences could be studied under the most eminent professors.

Nalanda was another centre of learning which flourished from the fifth to twelfth century A.D.

Great care was taken in the selection of the candidates for admission in these centres of learning. The most capable teachers were on the selection committee whose members were called *Dwara Pandits, i.e.,* those who guarded the entrance. A candidate belonging to the family of physicians was preferred. The age at the time of admission to medical studies was 16.

The students were taught theory as well as practice of medicine equal importance being given to both.

Practical training of a student had three objectives ; (1) preparation of medicines, (2) training in surgery, and (3) examination of the patients. The student learnt the art of preparing flower juices and intoxicating liquors. Concocting different herbal combinations, making medicines using sugarcane or clarified butter *(ghee),* reducing to ashes stones, minerals and the like, preparing combination of minerals and herbs, combining and isolating minerals, making new compounds of minerals and extracting the alkalies out of the minerals. He was also trained in planting, grafting and general care of plants, as also recognising different herbs and when and how to cut and preserve them.

For practical training in surgery, different surgical procedures were taught on different objects : incisions were taught by making cuts on gourds (*pushpaphala, alavu),* watermelon, cucumber; excisions were demonstrated by making openings in the body of a full water bag or in the bladder of a dead animal or in the side of a leather pouch full of slime or water; scraping was taught on a piece of skin on which the hair has been allowed to remain; venesection *(vedhya)* was taught on the vein of a dead animal, or with the help of a lotus stem; probing and stuffing was taught on worm eaten wood, on the reed or bamboo, on the mouth of a dried *alavu* (gourd); extracting was taught by withdrawing seeds from the kernel of a *vimbi, vilva* or jack fruit, as well as by extracting teeth from the jaws of a dead animal; evacuating was taught on the surface of a *shalmali* plant covered over with a coat of bee's wax; suturing was taught on pieces of cloth, skin or hide; bandaging or ligaturing by tying bandages round the limbs and on a full -sized doll made of stuffed linen; tying up a severed ear lobe *(karna-sandhi)* was demonstrated on a soft severed muscle or on flesh, or with the stem of a lotus lilly; cauterising or applying alkaline preparations (caustics) was demonstrated on a piece of soft flesh; the art of inserting syringes and injecting enemas into the region of the bladder was taught by asking the student to insert a tube into the mouth of a gourd *(alavu).*

After the period of training was over, there was an examination consisting of theory as well as practicals. An example of a practical examination is found in Jivaka's biography. Here Atreya asked his pupils "to go to the pine hill and fetch from it that which is no remedy." While other students did bring certain things, Jivaka came back empty handed, saying there was none that was not a remedy for one disease or the other. Jivaka was declared successful.

Theoretical examination was conducted by asking the candidate to explain a page from a manuscript. This particular page was lifted out by means of a rod; hence this test came to be known as *shalaka* test. Degrees were awarded to the successful candidates at a special ceremony (*samavartana),* during which they were charged with the following oath.

Acting at my behest, thou shalt conduct thyself for the achievement of the teacher's purpose alone, to the best of thy abilities.

If thou desirest success, wealth and fame as a physician and heaven after death, thou shalt pray for the welfare of all creatures beginning with the cows and Brahmins.

Day and night, however, thou mayest be engaged, thou shalt endeavour for the relief of the patient with all the heart and soul. Thou shalt not desert or injure thy patient even for the sake of thy life or thy living. Thou shalt not commit adultery even in thought. Even so, thou shalt not covet others's possessions. Thou should not be a drunkard or a sinful man, nor shouldst thou associate with the abettors of crimes. Thou shouldst speak words that are gentle, pure and righteous, pleasing, worthy, true, wholesome and moderate. Thy behaviour must be in consideration of time and place and heedful of past experience. Thou shalt act always with a view to acquisition of knowledge and the fullness of equipment.

No person who are hated of the king or who are haters of the king or who are hated by the public or who are haters of the public, shall receive treatment; similarly those that are of very unnatural, wicked and miserable character and conduct those who have not vindicated their honour and those that are on the point of death, and similarly women who are unattended by their husbands or guardians shall not receive treatment.

No offering of meat by a woman without the knowledge of her husband or guardian shall be accepted by thee. While entering the patient's house, thou shalt be accompanied by a man who is known to the patient and who has his permission to enter, and thou shalt be well-clad and bent of head, self-possessed, and conduct thyself after repeated consideration. Thou shalt thus properly make thy entry. Having entered, thy speech, mind, intellect and senses shall be entirely devoted to no other thought than that of being helpful to the patient and of things concerning him only. The peculiar customs of the patient's household shall not be made public. Even knowing that the patient's span of life has to come to its close, it shall not be mentioned by thee there, where if so done, it would cause shock to patients or to others.

Though possessed of knowledge, one should not boast very much of one's knowledge. Most people are offended by the boastfulness of even those who are otherwise good and authoritative.

There is no limit at all to which knowledge of Ayurveda can be acquired; so thou shouldst apply thyself to it with diligence. This is how thou shouldst act. Again thou shouldst learn the skill of practice from another without carping. The entire world is the teacher to the intelligent and the foe to the unintelligent. Hence knowing this well, thou shouldst listen and act according to the words of instruction of even an unfriendly person, when they are worthy and such as bring fame to you, and long life, and are capable of giving you strength and prosperity.

Before a qualified physician could start practice, he had to have the permission of the king. This was to safeguard the people from the nuisance of the quacks.

Anatomy

Description of the human anatomy, as it appears in samhitas, is fairly rudimentary. Total number of bones, inclusive of teeth and nails in the body, according to Charaka, is 360, but according to Susruta, it is 300.

Muscles of the body are just mentioned as fleshy masses. Heart was supposed to have only one cavity in it and ten vessels ran from it to different parts of the body. Mention of the structure of function of the brain is negligible. Though lungs are mentioned, they are not supposed to be concerned with breathing. Knowledge of *marmas,* the vital spots or centres where a hurt or injury could prove very dangerous, was widely prevalent.

Embryology

Indian physicians state certain views and record observations about the conception and development of the fectus in the uterus of the mother. Their views on the subject of embryology have not stood the test of time; on the other hand, what they observed themselves and recorded is substantially correct. Here are some of the observations in this regard:

If at the time of fertilization, the blood (*sonita)* of the mother predominates in the embryo, the result is a girl; if the semen predominates, it is a boy; a hermephrodite is born when the semen and the blood are in equal measure, or if the productive power of the semen has been burnt up. If the seed gets divided into two or more portions, then two or more children are born.

If the conception occurs during the even days of menstrual cycle, a male child is born; on odd days, it is female. The reason for this is the fact that the menstrual fluid flows less on even days, hence a male; it is more on odd days, hence a female. As a corollary to that, if a couple desire a son, they should have intercourse on the 4th, 6th, 8th, 10th or 12th night, and for a daughter on the odd nights.

Intercourse on the 13th and subsequent nights is deprecated. The fourth night after the start of the menstrual period in a woman is considered as the most auspicious for having intercourse. This, however, is contrary to modern scientific views which state that ovulation occurs between the 13th and 17th days after the start of menstruation, and accordingly on the fourth and many subsequent days till ovulation occurs, the intercourse would be without conception.

Whether a son or a daughter would be born to a pregnant mother, has excited the curiosity of all concerned at all times. Ancient Indian texts describe observations which, according to them, can clarify this mystery. Birth of a male child is predicted if the pregnant woman raises the right foot first while walking; if the right eye looks larger; if she evinces a longing for thigs with a masculine name; if she dreams of receiving flowers of any masculine name; if her face becomes brighter; if the milk is first detected in the right breast.

Desire for the company of females, bulging of the foetus on the right side of the abdomen, manly temper and actions also indicate a male child. Conditions opposite to the above indicate a female child. If the sides of the abdomen become raised, and the forepast is found to bulge out, a sexless child is predicted. If the middle part of the abdomen is sunk or divided in the middle like a leather bag, twins may be expected.

Charaka and Susruta describe the gross development of the foetus during each month of pregnancy. These observation they must have made on the foetuses passed out in abortion cases.

Physiology

According to Ayurveda, the food which we take and also our bodies, are composed of five elemental entities (*bhutas)* namely, earth (*prithvi),* fire (*teja),* water (*apa),* wind (*vayu)* and ether (*akasha).* These five elemental entities in the body exist in the form of substances (*dhatus),* namely, *rasa,* blood, flesh, fat, bone, marrow and semen. Function of the food is to nourish these *dhatus,* maintain their equilibrium and sustain the digestive function. Food which is taken, is first converted into *rasa* and then in turn, into blood, flesh and other *dhatus.* During the process of digestion, a sweet reaction set in. This gives rise to the production of foamy phlegm (*kapha).* A little later, when food is half-digested, sour reaction sets in and from the food in the intestine is produced a liquid substance called (*pitta)* (bile). Lower down in the intestine, the digested food is converted into a dry mass and during this process, a bitter and astringent reaction sets in, which gives rise to the production of wind (*vata).* This is how the three above-mentioned *dosas* namely, *kapha, pitta* and *vata* are produced.

Function of Dosas. The three *dosas* perform very useful functions in the body. The role of wind (*vata*), which is of five types, is to provide active energy to perform the function of movements, inhalation and exhalation of breath, speech, throwing out of urine and faeces, *pitta* (bile) helps in digestion, provides heart to the body and gives good eye sight, good complexion, cheerfulness of mind and intelligence, *kapha* (phlegm) gives normal oiliness to the body, sprightliness to the joints and body, normal weight, sexual power strength, capacity to bear or endure.

The three *dosas* may exist either in equilibrium or any one of them may predominate in a person. While in a person's constitution phlegm predominates, he has a body which is oily, smooth, delicate, clean and agreeable to look at. When bile predominates, the person is incapable of bearing heat, the body is dry and delicate. When wind predominates, the person has body which is dry, lean and small-sized. Possessor of a body in which different *dosas* are in equilibrium remains generally healthy.

Causation of Diseases

Excessive, deficient or faulty exposure of the senses (touch, taste, smell, hearing and sight), inclement weather conditions, misuse of intelligence such as it witnessed in taking improper dict, act on the three humours, namely, wind, bile and phlegm and lead to their dis-equilibrium which in turn reacts upon various substances (*dhatus)* of the body. This gives rise to the production of various diseases. This is called the *tridosa* theory.

Diseases have been classified in various ways. The internal diseases are due to the predominance of any one of the humours and these may be easily curable, curable with difficulty and incurable. They may be accidental, caused by demons. They may be violent or mild.

The following interesting mythological story tells as to how consumption descended on human beings and animals. Daksha Prajapati, married his 27 daughters to the god Moon. Moon, however, loved only one of his wives and gave all attention to her. The other wives, in frustration, reported the matter to their father who rebuked his son-in-law for his unworthy monogamous habits. But it had no effect. Eventually, the father-in-law lost his temper and created a demon of consumption to eat away and destroy Moon. Moon, when he realised his predicament, promised to lead the desired married life and thus though saved yet remained liable to periodic progressive consumption. The demon of consumption descended on the earth to find his pray among human beings and animals.

Diagnosis

Charaka laid great stress on the proper examination of the patient and his environments with a view to arriving at the diagnosis of the diseases, before the treatment was prescribed. According to him, a physician who failed to enter the body of the patient with the lamp of knowledge and understanding could never treat diseases. The physician should pay heed to inducing causes, prodormal symptoms, constitution of the patient, the diseases which he is generally liable to suffer, age of the patient, his vitality, the season in which he got the disease and all other relevant factors while prescribing medicine, diet and routine for the patient to follow.

Prognosis

Prognosis of the patient suffering from any disease was made after keeping in view the physical state of the patient, diagnosis of the disease, the accompanying environment as well as the omens and the dreams which the patient had.

Materia Medica

Charaka's Materia Medica consisted chiefly of vegetable products, though animal and mineral products were also used. All these drugs were classified into 50 groups on the basis of their action on the body. The drugs were given in various forms such as powder, paste, infusion, decoction, pill, confection, roast, fermented, distilled, medicated and alcoholic drinks, medicated oil or *ghee* and inhalants as well as injections into the rectum, urethra and female genital organs. The aim of the drugs or other regimens was to help maintain or being back normal balance between various *dhatus* and *dosas.*

Treatment

While proper drugs and diet are essential in bringing about a cure, they by themselves are not enough. There are other factors, too, upon which depends the success or otherwise of the treatment. *Kasyapa Samhita* describes all the factors upon which the outcome of the treatment depends.

According to it, there are four pillars of treatment. When these four pillars have the requisite qualities, then a curable disease will not be left uncured. These four pillars are : physician, medicine, patient and attendant.

Drugs and other therapeutic measures can be administered not only by mouth but through other routes also. Indian physicians administered liquid medicines into the rectum, the urethra and the vagina, and the inhalations and fumigations in the nose. They are applied dry and wet heat to the body by means of different ingenious procedures.

Application of caustics, in many cases, was considered, as a better procedure than surgery. This was recommended in different skin diseases, haemorrhoids, fistula-in-ano, other fistulas, abscesses, mouth and throat diseases etc.

Alkalies were prepared from vegetable products, essentially from the ashes of the burnt wood of certain trees. The final product was of mild, medium or strong potency depending upon the need.

Cauterization (burning the part) was considered even better than the application of alkalies in certain cases. According to *Susruta Samhita,* a disease burnt with fire is cured for good and knows no recrudescence : and diseases which ordinarily baffle the skill of a surgeon of a physician; and never prove themselves amenable to medicinal or surgical remedies, are found to yield to fire. Burning the part — cauterization — is particularly prescribed in cases of tumours, fistula, swelling of testicles, elephantiasis, swollen glands, decolourisation of the skin, bad wounds or ulcers, ophthalmia, headache, haemorrhoids and other diseases. This was done by means of red hot iron of various shapes, burning medicinal sticks *(varti),* cow's tooth *(godanta)* and different crystalline stones *(surya kanta).* Fluid substances like honey, syrup, oil and wax brought to a boiling point, were also used. The part could be cauterized in circles, points, lines or the whole surface depending upon various indications and contra-indications.

Indian physicians bled the patients suffering from abscesses, enlargement of the spleen, and inflammations of different parts of the body. This they did by applying leeches, by cupping, sacrification or by cutting the superficial veins.

Application of leeches was the safest method of letting out the blood, and caused no pain. This was used in infant and old people of those of timid nature, or where the patient was too weak to stand any operation.

Careful attention was given to recognizing whether an inflamation had supporated or not, as successful treatment, according to them, depended largely upon that. Signs and symptoms of a suppurated abscess are described in great detail. An abscess was opened only when it had suppurated and was localised. The physician who opened an unsuppurated or unripe swelling out of ignorance, as well as a man who neglected a fully suppurated one, was looked upon as the vilest *chandala* (low born) for his wrong or incorrect diagnosis.

Susruta Samhita describes 14 different types of bandages. Fifteen different materials were used for bandages, including the barks of the trees. Knots of the bandages were advised to be tied away from the wound. The students practised tying the bandages over the dummies provided for the purpose.

There are certain wounds over which bandage is contra-indicated. There are leprosy wounds, those caused by burns, diabetic carbuncles, wounds caused by the bite of rats, alkali wounds, poisoned wounds, those having severe inflammation of the muscles, decaying wounds, spreading wounds and those at the anal region.

According to *Susruta Samhita,* a bandage plays a more important part than a medicinal plaster as regards its healing and curative efficacy, inasmuch as it materially contributes to the purification and healing of an ulcer and keep the joint steady.

Management of fractures is dealt with elaborately in *Susruta Samhita.* Immobilization was provided by means of splints.

Susruta describes some of the major surgical operations with precise skill and steps. While only limited means were available at that time yet these operations looked nothing less than marvels even now.

Abdominal Operations. In a case, where the abdomen has perforated and the intestines are protruding, as a result of injury to the abdomen, Susruta recommends that "they (the protruded intestines) be gently re-introduced into the abdominal cavity and placed in their original position. In case the intestines have perforated, according to some practitioners, large black ants should be applied to the perforated part. After they have firmly bitten the perforated parts with their claws, their bodies should be separated from their heads. After that the intestines should be rinsed with milk so as to remove any foreign body attached to them such as grass, dust, blood, cloth etc., and lubricated with *ghee* and gently pushed back into the cavity and reinstated in their original position."

Removal of the stone from the urinary bladder was practised. To remove fluid from the abdomen, paracentesis was done. Craniotomy of the foetus was undertaken if the foetus died inside the uterus. In case of cataract, the lens was displaced in the vitreous.

Plastic Surgery. The surgical techniques of Susruta, which attracted the attention of the world most, were those which we now categorize under plastic surgery. Making a new nose or a new ear out of the flesh from the adjoining parts in cases where the original had been cut off, is described by Susruta. "For making a nose, the leaf of a creeper, long and broad enough to fully cover the whole of the severed or clipped off part, should be taken, and a patch of living flesh, equal in dimension to the preceding leaf, should be sliced off (from down upwards) from the region of the cheek, and after sacrifying it with a knife, swiftly adhered to the severed nose. Then cool-headedly, the physician should tie it up with a bandage decent to look at and perfectly suited to the end for which it has been employed. The physician should make sure that the adhesion of the severed parts has been fully effected, and then insert two small pipes into the nostrils to facilitate respiration, and to prevent the adhesioned flesh from hanging down. After that, the adhesioned part should be dusted with the powders of *pattanga, yashtimadhukam* and *rasanjana* pulverised together; and the nose should be enveloped in cotton and several times sprinkled over with the refined oil of pure sesamum.

"Clarified butter should be given to the patient for drinking and he should be anointed with oil and treated with purgatives after the complete digestion of the meals he has taken. Adhesion should be considered complete after the incidental ulcer had been perfectly healed. The nose should be again sacrified and bandaged in the case of a semi or partial adhesion. The adhesioned nose should be tried to be elongated where it would fall short of its natural and previous length, or it should be surgically restored to its natural size in the case of an abnormal growth of its newly formed flesh."

Śusruta's technique of making the new nose was being practised in India till lately. Description of this operation was published in the *Gentleman's Magazine* in 1794, and after that a leading surgeon of London, Joseph Constantine Carque, published his results in 1816, which led to the world-wide publicity for the technique. Later on, many modification of the technique were adopted and a new science of plastic surgery took birth.

Rasāyana and Vajikarana

Besides the drugs and prescriptions for the treatment of diseases brought about by *dhatu vaisamya,* Indian medical treatises describe two other classes of medicines called *rasayana* and *Vajikarana* for the general toning up of the system of healthy persons.

These medicines are not specifics for any particular disease but are intended to improve the strength of the patients and to alleviate diseases in general.

Rasāyanas have the capacity to impart superior *rasa* and *dhatus* to the body. They are elixirs of life for preserving and increasing vigour, restoring youth, improving memory and preventing diseases. About them, *Susruta Samhita* states: " A wise physician should (invariable) prescribe some sort of tonic (rasayana) for his patients in their youth and middle age after having their systems (properly) cleansed by the applications of a *sneha* and purifying remedies (emetics and purgatives); he should not, in any case, have recourse to such tonics inasmuch as they would fail to produce the wished for result, just as the "application of dye to a piece of dirty cloth will prove non-effective."

"Vajikarana is for increasing virile strength. A youth in sound health taking regularly some sort of vajikrana remedy may enjoy the pleasures of youth every night during all the seasons of the year. Old men, those wishing to enjoy sexual pleasures or to secure the affections of women as well as those suffering from senile decay or sexual incapacity, and persons weakened with sexual excesses should do well to submit themselves to a course of vajikarana remedies. They are highly beneficial to gay, handsome and opulent youths and to the persons who have got many wives. If duly taken, vajikarana remedies make a man sexually as strong as a horse (*vaji)* and enable him to cheerfully satisfy the heat and amorous ardours of young maidens, a fact which has determined the nomenclature of this class of (medicinal) remedies".

Surgical Instruments

Susruta Samhita describes surgical instruments under two main heads : Blunt (*Yantra*) and Sharp (*Sastra)*.

There are 101 blunt instruments, each one having a specific name. They are divided into six categories as follows :

1. Cruciform (*Swastika),* 2. Forceps (*Sandamsa),* 3. Pick Lock like (*Tala*), 4. Tubular, 5. Probes (*Salaka),* 6. Accessory instruments (*Upayantra).*

There are 20 sharp instruments.

According to *Susruta Samhita,* a good instrument should have a well made handle, affording a firm grasp; it should be made of iron of good quality; it should have a fine edge, a pleasant shape and a well finished point; and it should not be dented (except the saw). It should not be bent, or broken or jagged, or too thick, or too thin, or too long, or too short.

For keeping the instruments properly, boxes or covers made of wood, silk, leather or wool were used, each instrument being properly separated from the other.

Toxicology. Effects of poisons, of vegetable or animal origin, on human body were studied extensively by Indian physicians in ancient times. For this aspect of medicine, they were famous throughout the world. The most renowned medical man in the kingdom, the royal physician, was always an expert toxicologist. One of his main duties was to protect the king against being poisoned. He resided inside the palace compound and checked all the dishes served to the king. Whenever the king, with his army, went on a battle, it was the duty of the royal-physician to go with him and to keep a check on the kitchen. He also tested drinking water from tanks and wells to see that it was free of any poisonous matter that might have been put in by the enemy agents.

Veterinary medicine

Animals received good medical care in ancient India. They were cared for because they were of paramount importance to the individual, the society and the king, in times of peace as in times of war. Upon cattle depended life in the homes of milk, as much as in the fields for gricultural operations. In the battle fields, many a time, victory depended upon the superior force of the elephants and the horses. Not only the physicians but also the kings and the princes, were well-versed in veterinary sciences. King Nala had a surname Ashvavit, *i.e.,* one who is well-versed in the science and care of the horses. Nakula and Sahadeva, the twin sons of Madri, were taught by Drona the art of curing, training and managing the horses and the cattle. To Nakula is ascribed the work called *Ashva-Chikitsa,* which is still extant. King Romapada, the contemporary of Dasaratha of Ayodhya, is known to have learned *Gajayurveda* or *Hasti Ayurveda* meaning the treatment of the elephants, from the sage Palakapya.

During those days, physicians treating human beings were also trained in the care of the animals. Indian medical treatises like *Charaka, Susruta* and *Harita Samhitas* contain chapters or references about care of the diseased as well as the healthy animals. There were, however, physicians who specialised only in the care of the animals or even in one class of animals; the greatest of them all was Shalihotra, the father of veterinary sciences.

Shalihotra is described to be the son of a Brahmin sage, Hayagosha. He is said to have lived in Sravasti (modern Sahet Mahet on the borders of Gonda and Bahraich district in the Uttar Pradesh). Some other sources describe Salihotra to have lived in Salatur, a place near Kandahar. Shalihotra and Agnivesha are described to be the pupils of the same teacher; others say that Susruta was Shalihotra's pupil.

Shalihotra is known to have been a specialist in the treatment and other aspects of the horses. He composed a treatise called *Haya Ayurveda* or *Turangama-Sastra* or

Shalihotra samhita, a work on the care and treatment of the horses. True to Indian tradition knowledge embodied in *Haya Ayurveda* is also said to have been revealed to Shalihotra by Brahma himself, the fountain head of all knowledge. Two other works, namely *Asva-prashnsa* and *Asva-lakshana sastram* are also attributed to Shalihotra.

Haya-Ayurveda was accepted as a standard work on the subject in ancient times. Some chapters of it have been quoted in *Agni-Purana, Matsya* and *Garuda Puranas* also refer to this treatise. This work of Shalihotra was later translated into Persian, Arabic, Tibetan and English languages. The fame of Shalihotra and his work spread so much that in certain places the word Salotri still stands for a horse doctor. Some of the later authors have named their veterinary works after Shalihotra and others have based their work on his saṁhitā.

Hasti Ayurveda or Palakapya Samhita, composed by Palakapya, is devoted solely to the care and description of the elephants. It is divided into four sections and 152 chapters. It contains more than 10,000 verses or 20,000 lines and is almost as big as *Charaka Samhita.* It gives detailed information about the anatomy, physiology, pathology of diseases, surgical and medical treatment, and care and diet of the elephants.

The Indian and the Greek Systems of Medicine

Some of the similarities between the Greek Medicine and the Indian Medicine are so striking that exchange of ideas between the two or the influence of one on the other, is difficult to deny.

Historical tradition suggests that the ancient Indians and the Greeks knew about each other, to a certain extent, even before the sixth century B.C., if not directly, at least through an intermediary. About 519 B.C., the Achaemenidean king, Darius I, is known to have sent a

Greek sea-faring man, Skylax of Karyanda to the Indus Valley to explore the possibility of conquering the region. Since that time and after the conquest of the Indus region by Darius I, the Indians and the Greeks came in close contact with each other as both had parts of their lands and peoples under the Persian empire.

The Greek physicians are known to have lived at the court of the Persian kings and the Indian troops were among those whom Xerxes led against Greece in 480 B.C. Such contacts between the two proples continued till the time of Alexander. It was during this period that Hekatcus of Miletus, Ktesias, Herodotos and others heard about India. Herodotos even describes a meeting in the presence of the king at the court of Susa between Greeks and Indians discussing through interpreters the best way to treat corpses.

Further evidence of the exchange of medical ideas between the two civilizations is witnessed in their medical treatises. Study of the samhitas of Charaka and Susruta reveal many analogies between the Indian and the Greek systems of medicine.

Hyppocratic treatises do not quote any Indian medical doctrine while they mention Indian drugs, *e.g.,* Kardomomen, Amomon, Peperi, Kinnamonos, Akoras, Sesamon etc. Nevertheless, we may admit the probability of an exchange of doctrines as we find in other books of Hippocratic collection, teachings closer to the Ayurvedic system than to most of the Greek ones. It is most clear in the case of a treatise, called *Peri-Phuson,* which means 'About the winds'.

At the time of Alexander's invasion of India, the Greeks knew thoroughly well the achievement of Indian physicians on the subjects concerning hygiene, diet, snake bites and also the veterinary Indian art regarding elaphants.

Some similarities between the Indian medical theory of *tridosa* and the Greek humoural theory have led to many comments and controversies as regards the borrowings of one from the other system of medicine.

There are many fundamental and essential differences between the Greek theory of humours and the *tridosa* theory. The Indian theory starts with *pancha bhutas* or five elements, *viz.,* air, earth, fire, water and ether. The Greek theory starts with four elements, *viz.,* air earth, fire and water. The Indian *dosas* form a triad (except with Susruta), whereas the Greek humours form a tetrad. The *dosa* are *vayu* (air), *pitta* (bile) and *kapha* (phelgm); the humours are blood, phlegm, yellow and black bile. Blood is an important humour in the Greek theory, while it is considered as a *dhatu* in the Indian theory. Air does not form one of the Greek humours, while it is the most important in the Indian theory. Besides, there is a fundamental difference in the conception of the production of diseases by the humours. The *dosas* by themselves cannot produce any disease; they must be disordered by their respective *nidanas.* After they are disordered, they vitiate the *dhatus* or the constituents of the body and produce disease in them. In the Greek theory, it is the disequilibrium of the humours that constitutes disease. Thus it will be seen that while the similarities are superficial, the differences are fundamental.

The Indian and the Arabian System of Madicine

During the reign of Harun-al-Rasheed (786-814 A.D.), the Abbasid Caliph, Baghdad was the most important city of the Arab world, and one of the most important cultural centres of the world. The Barmecid family of Indian physicians then occupied a very important place in his court. The Barmecids were the descendants of the chief priest (Pramukh, Arabicized Barmak) of the Buddhist temple at Balkh. The first Barmak to acept Islam was probably Khalid. The Barmecids encouraged the Indian physicians to come to Baghdad. They also translated into Arabic and Persian many of the Indian medical classics.

Indian physicians occupied high positions in Baghdad hospitals. They were popular both among the chiefs as well as the common people. Many stories are recorded of the cures they brought about when others had failed. It is said Harun-al-Rasheed himself once suffered from some serious disease which baffled the talents of the practitioners of the Greek system of medicine in Baghdad. At last, at the suggestion of his courtiers, a physician from India was called by the Caliph who was treated by him and cured.

Manka was one of the most well known Indian physicians. He knew the Persian language and culture as well as his own. He was attached to the hospital of the Barmecids and had cured many a noble with his remarkable skill in healing. He translated many Sanskrit books into the Persian and Arabic languages and was amply rewarded by the Caliph. Later on the embraced Islam.

Ibn Dhan was another prominent Indian physician, contemporary of Manka. He was called to Baghdad by Yahya, the Barmecid, and was made director of a hospital. He also translated many works.

During the ninth and the tenth century A.D., Indian medicine and medical men were held in high position. This is also stated in the works of some of the Arabian scholars of this period.

That the Arabians regarded highly the achievements of Indian medicine, is also witnessed by the fact that since the early part of the ninth century, many of the Arabic and Persian treatises on medicine devoted chapters to the Indian system of medicine as well.

The Yoga Doctrine and Patanjali

The aim of Yoga, as given in the beginning of the *Yoga*

Sutras, is the intentional stoppage of all the spontaneous activities of the mind, which by its very natural is in constant agitation like the surface of a pond broken by a breeze. In order that it should stand still, it is necessary that all the sense impressions coming from outside as well as the stimuli from within should stop completely. When this is achieved, the God stands revealed like a jewel lying at the botton of a quiet pond.

To achieve this end, Yoga doctrine recommends certain physical and mental disciplines which can be undertaken in eight successive stages. The first two stages are of self-restraint (*yama*) and observance of the rules of conduct (*niyama*), which are intended to overcome egoistic impulses and to lead to detachment from worldly objects. This having been achieved through constant practice, the next three stages, namely right and steady posture (*asana*), regulation of breathing (*pranayama*) and withdrawal of senses (*pratyahara*) are designed to gain control over mind. The essential point about different postures is to keep the backbone straight. As patterns of breathing and different thought processes such as agitation or calmness were noticed to be inter-related, control over breathing was considered to confer control over thought processes.

Withdrawal from distractions arising from within or from without by different sense perceptions such as of touch, taste, smell, hearing and seeing was considered analogous to the withdrawl of its limbs by the tortoise and thus its protection from the outside world.

After this has been attained, the next two stages, namely, steady mind (*dharana*) and contemplation (*dhyana*) are meant to assist in getting a gradual mastery over the fitful mind.

For contemplation, the object chosen may preferably have certain definite qualities (*saguna*); it may be an image or an idea. During this stage, the outside world for a yogi vanishes and the senses no longer perceive it. In the next and final stage (*samadhi),* the mind merges with the object of contemplation and time and space are said to be overcome.

Different stages in this process are regulated and adjusted by the preceptor (*guru)* according to the fitness of the disciple. The last stage can be achieved only by very few.

Hatha Yoga texts state that from the base (*muladhara)* in the perineal region, there run upwards towards the nose two channels (*nadis)* along the left and right side of the back bone. The left channel is called the *pingala* or the solar channel (*surya nadi)* and the right channel the *ida* or lunar channel (*chandra nadi).* There are also a series of six centres (*chakra),* from below upwards situated along the back bone whose locations are as follows : in the sacral region (*muladhara),* a little above lumber region (*svadhisthana),* opposite the naval (*manipura),* near the heart (*anahata),* in the throat (*visudha),* and opposite the junction of the eye brows (*agya).* There is a very final channel (*sushumna)* travelling in the centre of the back bone which enters the head through a hole in the skull.

During the stage of *pranayama,* the sponataneous activity of breathing becomes more and more infrequent and *prana* withdraws itself from the mouth to inside the body and is stored in the two channels the *ida* and the *pingala.*

By the pressure of its presence at the base (*muladhara)* of these channels *prana* awakes the pent up and coiled energy (*kundalini),* which resides there. Then in the successive stages of Yoga, this energy rises up step by step through the central fine channel (*sushumna)* and the various centres along the backbone and goes into the centre in the head (*brahmandhra).* When this happens, the yogi attains illumination.

Such a theory, describing the two channels starting at the nostrils and ending near the lower end of the back, where they enter in the spinal marrow, is not intended to convey the anatomy of the respiratory organs. This theory resulted from experiences during the process of yoga practice.

In praise of the Yoga practice, Swami Vivekananda said: "There is not a single muscle in the body over which man cannot establish perfect control by practice; even the heart can be made to stop or go on at yogi's bidding."

This long and arduous course of physical and mental discipline is, no doubt, known to benefit its enthusiasts in various ways. *Asanas* and *pranayama* are said not only to lead to a healthy youthful body and prolong life, but also to give relief from or even cure many bodily ailments. Some yogis have been seen stopping the beating of their hearts and holding their breath completely. They could maintain themselves alive and healthy for days together in underground chambers and then they could revive themselves after a stipulated period.

It has been shown under precise experimental conditions that yogis can voluntarily manoeuvre their body in such a way that their heart sounds cannot be heard and the pulse cannot be felt. This they have been shown to do by forcefully rataining in the inspired breath which tremendously increases the pressure in the chest cavity so that the veins which take the blood to the heart are completely obstructed by this pressure.

The heart thus gets and in turn pumps out less blood and its feeble beat is not heard or felt as pulse in the forearm or anywhere else. The heart in X-ray looks smaller but it does continue beating, though feebly, as has been recorded on the electrocardiogram. It has also been shown that the yogi when placed in hermetically sealed chamber reduced the consumption of oxygen or production of carbondioxide by reducing very much the essential activity of the body organs by means of some control over the functioning of the autonomic and endocrine systems which are regulated by the brain.

Control over the physical and mental processes of the body by the yoga practices is an idea and technique perfected and given by ancient India to the world. It carries with it potentialities of understanding some of the so-called supernatural phenomenon which are now being actively studied in India and abroad under the science of parapsychology.

Patanjali, the expounder of *Yoga Sutras,* is known to us through different legendary descriptions, in some of which he has been identified with and in others distinguished from his name-sake who composed the great commentary *Mahabhasya* on Panini's Sanskrit Grammar. He probably lived and composed *Yoga Sutras* in the second century B.C. The basic ideas and techniques of Yoga are, however, found in some of the earlier Upanishads and can ever be traced back to the *Atharvaveda.*

Atomic Theory of Kanada

Kanada, also known as Aulukya and Kashyapa, was son of sage Uluka. He lived around sixth century B.C., at Prabhasa in Allahabad. He was the pupil of Soma Sharma, who was said to be an incarnation of Lord Siva. Kanada lived the life of an ascetic and for his daily bread collected grains from the public streets. That is why he came to be known as Kanada, Kanabhuk or Kana-bhaksha, meaning one who feeds on particles. A mythological story says that by such severe austerities, he pleased Lord Siva, the Omniscient, who imparted to him the knowledge about the constituents of which the universe was made of and also asked him to make a treatise embodying those truths for the benefit of mankind. Thus Kanada composed the *Vaiseshika Sutras* the first systematic work of the Vaiseshika philosophy.

According to Kanada, everything in the universe is made up of *pramanus,* the real entities which are obtained when a thing is divided and sub-divided until further division is not possible. *Pramanus* of different kinds have different characteristics but individually they cannot be perceived through any of the organs of sense perception not can they exist in a free state. They are eternal and indestructible. (By the above characteristics, the word atom in English language is the approximate equivalent of *pramanu.) Pramanus* combine together in various fashions and it is by their combination that they give rise to the creation of the universe and its contents which we see and perceive. Elaborate discussions of the peculiar characteristics (*vasisha* means peculiarity) of the different kinds of *pramanus* and their various combinations give the name Vaiseshika to this philosophy.

In Kanada's view, whatever is in the universe, can be broadly placed under six categories, namely, substance (*Dravya),* Quality (*Guna),* Action (*Karman),* Generality (*Samanya),* Particularity (*Visesha),* and Co-inherence, *i.e.,* intimate relation of the constituent part (*Somavaya).*

Further, substances can be subdivided into nine entities, namely Earth (*Kshiti),* Water (*Apa),* Fire or Heat (*Teja),* Air (*Vayu),* Ether (*Akasha),* Time (*Kala),* Space (*Dik),* Mind (*Mana),* and Soul (*Atman).* The words earth, water and air denote all substances which are solid, liquid and gases, Earth, water, fire, air and ether have respectively the specific and distinguishing properties of smell, taste, colour, touch and sound. The first four are composed of four kinds of *pramanus.* Ether, space and time are imperceptible substances, each of which is eternal and all pervading. Combination and separation of the *pramanus* explain the origin and destruction of various objects in the world.

Different substances are endowed with different qualities which are represented by 24 varieties, *viz.*, colour, taste, smell, touch, sound, number, magnitude, distinction, conjunction, disjunction, remoteness, nearness, fluidity, viscocity, cognition, pleasure, pain, desire, aversion, striving, heaviness, tendency, merit and demerit. Action in a substance is a movement which may be of various kinds. Generality is the eternal essence common to all the things of a class and Particularity is the unique individuality of the eternal entities. Co-inherence is the intimate relation of the constituent part of the whole.

Kanada also propounded his views regarding the way in which combination of *pramanus* of one or different class of substances occur. One pramanu unites with another under an inherent impulse to form what we may call as binary molecules (*dvynukas*). *Pramanus* of the same type of substance uniting in pairs give rise to molecules with homogeneous qualities corresponding to the original qualities of the *pramanus,* provided no chemical change under the action of heat (*teja*) takes place. The binary molecules then combine among themselves by groups of three, four, five etc. to produce larger aggregates and thus a variety of elementary substances are created. *Pramanus* may also unite in pairs, triads, tetrads, etc. either directly or by the successive addition of one *pramanu* to each preceding aggregate, leading to the formation of binary, tertiary and quaternary molecules etc. The variety of elementary substances of the same class. *e.g.,* of earth is thus the consequence of the difference in their molescular composition and configuration.

Elementary substances thus produced by primary combination may, however, undergo qualitative transformation (chemical change) due to combination with heat *(teja),* by the process of decomposition into original *pramanus,* a transformation of the character of the *pramanus* and the reunion of the transformation *pramanus* into different groups or arrangements with development of new characteristic properties. This is witnessed when a newly made earthen pot is originally put into fire and it changes its colour and other characteristics or when a raw mango is kept covered under some thick warm cloth and it changed its colour, taste, smell and consistency; each change being due to differences in combination with heat *(teja).*

Combination may also take place between molecules of two or more substances belonging to the same or different class, leading to the formation of a variety of compounds which constitute various natural products.

This is how, in a nutshell and simple way, the universe is formed out of the different *pramanus,* according to Kanada's theory.

4

Origin Of Vedic Medicine

The art and science of medicine is as old as the mankind itself. Disease and injury have been part of our life and the measures taken to treat them coincided with the march of civilization.

As yet we know very little about the practice of medicine during the Harappā Civilization in India. In the absence of decipherment of the Harappā seals, a few snippets of information point out to the practice of primitive medicine at the time. A few medicinal finds which might have been used to treat patients are *śilajātu,* leaves of *neem* tree [*Ȧzadirachta indica*], antlers of the red deer, etc. Skull bones into which holes had been drilled when the persons were alive (trepanning) have been recovered from the Harappā sites. Possibly they were the cases of first surgery on human body.

We are, however, better informed about the preventive aspects of medicine in this period. The discovery of an advanced drainage system, both inside the house and outside, with properly covered drains, toilets in the corner of the house, straight and wide paved streets in a planned township establish the awareness about sanitation and hygiene for healthy living among the Harappans.

It is possible that when the Harappan seals are deciphered, we know more about the curative aspect of medical practice of the period.

We are much better informed about the concepts and practice of medicine during the Vedic period. No medical text as such pertaining to early Vedic period is available. But the latter-day Vedic Samhitās, Brāhmanas and Upaniṣads throw light on the concepts of origin of life, birth, death, disease and suffering.

Two main sources of early medical knowledge are the *Rigveda* and the *Atharvaveda.* The *Kauṣika sūtra,* the *Śatapatha Brāhmana* and the various upaniṣads also contribute to knowledge. However, much of what we learn is a mixture of myth, legend and empirical knowledge and it requires proper screening to sort out valid facts.

The following account gives an idea about the concept and practice of medicine in this period. It also reveals the beginning of the Āyurvedic system of medicine.

Cosmic Nature of the Human Body

Through the ages, in India, the human body has been considered as the manifestation of divine energy. The principal forces and faculties which abide in the body, giving it life and supporting its processes, are considered microcosmic counterparts of the powers which pervade the cosmic body, the universe. Such a concept is witnesed in a variety of myths and speculations. An hymn in the *Rigveda* describes the origin of the universe from the body of a primeval being, the Puruṣa.[1] According to it, the gods, in the beginning of time sacrificed Puruṣa. As they divided him, his head became heaven, his feet earth, his ears became space, his eyes the sun, his breath the wind-god, and so on.

Another Vedic source describes that at the dawn of Creation, the divine guardians of the world spheres, *loka pālas,* emanated from the body of Puruṣa and entered as sense-faculties and life-forces of the human body. Fire became speech and entered the mouth, wind became breath and entered the nostrils, the sun became sight and entered the eyes, the quarters of space became hearing and entered the ears, plants and trees became hair and entered the skin, the moon became mind and entered the heart, death became breathing down *(apana)* and entered by navel, waters became semen and entered the male organ.[2]

The following hymn for the *Atharvaveda* describes this process more elaborately.[3]

When (in the beginning of time) the Divine Craftsman drilled the apertures (which are the outlets for the sense faculties and vital processes of the human body), the gods took the mortal for their house and entered man.

Sleep, forsooth, weariness, bane, the divinities evil by name old-age, baldness, hoariness entered the body, one after another.

Theft, ill-doing, wickedness, truth, sacrifice, and great fame, strength and valour and force entered the body one after another.

Luck and ill-luck, increase and waning liberalities and illiberalities whatever there are, and all hungers and thirsts, entered the body, one after another.

Blaming and not-blaming and what is "Well" and "No", what is known and unknown, and what else is to be taught, entered the body one after another.

Delights, joys, enjoyments, laughing, dancing addressing and prating; breathing forward and breathing downward, sight and hearing, the indestructible and destruction, breathing asunder and breathing upward, speech, mind, entered the body, one after another.

Whatever waters there are and whatever divinities, the Lordly Power (of the Highest Being : Virāj), together with Brāhmana (the Supreme Essence) entered the body : the Lord-Creator dwells in the body [as the generative principle].

The Sun took possession of the eye, wind of the breath, each one as his own share [while the other forces of nature found their places in the organs and functions of the human body which correspond to them].

Then the divinities bestowed man's other [mortal] self [which is consumed on the funeral pyre] upon the Fire God.

Therefore, indeed on who knows man thinks "this is Brāhman' [the divine principle manifesting itself in al forms and activities of the universe], for all divinities have their abode in man, as cows in a cow-pen.

The concept of *prāna,* the sustainer of life processes in the microcosm, human body, as well as in the macrocosm, the world, is well described in an hymn, sung in its praise in the *Atharvaveda.*[4]

Reverence to *Prāna,* to whom all this (universe) is subject, who has become the lord of all, on whom the all is supported.

Reverence, O *Prāna,* to the roaring (wind), reverence, O *Prāna,* to thy thunder, reverence, O *Prāna,* to thy lightning, reverence, O *Prāna,* to thy rain.

When *Prāna* calls aloud to the plants with his thunder, they are fecundated, they conceive, and then are produced abundant (plants).

When the season has arrived, and *Prāna* calls aloud to the plants, then everything rejoices, whatsoever is upon the earth.

When *Prāna* has watere the great earth with rain,

then the beasts rejoice; (then think) : strength, forsooth, we shall now obtain.

When they had been watered by *Prāna,* the plants spoke in concert : 'Thou hast, forsooth, prolonged our life, thou hast made us all fragrant'.

Reverence be, O *Prāna,* to thee coming, reverence to thee going; reverence to thee standing, and reverence, too, to thee sitting.

Reverence be to thee, O *Prāna,* when thou breathest in, reverence when thou breathest out. Reverence be to thee when thou art turned away, reverence to thee when thou art turned hither; to thee entire, reverence be here.

Of thy dear form, O *Prāna* of thy very dear form of the healing power that is thine, give unto us, that we may live.

Prāna clothes the creatures, as a father his dear son. *Prāna* truly is the lord of all, of that breaths, and does not breathe.

Prāna is death, *Prāna* is fever. The gods worship *Prāna. Prāna* shall place the truth-speaker in the highest world.

Prāna is Virāj (power, lustre), *Prāna* is Deshtri (the divinity that guides) : all worship *Prāna. Prana* verily is sun and moon. They call *Prāna* Prajāpati (the creator of all beings).

Rice and barley are in-breathing and out-standing. *Prana* is called a steer. In-breathing, forsooth, is founded upon barley, rice is called out-breathing.

Man breathes out and breathes in when within the womb. When thou, O *Prāna,* quickenest him, then is he born again.

They call *Prāna* Mātarisvan (that swells in the womb); *Prāna* forsooth, is called *Vāta* (the wind) the past and the future, the all, verity is supported upon *Prāna.*

The holy (*atharvana)* plants, the magic (*angirasa)* plants, the divine plants, and those produced by men, spring forth, when thou, O *Prāna,* quickenest them.

When *Prāna* has watered the great earth with rain, then the plants spring forth, and also every sort of herb.

Whoever, O *Prāna* knows this regarding thee, and (knows) on what thou art supported, to him all shall offer tribute in yonder highest world.

As all these creatures, O *Prāna,* offer thee tribute, so they shall offer tribute (in yonder world) to him who hears thee, O farfamed one.

He moves as an embryo within the gods; having arrived, and being in existence, he is born again. Having arisen he enters with his mights the present and the future, as a father (goes to) his son.

When as a swan he rises from the water he does not withdraw his one foot. If in truth, he were to withdraw it, there would be neither today, nor tomorrow, no night and no day, never would the dawn appear.

With eight wheels, and one rim, he moves, containing a thousand sounds (syllables), upward in the east, downward in the west. With (his) half he produced the world : what is the visible sign of his (other half).

He who rules over this (all) derived from every source, and over everything that moves — reverence be to thee, O *prāna* that wieldest a swift bow against others (the enemies).

May *Prāna,* who rules over this (all) derived from every source, and over everything that moves, (may be) unwearied, strong through the Brāhma, adhere to me.

Erect the watches in those that sleep, nor does he lie down across. No one has heard of his sleeping in those that sleep.

O *Prāna,* be not turned away from me, thou shalt not be other than myself. As the embryo of the waters, (fire) thee, O *Prāna,* do bind to me, that I may live.

In the above hymn, the devotee in paying homage to his own *prāna,* first adumberates it as the cosmic life-principle, the Lord of all, whose enlivening forces manifest themselves most impressively at the rainy season. Then from the macrocosmic aspect of breath, the hymn turns to its activity in man. It mentions that *prāna* maintains beings as a father does a son. But since it is the paramount principle of nature, it incorporates the negative as well as the positive aspects of existence. *Prāna* is regarded as the unity of antagonistic principles. It is *prāna* that enables man to live while in the womb, and to be reborn. The hymn then announces the reward which is in store for the initiated who becomes aware of the power of breath and worships all its aspects, revering its very sound as perceived in its ceaseless rhythmical flow in his own organism and in the universal body. The hymn delves again into the secret nature of *prāna* as the supreme principle in man and the universe, enlarging on its different aspects. *Prāna* excels over the other divine powers which animate the human body as sense faculties and active 'agents'; for *prāna* alone partaking of the wisdom of Brāhma, remains unwearied and ceaselessly active, while the other tire and lie down, when man falls, asleep. *Prana,* man's inner swan (a bird which freely wanders between the water below and air above), remains faithful to the abode it has chosen in man's body, and if properly honoured, it never withdraws completely though free to do so.[5]

Structure of the Human Body

There are many instances in the Vedic texts that deal with the structure of various parts of the human body. The observations, however, are rather rudimentary. The following hymn in the *Atharvaveda* in a general way refers to different parts of the human body.[6]

By whom were brought the two heels of a man (*puruṣa),* by whom was his flesh put together, by whom his two ankle joints, by whom his cunning fingers, by whom his apertures, by whom his (two) *uchlakhas* in the midst, who (put together) his footing.

From what, now, did they make a man's two ankle joints below his two knee-joints above, separating his two back-things. Where forsooth, did they set him in, the two joints of his knees — who indeed understands that.

There is joined, fourfold, with closed ends, above the two knees, the pliant trunk; that the hips are, the thighs — who indeed produced that, by which the body became very firm.

How many gods (and) which were they, who gathered the breast, the neck-bones of man, how many disposed the two teats, who the two collar bones, how many gathered the shoulder-bones, how many the ribs.

Who brought together his two arms, saying "he must perform heroism", what god set on his two shoulders upon the body.

Who bored out the seven apertures in his head — these ears, the nostrils, the eyes, the mouth, in the might of whose conquest in many places quadrupeds (and) bipeds go their way.

Since in his jaws he put his ample tongue, then attached (to it) great voice : he rolls greatly on among existences, clothing himself in the waters who indeed understands that.

Which was the god who (produced) his brain, his forehead, his hindhead, who first his skull, who, having gathered a gathering in man's jaw, ascended to heaven.

The following verse from *Śatapatha Brāhmana* gives

direction for the construction of an altar in shape of a human figure. This indicates that an altar-maker was supposed to possess a fair amount of knowledge about human anatomy.[7]

The *trivrit* (stoma) is its head, whence that (head) is three-fold *(tri-vrit)* — skin, bone and brain.

The *pankadaśa* (fifteen-versed hymn-form) is the beck-joints — for there are fourteen of these (joints), and the vital force is the fifteenth; hence by means of that (neck), though being small, man bears heavy burden : therefore the *pankadaśa* is the neck.

The *saptadaśa* (seventeeen versed hymn-form) is the chest; for there are eight *gatru* on the one side, and eight on the other, and the chest itself is the seventeenth : therefore the *saptadaśa* (stoma) is the chest.

The *ekavimśa* (twenty-one versed hymn-form) is the belly, for inside the belly there are twenty *kuntapa,* and the belly is the twenty-first, therefore the *ekavimśa* (stoma is the belly.

The *trinava* (thrice-nine-versed hymn-form) is the two sides *(parśava);* — there are thirteen ribs *(parśu)* on the one side and thirteen on the other, and the sides make up the thrice ninth : therefore the *trimava* (stoma) is the two sides.

The *trayastrimśa* (thirty-three versed hymn-form) is the spine; for there are thirty-two *karukara* of that (spine) and the spine itself is the thirty-third : therefore the *trayastrimśa* (stoma) is the spine.

Following is the famous hymn of *Śatapatha Brāhmana* which gives the total number of bones in the human body. The relevant stanzas are as follows :[8]

And there are three hundred and sixty nights in a year, and three hundred and sixty bones in man, and these (two) now are one and the same; — there are three hundred and sixty days in the year, and three hundred and sixty parts of marrow in man and these (two) now are one and the same.

And there are seven hundred and twenty days and nights in the year and seven hundred and twenty bones and parts of marrow in man and these (two) now are one and the same.

The 360 bones are enumerated as follows : (1) heels, two in feet, (2) ankle bones, two, (3) digits, in pleural number, (4) matacarpal and metatarsal bones of hands, and feet, (5) base (*pratishtha),* (6) the knee caps, two, (7) the knee joints, (8) the shanks, two, (9) the pelvic cavity, (10) the thigh bones, two, (11) the breast bones, two, (12) the windpipe, in the pleural, (13) the breast, two, (14) the shoulder-blade, two, (15) the shoulder-bones, pleural, (16) the back bones, pleural, (17) the collar-bones, two, (18) the brow, (19) the central facial bone, (20) the pile of the jaw, the cranium with temples.

The *Śatapatha Brāhmana* mentions 26 ribs (*parśus)* which are fastened at either end to the thoracic vetebra at the back and anteriorly to the costal cartilages.[9] According to it, the vertebral column has three subdivisions : (1) the cervical (2) thoracic and (3) the lumber.[10] Ideas about the structure of the heart are rudimentary. Heart is said to be of shape of lotus with nine openings in it.[11]

Some of the upaniṣads describe the heart rather elaborately. It is said to be made up of flesh with a net-work structure.[12] It is like the wheel of a chariot, the spokes of which are like arteries emanating from it, the number of which is variously described as 101[13] and 72000[14] [along with the sub-branches], which pass out from the heart through the pericardium, with which the heart is covered.[15] Its weight is described to be 8 *palas* (870 grams) in *Garbha Upaniṣad.*[16]

Other organs mentioned in the *Atharvaveda* are the lungs, bronchi, gall-bladder, kidneys, liver, stomach, intestines, colon, rectum, urinary bladder. Semen was considered as "the thread of life".

As regards its function, in a prayer it is requested, "O Mitra and Varuna, take away the thinking power [*chit*] from the heart.

There are many references to the different types of channels that convey different types of body constituents. The *Brihadāraṇyaka Upaniṣad* describes that there is the finest essence of food juice inside the cavity of the heart. It is this essence which by penetrating into the finest *nādis* serves to support the body. Heart is surrounded by a net-work of *nādis* and from it (food essence) rushes upwards through the extremely find *hita nādis.*[17] The same *Upaniṣad* mentions that the *hita nādis* of the heart are as fine as a thousandth part of a hair and they carry white, blue, yellow and green liquids. The *Chhāndogya Upaniṣad* states that 101 *nādis* proceed from the heart.[18] The *Māṇdukya Upaniṣad* also speaks in the same tune when it states that like spokes in a wheel, *nādis* are connected to the heart.[19] The *Praśna Upaniṣad,* however, states that *vyana vāyu* (air) flows through 100 *nādis* connected with the heart.

The *Maitrāyaṇi Upaniṣad* mentions of a *sushumnā nādi* proceeding upwards towards the head through which flow *prāṇa.* The *Atharvaveda* mentions of two *gavinyān nādis* which carry urine from the kidneys to the bladder.[20] The words *dhamani* and *śira* have also been used on different occasions to denote the same meaning as *nādi* but it is difficult to assign a particular specific and different meaning to each of these terms.[21] In certain references the term *dhamani* has been used to denote a larger channel than the other two.

It was observed that the contents of the channels moved. A verse in *Atharvaveda* states : "Who stored in him floods turned in all directions moving diverse and formed to flow in rivers, quick, rosy, red and copper dark, running always in a man upward and downward".[22]

Diseases and Their Treatment

Generally speaking, different diseases, even accidents, were attributed to super-natural causes. Committing a sin in the present or even past life, transgression of the normal divinely-prescribed course of life, disrespect to gods, and the witchcraft of the enemies were some of the major factors that led to different diseases. Different gods, singly or collectively, by themselves or through the agency of various demons, made man suffer for the wrongs he did. Hereditary diseases were considered to be caused as a result of the sins committed in the past life by patient himself or by his parents.

Varuna, the cloud god could cause many diseases, but the one particularly attributed to him was dropsy, i.e., the swelling up of the whole body. Rudra's special way of inflicting illness was to shoot arrows at the victims, thus causing acute pain.

Takman was the god that caused fever.

While many of the symptoms themselves were considered as diseases, for example, dropsy, jaundice, retention of urine and cough, combinations of symptoms in a patient led to the diagnosis of a particular disease. Fevers that occurred on particular days, or those occurring continuously, diarrhoas of varying severity; consumption, leprosy, epilepsy, madness, and some of the diseases frequently mentioned in the *Atharvaveda*.

Fevers of different kinds seem to have been a common ailment. There were fevers preceded or accompanied by cold, or marked by a burning sensation all over the body, or occurring every alternate day, or leaving two afebrile days in between. Some fevers were accompanied by jaundice, and some others by cough and consumption. Some occurred only in the summer or in the autumn, and some others throughout the year. A very interesting observation from epidemiological point of view is that the regions named as Gandhara, Mahāvrisa, Maunjavan, and more particularly Balhika (Balkh) were regarded as the home of all sorts of fevers.[23]

In the *Rigveda* the mythical Aśvins were called the divine physicians.[24] They had remedies against various diseases.[25] They could even ward off death.[26] Their devotees reached old age with bright eye-sight and were blessed with riches and lots of children.[27] In the mythical account of their marvels, it is said that they could restore youth to the old. The debilitated body of the sage Chyavana was fortified with youth and made desirable to his wife again by the Aśvins.[28] In the same way they also invigorated aged Kāli.[29] Sage Rebha, after being stabbed, was hidden under the waters for ten days and nights, when the Aśvins pulled him up and revived him to health. They saved Vandana from a calamity, drew him out of a pit where he had been hidden away as dead and restored him a normal life.[30] They saved Sage Atri Sapta-Vadhri who, along with his companions, was thrown in the burning fires by a demon. They restored eye-sight to Rijrasva who had been blinded by his father because he had killed his father's hundred and one sheep to quench the appetite of a she-wolf.[31] They provided an iron leg to Viṣpalā, wife of khela king, whose own leg had been cut off in a battle.[32]

In the *Atharvaveda* are mentioned the procedures adopted to cure different diseases. They include incantations, charms, amulets, and herbs, both for external and internal use.

For the long life of a boy, the parents payed thus :

For thee alone, O (death from) old age, this (boy) shall grow up: the other hundred kinds of death shall not harm him! Like a provident mother in her lap. Mitra shall befriend him, shall save him from misfortune ! Lead this dear child to life and vigour, O Agni, Varuna and King Mitra ! As a mother, afford him protection, O Aditi, and all ye gods, that he may attain to old age ![33]

A cure was countered by a curse. A curse would be induced by giving a white lump of earth to a dog, an amulet tied to the cursed person, and oblation poured, or faggots of a certain plant consigned to fire,[34] and the following verse chanted.[35]

The thousand-eyed curse having yoked his chariot come hither, seeking out him that curses me, as a wolf the house of him that owns sheep.

Avoid us, O curse, as a burning fire (avoids) a lake! Strike here him that curses us, as the lightning of heaven the tree !

He that shall curse us when we do not curse and he that shall curse us when we do curse, him do I hurl to death as a bone to a dog upon the ground.

In order to cure dropsy, the following hymn mentioned in the *Atharvaveda* was recited to propitiate Varuna :

The golden chamber, King Varuna, is built in the waters.

Thence the king that maintains the laws shall loosen all shackles.

From every habitation (of thine). O king Varuna, from here do thou free us : If 'O waters, inviolable ones', if 'O Varuna' we have said, from this (sin) O Varuna free us...

Loosen from us, O Varuna, all fetters, the uppermost, the nethermost and those imposed by Varuna! Evil dreams and misfortune drive away from us : then may we go to the world of the pious.[36]

Besides the chanting of the hymn, a few rituals were obligatory for effective treatment. A hut was built at the confluence of two rivers. The dropsical patient was placed in this hut. An offering was made while the prayer was being recited. Then the patient was washed with the help of three bunches of grass, dipped in water.[37]

In order to get relief from the pain caused by Rudra's arrows, the following incantation was sung :

The arrow that Rudra did cast upon thee, into (thy) limbs and into thy heart, this here do we draw out away from thee.

From the hundred vessels which are distributed along thy limbs, from all of these do we exercise forth the poisons.

Adoration be to thee, O Rudra as thou casteth (thy arrow); adoration to thee (arrow) when it has been placed upon (the bow); adoration to it as it is being burled; adoration to it when it has fallen down.[38]

In order to get relief from fever caused by Takman, the following verses were recited:

When Agni having entered the waters, burned, where the (gods) who uphold the order of (the universe) rendered homage (to Agni), there, they say, is thy origin on high; do thou feel for us and spare us, O Takman:

Whether thou art flame, whether thou art heat, or whether from licking chips (of wood), thou hast arisen. Hrudu by name art thou, O god of the fiery, do thou feel for us, and spare us, O Takman:

To the cold Takman, and to the deliriously hot, the glowing, do I render homage. To him that returns on the morrow, to him that returns for two (successive) days, to the Takman that returns on the third day, homage, shall be.[33]

In the following hymn, Takman is propitiated as a god and then rebuked and asked to go away and live in the frog.

Homage (be) to the deliriously hot, the shaking, exciting, impetuous [Takman]! Homage to the cold (Takman), to him that in the past fulfilled desires ! May (the Takman) that returns on the morrow, he that returns on two (successive) days, the impious one, pass into this frog.[40]

To treat obstruction of urine and stool, the patient was made to drink water out of a rat's hole, or a certain plant, or sawdust from old wood. He was made to ride an elephant or a horse, and to shoot an arrow. A fine iron needle was then passed through the urethral canal. The following verse was then chanted :

I open your urinal path like a canal through which the waters rush. So may the urine come out with a whizzing sound.[41]

In order to stop bleeding and to check the flow of blood after an injury, the incantation recited was:

The maidens that go yonder, the veins, clothed in red garment, like sisters without a brother, bereft of strength, they shall stand still.[42]

At the bleeding spot a handful of dust was applied or bandaged over.[43]

The treatment of jaundice consisted of imparting the redness from the red objects and animals, preferably a red bull, to the patient. An elaborate ritual had to be undergone. An amulet consisting of a piece of bull's skin, soaked in cow's milk and anointed with the dregs of *ghee,* was tied around his neck. He was to drink milk and eat prescribed foods, the following hymn was recited :

Up to the sun shall go the heart-ache and thy jaundice: in the colour of the red bull do we envelop thee !

We envelop thee in red tints, unto long life. May this person go unscathed and be free of yellow colour :

The cows whose divinity is Rohini; they who, moreover, are (themselves) red (rohinih) — (in their) every from and every strength we do envelop thee.

Into the parrots, into the *ropanakas* (thrush) do we put the jaundice, and furthermore, into the *haridravas* (yellow wagtail) do we put thy jaundice.[44]

It is prayed that may the red colour of sun and the bull enter the patient's body and the yellow colour of jaundice go to the birds of yellow colour.

In a charm against various diseases owing to infestation by worms, the priest, while uttering the incantation, held dust in his left hand and pressed it with his right hand, and then threw it on the patient.[45]

The worms are described as visible and invisible. Some of them are called *algandu* and other *saluna.* They generate in the intestine, head and heels, and go about through the body, and cannot be killed even with different kinds of herbs. They sometimes reside in the hills, and forests, in herbs and animals, and they enter into the body and through sores in our body and through various kind of food and drinks.

In another charm against worms, the patient is given the juice of the twenty different kinds of roots.[46]

The hymns not only describe an empirical or perhaps rational treatment but also give a very good description of the worms that infest the intestine and other parts of the body. The knowledge that they enter our body through food and drinks is highly creditable as a scientific fact.

In order to treat leprosy, the priest-doctor chanted the following hymn addressed to a dark coloured plant, to drive away the white spots.

The leprosy and the gray spots drive away from here — may thy native colour settle upon thee — the white spots cause to fly away! The leprosy which has originated in the bones and that which has originated in the body and upon the skin, the white mark begotten of corruption, I have destroyed with my charm.[47]

A verse describes the application of an ointment made up of cow-dung and different herbs on those white spots until they turn red.[48]

Against hereditary leprosy (that appered in early childhood), an amulet consisting of *arjuna* wood, barley, seasmum and its flowers was tied on the patient.[49]

Another amulet for the same disease containing the born of a deer.[50]

In a mad and maniac patient who shouted wildly and who is 'bound and well-secured', Agni is invoked to calm down his mind which has been maddened by the sin of the gods or been robbed of sense by the demons. It is further prayed, "May the Apsaras restore thee, may Indra, may Bhaga restore thee, may all the gods restore thee, that thou mayest be freed from madness".[51]

For eye diseases, patient was given different kinds of vegetable leaves fried in oil;[52] for helping the growth of hair on the head, the hair was sprinkled with a decoction made up of different herbs;[53] a consumptive was asked to eat rotten fish;[54] for virility the root of a (*kapittha)* tree boiled in milk was given for drinking; for poisoning due to some vegetable, the essence of a (*kumuka)* tree was given for drinking.[55] For conception,[56] for causing sterilty,[57] for conceiving a son,[58] for preventing miscarriage,[59] and for easy delivery,[60] there are verses and formulae in the *Atharvaveda.*

Following is a verse that a sick man should chant himself.

O Soma and Rudra, eject asunder the disease that has entered our household, drive far to a distance perdition any committed sin put away from us. O Soma and Rudra, do ye put all these remedies in our bodies, unite, loosen from us what committed sin may be bound in our bodies.[61]

Evil omens that come in the form of pigeons, owls and black birds or evil dreams were warded off by reciting verses and wearing amulets of pearl, shell, etc. At night a person was thought to be very susceptible to being overpowered by evil spirits; so he prayed thus before going to bed :

O Night, the earthly space hath been filled with the father's orderings, great thou spreadest thyself to the seats of sky : bright darkness come on. . . uninjured may we, O wide darksome night, attain thy further limit. . . Let no darksome night, attain thy further limit, no demon, [no] mischief-plotter master us; let no evil-plotter master us.[62]

Herbals in the Cure of Disease

Plants and their products formed part and parcel of the practice of medicine in Vedic times. Quite often their use in different diseases appears to be rational based upon proper understanding of their action and effect; but more often it is just empirical based upon the previous experience of their having been found useful in similar conditions.

Different plant products were not only prescribed to be taken internally or applied externally, not also amulets made out of them were worn. Vedic Aryans were familiar with hundreds of different plants that were useful either single or in combination with others, in different diseases. They revered them, propitiated them and also actively cultivated them so that they may be available abundantly.

In the following incantation in the *Rıgveda,* the physician *(bhisaja)* praises such medicinal plants, ascribes a hundred-and-seven virtues to them and requests them to help him cure the patient.[63]

These herbs, the first-born of the gods,
three ages of the world age,
these will I worship in my thought
the hundred-and seven virtues of these
(with new) tawny (sprouts).

Hundred, O mothers are your virtues,
and thousand, your shoots,
ye, of hundred potencies, then,
make me hale this man.

Rejoining, herbs, respond,
Ye with flowers, ye with shoots,
like mares, winning the race
eager, the plants to ferry over to the side of safety.

Herbs :— thus I addressed you, mothers, goddesses,
may I win horse, cow, clothes,
. . . thy life-spirit (*atman),* O man !

In the *Aśvattha* (tree) your seat,
your abode made in its leaf
ye like milking cows would be
when you better me this man!

With whomever the herbs have come together
like kindly chiefs unto the gathering,
that Brahmana is called a 'healer' (*bhiśaja),*
A demon-killer, a disease-dispeller.
The rich in mare-like waters, the rich in *Soma,*
the invigorating, the one excelling in strength :

all herbs found I for this man
to free him from harm.

Like cows from the cow-pen,
stream forth the virtues of the herbs,
eager to secure rich fee (for me).
(for thee) thy life-spirit (*atman),* O man !

Weal-working is your mother's name,
hence you are woe-expellers.
Winged streams are you :
you expel what ails.

Over all enclosures they have climbed
like a thief into the cow-pen.
The herbs have driven away
all defects of the body whatever.

Since, strength-imparting, I hold
in my hand these herbs,
the life-spirit (*ātman)* of consumption vanishes,
as if in front of Him who seizes the life-soul
(Yama, king Death).

Whom, herbs, you crawl along,
limb by limb, joint by joint,
from him consumption you divide asunder,
as, located at-the-center,
the mighty (king divides asunder
the ring of neighbour kings who
prey upon his realm).

Fly away, consumption, together with the jay,
with the blue jay,
with the blast of the wind
with the storm, vanish!

One of ye help the other,
one to the other be helpful,
ye all, of one consent,
help onward this my spell.

Those with fruit, those without fruit,
those flowerless and those with flowers,
impelled by the Lord of Magic Spell (*Vrihaspati),*
may they deliver us from ill.

May they deliver me from imprecation
and from (the dropsy), that comes from Varuna,
and from the Tamer's fetterlock (sickness unto death),
from all god-sent diseases.

Flying down from heaven the herbs spake :
whom, alive, we reach,
that man does not perish.

Whatever herbs there are in *Soma's* kingdom,
the many, wise a hundred-wise.
Of these thou are the best
ready to desire, weal to the heart.
Whatever herbs ye be in Soma's kingdom,
spreading earth-wide,
impelled by the Lord of Magic Spells,

lay your strength together in this herb.

May he not come to harm who digs you;
nor he, for whom I dig you;
our two-footed, our four-footed
all uninjured be.

Whatever plants hearken to this spell,
and those gone out of reach,
all flocking here together,
shall give their strength together in this herbs.

The herbs consult with Soma, with their king :
'For whom a Brahmana works a charm
him O King, we ferry over to the side of safety'.

Thou art the best, O herb,
the trees to thee are servents;
Be subservient unto us.
He, who seeks to do us harm.

In this incantation, all existing herbs are invoked to lend aid. They are blended into an arcanum to conquer consumption, the wasting disease. The herbs are propitiated and also appeased for being uprooted. the high cost of the medicinal preparation and the deep knowledge of the physician is emphasized upon. His closeness to the healing divinities is publicised. Lastly, after the administration of the drug, it is forcefully suggested that "the herbs have driven away all defects of the body whatever".[64]

The following long hymn in the *Atharvaveda* was chanted when out of the many herbals, a medcine is prepared for a patient suffering from consumption (*yakshma*).[65]

These that are tawny that are bright,
the red and the spotted,
the swarthy, the black herbs,
all do we conjure hither.

Let them save this man
from consumption sent-by-the-gods,
these plants, fathered by Heaven, mothered by Earth,
whose root is the primal cosmic ocean.

The divine herbs in the beginning were the primal waters
they have made depart from thee, from every limb,
they sin-born consumption.

The spreading, the bushy, the one-spathed,
the extending herbs, I conjure hither,
those with shoots, those with joints, those with spreading branches,
I call for thee the plants that are of all gods,
mighty, life-giving unto man.

Whatever power is yours ye powerful ones,
whatever valour and strength is yours,
therewith free ye this man from this consumption.
O herbs, Now do I make a remedy.
The lively, by no-means harming, living herb,
the non-obstructing upward-leading,

nourishing flower, rich in sweets,
do I call hither,
to make this man free from harm.

Hither shall come the forethoughtful ones,
the allies of my spell,
that we may safely ferry over this man from Distresser.

Food of Fire, from the womb of waters.
growing up renewed, firmly rooted, named a
thousand names,
be they remedial in being brought.

With *avakā* (*Blyxa octandra Rich)* as their full
with the waters as their nature
May the sharp-horned herbs rend distress asunder.

These that release, dispel *varuna* (dropsy),
the mighty, the poison-destroyers,
the swelling-dispellers as well,
the spoilers of witchcraft,
may these herbs come hither!

The purchased, and praised, most powerful plants,
May they protect in this village
Cow, horse, man and beast.

Rich in sweet the root, rich in sweets the tip,
rich in sweets has grown the middle of these plants;
rich in sweets the leaves, rich in sweet the flowers of these

partaking of honey, drink of the elixir of Immortal life (*amrita).*

May they milk forth melted butter, food,

and first of all, milk.

How many and whatsoever be these herbs upon the earth
May that, the thousand-leafed,

released me from death, for peril.

May the tigerish amulet of plants,
protecting, guarding against imprecations,
smite far from us diseases and all demons.

As at the lion's roar,
they start with fear,
as at fire, they start fearing the herbs brought hither;
May consumption of kine, of men, be gone,
driven out by the plants, beyond the navigable streams.

Herbs, released from the fire who-dwell-with-all
men (*Vaisvanara),*
go ye stretching over the earth,
ye whose king is the forest-tree.

Those herbs, related to the Angirasas (the semi-divine first Brahmanas),
which grow on mountains and plains,
may they be rich in milk, propitious,
weal to our heart.
Those plants I watch, those with the eye I see,
the unknown and the ones we know of,

and these in which we wit the virtues brought together.

May all herbs together note my spell

that we may safely ferry over this man out of distress.

The *asvattha* (tree, *Ficus religious Indica),* the *darba grass* (*Sacchorum cylindricum),*

Soma, the king of plants, oblation, the immortal dish,

rice and remedial barley, ye twain immortal sons of Heaven.

Rise ye up; it thunders and roars at (you), O herbs,

when Parjanya (the god of rain) favours you with seed,

O ye children of the spotted Cow (the earth).

Of this divine elixir of immortal life (*amrita),*

we make this man drink strength;

now I do make a remedy,

that he come to a hundred years.

That plant the boar knows'

that remedial herbs the monogoose knows,

(the genii of the *amrita*-containing

moon cup, gurrdians of the vegetative lunar cycle), those I call to his aid.

Whatsoeve herbs, related to the Angirases, the eagles,

whatsoever divine one the bees (?) know.

Whatsoever the birds, the swans know, and all winged ones,

Of however many herbs the inviolable kine eat,

Of however many the goats and sheep,

May all these herbs, brought hither,

extend protection unto thee.

In however, many herbs the human physicians find a remedy,

So many, all remedial, do I bring unto thee.

Those rich in flowers, rich in shoots
rich in fruits, these fruitless ones as well,
like mothers assembled, let them yield milk
upto this man for freedom from harm.

I have snatched thee away from the Him-with-the five-stings,

and from Him-with-the-ten-sitings as well,

also from the fetterlook of the Tamer (Yama, king of Death)

from all sickness sent by the gods (in retribution for offences).

In this incantation, consumption is sought to be expelled from the patient's body through the dual effect of the incantation and of powerful plants, all combined into one medicinal portion for the patient. The herbs are propitiated and flattered and reminded of their healing power. This last point is equally intended for the patient and his relations that he is being treated with such effective medicine. The patient is not only given the herbal preparation to drink, but also an amulet made out of them is tied on his arm, whose 'tiger-like' strength is extolled. Finally, and in anticipation, the physician remarks that through the administration of this drug, he has already snatched away the patient from the disease.[66]

The foregoing two hymns, one from the *Rigveda* and the other from the *Atharvaveda*, give us an insight into the whole procedure about the use of different herbals for treating diseases during vedic times.

There are several other hymns in the *Atharavaveda* which provide us information about the specific uses to which different herbals were put to against various diseases.

Classification of Medicinal Plants

A classification of the medicinal plants according to the type of diseases they were employed to cure, mentioned in the *Atharvaveda* is as follows :

1. Those that cured different diseases of the body (*kāyachikitsā).*
2. Those that cured diseases of the mind (*bhutavidyā).*
3. Those that helped in the procreation and protection of children (*kaumāra-vidyā).*
4. Those that were used against wounds (*śalyavidyā).*
5. Those that were used as antidotes against the bite of snakes, etc. (*vishavidyā).*
6. Those that were used for securing prosperity and prolongation of life (*rasāyana).*
7. Those that were used for virility and erotic success (*vajikarana).*
8. Miscellaneous.[67]

1. Plants for Diseases of the Body

For Leprosy. The plant used was *haridra (Circuma longa),* and the following verses were chanted along with.

Night-born are thou, O herb, O dark, black, dusky one; O colourer, do thou colour this leprous spot and what is pale.

Of the bone-born leprous spot, and of the body born that is in the skin, of that made by the spoiler-by incantation have I made the whole mark disappear.[68]

The Asura-woman first made this remedy for leprous spot, this effacer if the leprous spot; it has made the leprous spot disappear, has made this skin uniform.[69]

For Fevers. The plant used is identified as *Costus specious* or *arabicus (kuśttha)* and the following verses were chanted.

On an eagle-bearing mountain, born from the snowy one, for they go to it with riches, having heard of it, for they know the effacer of fever.

The Aśvattha, the seat of the gods, in the third heaven from here; there the gods won the Kuśttha, the sight of immortality.

Born in the north from the snowy mountains, thou are conducted to people in the eastern quarter, there they have shared out the highest names of the Kuśttha.

Head diseases attack, evil of the eyes, of the body all that may Kuśttha relieve, verily a divine virility.[70]

Thou are born upon the mountains, as the most potent of plants, come hither, O Kuśttha, destroyer of the Takman, to drive out from here the Takman![71]

Thou are born of the gods, thou are Soma's good friend. Be thou propitious to my in-breathing and my out-breathing, and to the eyes of mine !

Superior O Kuśttha, is thy name; 'superior' is the name of thy father. Do thou drive out all diseases; and render the Takman devoid of strength!

Pain in the head, affliction in the eye, and ailment of the body, all that shall the Kuśttha heal — a divinely powerful (remedy) forsooth!

2. *Plants for Diseases of the Mind*

The plants that were used for the purpose included *sahadevi (Sidacordifolia* and *Rhombifolia)* and *apāmmārya*

(*Achyranthes aspera*). The following verses were chanted.

The truly-conquering, the curse repelling, the overcoming, the reverted one — all the herbs have I called together saying — may they save use from this.[72]

In the following verses meant for the same purpose, the plant identified, among others, in *ajasringe (Odina pinnata)*.

By thee do we expel the Apsrases, the Gandharvas : O goat-horned one, drive the demon; make all disappear by thy smell.

Where are the *aśwatthas*, the *nyagrodhas*, great trees, with crests — thither go away, ye, Apsrases; you have been recognized.

Higher hath come this mighty one of the herbs, of the plants; let the goat-horned *arataki*, the sharp-horned, push out.[73]

In the *avakā*-eating Gandhārvas[74], *avakā* is *Blyxa octandra*, a grass-like marsh plant.

The plant *Varana* mentioned in the following verses in *Crataiva roxburghu*.

The *Varana*, this divine, forest tree, shall ward off the Yaksha, that has entered this man — that have the gods warded off.[75]

3. Plants for Procreation of Children

In the following verses, the plants used are not mentioned, but the purpose is clear :

The plants of which heaven has been the father, earth the mother, ocean the root — let those herbs of the gods favour thee, in order to acquisition of a son.[76]

Whoever makes this woman one having a dead child or a miscarriage, him O herb, do thou make disappear, lustful for her, slippery.[77]

4. Plants for Wounds

The plants identified in the following verse are : *plaksha (Ficus infectoria), aświattha (Ficus religiosa), khadira (Acacia catechu), dhava (Anogeissus latifolia), nyagrodha (Ficus benegalensis), parna (Butea frondosa)* and *arundhati,* a climber.

If by a staff, if by an arrow, or if by flame as sore is made, of that thou are relief; relieve thou this man. Out of the excellent *plaksha* thou arisest, out of the *aświattha,* the *khadira,* the *dhaval,* the excellent *nyagrodha,* the *prana,* do thou come to us, O *Arundhati.*[78]

A preparation of these plants was perhaps applied locally over the injured area.

In the following verse, the plant identified is *pippali (piper longum).*

The berry remedy for what is bruised, remedy for what is pierced — that did the gods prepare; that is suficient for life.[79]

5. Plants as Antidotes

In the following verse, the plant mentioned is *madhuka (bassia latifolia).*

From the cross-lined (snake), from the black snake, from the adder (what is) gathered — that poison of the heron-joined one hath plant made to disappear.[80]

6. Plants for Prosperity

In the following verses, the plants intended to bring in prosperity are identified as follows :

Indra put thee *(aparajita)* on his arm, in order to lay low the Asuras; smite the dispute of (my) counter-disputants; make them sapless, O herb.[81]

The plant *aparajita* is *Clitoria ternata.*

Indra consumed the *patha,* in order to lay low the Asuras.[82]

The plant *patha,* is *Clypba hernendifolia.*

The *parna,* soma's formidable power, hath come, given by Indra, governed by Varuna, may I shining, greatly, wear it in order to lengthen life for a hundred autumns.[83]

The plant *parna* is *Butea frondosa.*

As thou, O *Aśwattha* didst break out the *knadira* within the great sea, so do thou break out all those whom I hate and who hate me.[84]

The plant *aśwattha is Ficus religiosa and khadira is Acacia catechu.*

Thou are the highest of herbs, *talisa,* of thee the trees are subjects : let him be our subject who assails us.[85]

The plant *talisa* is *Flacourtia cataphracta.*

Me with a portion of *simpasa,* together with Indra as ally, I make myself portioned; let the niggards run away.[86]

The plant *simsapa* is *Delbergia ṣisu.*

7. *Plants for Virility*

In the following verses, the plants intended to bring in virility are identified as follows :

About thee with an encompassing sugarcane have I gone, in order to absence of mutual hatred; that thou myest be one loving one, that thou mayest be one not going away from me.[87]

The plant mentioned is *madhuka (Bassia Latifolia)* or *yasthimadhy (Glycyrrhiza glabra).*

I dig herb, of plants the strongest, with which one drives off her rival; with which one wins completely her husband.[88]

The plant is *patha* or *vanaparni* (*Clypea hernandifolia).*

Of the horse, of the mule, of the he-goat and of the ram, also of the bull what vigors there arc — them do thou put in him, O selfcontroller.[89]

The plant is *kapitthaka (Feronia elephantum).*

As the black snake spreads himself at pleasure, making wondrous forms, by the Asura's magic, so let this *arka* suddenly make thy member altogether correspondent, limb with limbs.[90]

Wherewith they invigorate one who is lean, wherewith they incite one who is ill-with, that, O Brahmanaspati, make thou his member taut like a bow.[91]

(with amulet of *arka* wood).

The plant identified in the above two verses is *arka* (*Calotropis gigantea).*

A conciliator, a love-awakener, do thou, O brown, beauteous one : push together both you woman and me; make our heart the same.[92]

The plant identified with this verse is *Andropogon aciculatus.*

8. *Miscellaneous*

O thou of great leaves blessed one, rain increased, rigorous ! as a mother to her sons, be thou gracious to the hair, O Sami.[93]

Fix thou the old ones, genrerate those unborn, make longer those born.

What hair of thine falls down, and what one is hewn off with its root, upon it I now pour with the all-healing plant.

Fix thou the root, stretch the end, make the middle stretch out. O herb, let the black hairs grow out of thy head like reeds.[94]

The plants identified are *Prosopis specigera* and *Mimosa suma.*

Soma

Soma is an extract of the soma plant[95] which is said to have been brought to earth by the eagle from the heavens.[96] The plant is described to 'dwell' in mountains and name of the Mujavat mountain is specifically mentioned in this context.[97]

The colour of the plant, as also of the juice extracted from it, is said to be sort of brown or brownish green.[93] Extraction of the juice from the plant was done by crushing the stalk with a stone[99] or in a mortar and pestel.[100] The juice was strained by letting it ooze through sheep's wool.[101] Thus filtered, it was mixed with water, milk and honey and offered to gods. It was also mixed with barley and with *ghee.*[102] Soma juice from the plant was extracted at different times of the day for offering it to different gods.

Its reaction on the body, after taking it, is described as 'like roar of a bull'.[103] It acts swiftly.[104] It is exhilarating and invigorating. It stimulates speech also.[105] The worshippers, after taking, it exclaim, "We have drunk soma, we have become immortal, we have entered into light, we have known the gods".[106] After taking it, Indra slew all foes and no one could resist him in battle.[107]

The soma juice had medicinal powers also. It said to have healed the sick, made blind see and lame walk.[108] It bestowed long life[109] and increased fertility.[110] Soma is the lord of all plants.[111]

The soma plant has not yet been recognized botanically. Different conjectures have however, been made by many scholars. It probably belongs to ephedra family.

Nuclei of Ayurveda in Vedic Medicine

In the above-stated description of treating different diseases through incantations and the use of different herbal product, some fundamental principles of approach of the priest-physicians is discernible. The foremost is the simultaneous, many-sided approach to the disease, *viz.*, (1) to propitiate god, (2) to make the demon flee, (3) to use hebals as amulets, and (4) to make a medicine out of the herbals for internal administration. This clearly indicates that the clever priest-physicians of that era, utilized all the different approaches that had proved effective in their experience at one time or the other.

The second factor in the practice of Atharvavedic medicine is a lot of showmanship on the part of the physician. He prays, he chants, he shouts, threatens, even uses violent language, and makes fearful gestures. All this is to impress upon the people around, including the patient's kith and kins.

The third factor is the priest-physician's direct address to the patient himself. He convinces the patient that by his powerful charm the disease-producing demon is running away thereby preparing him psychologically to fight the disease.

The fourth factor is the use of variety of herbals in various forms, showing that the priest-physician had some idea of their action and efficacy.

The next step was only to discard the superstitious garb of the magic verse and to administer the medicine.

It appears that during Atharvavedic times, there existed two types of healing arts and their adherents. The first was the one which predominantly depended upon incantations of magical verses to cure the disease. The second type did use the magical formulae but also used empirically or even rationally, different herbals, their products and concoctions. The use of amulets was profusely practised by both. The *Atharvaveda* mentions that "there were hundreds of medical practitioners and thousands of herbals, but that which could be achieved by a collective effect of them all, could be done singly by a charmed amulet".[112] Also the one who binds the amulet is described as the best of all doctors.

It also appears that while in the earlier times, priestly and magical practice was appreciated better, in the later times this was not so. The herbal doctor had developed by then confidence in the effectiveness of his drugs and it was this which gained ground gradually and culminated in the establishment of the Āyurvedic medicine of the classical period.

There are many verses in the *Atharvaveda* which are devoted exclusively to extol the virtues of different plants. They also indicate their specific uses in specific diseases and conditions.

Information gathered on the different aspects of medicine culled from Vedic literature shows that there is a mixture of supernatural and the natural, empirical and the rational. Diseases, in general, are considered to be caused by supernatural factors, yet it is also stated that a disease may originate because of one of the three possible factors : *abharaja (aqueous), vataja (wind)* and *sushamaja* (desiccating agents).[113] The desiceating factor is also called *pitta.*[114] Acqueous factor is termed *sleshma* in *Śatapatha Brāhmana.* The term *tridhatu,* referring possibly to the three bodily humours, *vata, pitta, kapha or sleshma,* occurs for the first time in the *Rigveda.* different authors view these earliest references differently.

Writing about diseases in Āyurvedic medicine, S.N.Das Gupta said, "My own conclusion is that at least some Atharvavedic people had thought of a three-fold classification of all diseases, *viz.*, those produced by wind, those by water and those by fire or those that are dry and burning. This corresponds to the later classification of all diseases as being due to the three *dcṣas, vayu* (wind), *kapha, sleshma* (phlegm) and *pitta* (bile)."[115]

The later Vedic texts clearly accept that the human body (the microcosm) as also the universe (the macrocosm) is composed of the same five elements, *viz.*, *prithvi* (earth), *apa* (water), *vayu* (air), *jyoti* (fire) and *ākāśa* (ether).[116] The *vayu* in the human body is categorised into five types according to location and function.

Thus we see that the different aspects of the medical science and art mentioned in the Vedic literature from a nucleus around which was later built the science of Āyurveda.

Mythical Origin of Ayurveda

The *Charaka Samhitā* carries the following story about the origin of Āyurveda. The holy sages sat in a conclave on the slopes of the Himālayas. Among them were Angiras, Vasiṣta Kāśyapa, Bhrigu, Ātreya, Nārada, Agastya, Mārkandeya, Bhārdvāja, Chayavana, Gārgya, Kātyāyana and many others : an assembly of about fifty of the most eminent sages. The topic of discussion was : "How to get rid of the prevailing diseases which were causing so much ill-health among human beings, and interfering in the performance of their duties."

Collectively, they came to the conclusion that Indra, the Lord of the Immortals, be approached as he knew Āyurveda, the science of longevity (*ayu* means life, and *vida,* to know, to attain). They knew that Indra had learnt Āyurveda from the twin physicians of the gods, the Aśvins, who had learnt it from Dakṣa Prajāpati; the latter having learnt it in its entirety from Brāhma, the Creator.

Sage Bhāradvāja volunteered to go to Indra. The others agreed.

Bhāradvāja approached Lord Indra, bowed before him and in humility delivered the message of all the sages thus : "Diseases have arisen which are the terror of all human beings. Tell me, Oh Lord of the Immortals, the appropriate means of curing them."

Indra knew of the wide knowledge and understanding of sage Bhāradvāja, and hence could teach him the whole science of Āyurveda in brief.

After his return, Bhāradvāja passed on what he had learnt from Indra to the other sages, one among whom was Punarvasu Ātreya.

Ātreya taught Āyurveda to his six disciples, namely, Agniveśa, Bhela, Jātukarna; Parāśara, Hārita and Kṣparapāni. These disciples, on the basis of their own understanding of the subject, composed treatises and read them before the experts, one among whom was Punarvasu Ātreya himself. The sages whole-heartedly approved these works and blessed the authors. The treatises became popular and proved helpful in mitigating human suffering.[117]

There is another version of the origin of the Āyurveda. This is given in the *Suśruta Samhitā.* According to it when different types of diseases spread among human beings, and everyone felt helpless before this suffering and loss, Suśruta, along with some other sages approached King Divodāsa of Benares who was considered the incarnation of Lord Dhanvantari, and said : "Oh Lord, we are much grieved to see around us human beings suffering from bodily, mental, accidental and natural diseases. They lament and cry aloud like helpless beings without any friends or means. For curing these individuals, for the preservation of our own lives and for the good of all mankind, we have come here to be instructed in Āyurveda, and approach you as pupils."

Divodāsa assured Suśruta and other sages with these words : "You are welcome. You, my sons, are well educated and qualified to receive instruction in Āyurveda. The Āyurveda is a subsidiary branch of the *Atharvaveda.* Brāhma conceived it in one hundred thousand stanzas (*ślokas)* and a thousand chapters, before the creation of man. Afterwards in consideration of the short lives and the limited intellectual capacity of human beings, he divided it into eight chapters, viz., *śalya, śālākya, kayā-chikitsā, bhutavidyā, kaumāra-bhritya, agādatantra, rasāyana-tantra* and *vājikarana tantra.* Brāhma first expounded Āyurveda to Prajāpati, who taught it to the two Aśvins. From these twins, Indra studied the subject and from Indra, I obtained the knowledge. Now for the good of mankind, it is my duty to impart this knowledge to those who seek it in this world."[118]

Yet another vesion is found in *Kāśyapa samhitā.* It says : The Omniscient, Self-borne Brāhma, desirous of creating human beings, originated Āyurveda in the beginning for their protection, and later the elements and the universe. Afterwards, Brāhma expounded the holy, eternal, supporter of life, strengthening nectar Āyurveda to Aśvins; they two expounded to Indra, Indra to the four sages, *viz.*, Kāśyapa, Vasiṣta, Atri and Bhirgu, and the four sages to their sons and disciples for the maintenance and preservation of the four objectives of life : dharma, wealth desire and salvation.[119]

Such a mythical origin of Āyurveda, as described in different ancient medical texts, has similarity with the mythical origin of the healing arts of other contemporary or near-contemporary civilizations. Just as Brāhma revealed Āyurveda to the Indians, so did Thoth and Apollo reveal the Egyptian and Greek systems of medicines to their respective peoples.

The mythical stories about the origin of Āyurveda may have been circulated to make it acceptable to people. Just as good reviews or opinions expressed by eminent authorities make a book more acceptable to people now-a-days, it seems, in the same manner, in ancient times, manuscripts or knowledge said to have a divine origin or basis was more acceptable. This applies not only to ancient medical texts but to all books of knowledge in other fields as well. It was as true to Indian as to other civilised countries of the time.

Preceding Constituents of Ayurveda

These mythical stories apart, we can make an attempt to trace the origin of Āyurveda through bits of information available in medical and other manuscripts.

In the *Atharvaveda,* we find at least two systems of medical practice : one, the system predominantly of charms and magicoreligious medicine; two, the system of drugs used on an empiricorational basis.

We have no medical or related text between the end of the Atharvavedic and the beginning of the Āyurvedic periods about the sixth century B.C. We, however, know that many of the Brāhmanas and Upaniṣads were composed during this interval, and these scriptures themselves throw some light on the medical practices that prevailed in this period. The *Gopatha-brāhmana,* the Brāhmana of the *Atharvaveda,* mentions among other Vedas, the *Sarpaveda, Piśachaveda, Asuraveda;* it, however, does not mention Āyurveda. The *Chhāndogya Upaniṣad* which is later than the *Gopatha-brāhmana,* mentions among the subjects of study pursued in those days, the *Atharvaveda, Sarpavidyā, Pitriyavidyā,* and *Bhutavidyā,* but it does not mention Āyurveda. So it can be surmised that during the period of Brāhmanas and Upaniṣads, Āyurveda had not come into being as such. If that is so, then the concept and the applied science of Āyurveda must have been evolved roughly between 800 and 600 B.C.

The *Atharvaveda* mainly consists of *bhutavidyā* and *sarpavidyā (agada).* In the Brāhmanas and the Upaniṣads, besides the above two, there are also *rasāyana and vajikarna.* The Āyurveda contains, besides the above four divisions, another four, namely *śalya, śālākya, kayāchikitsā* and *kaumāra-bhritya.* Not that the knowledge about the latter four divisions did not exist before, but the existing knowledge was systematized, and thus originated the eight divisioned *(aśtānga)* Āyurveda.

The question now arises as to what led to this systematization of knowledge ? What were the conditions or compulsions that made people think of it? How is it that a predominantly magico-religious system of medicine changed into a rational system of medicine with a broad-based theoretical background ?

One thing we know for certain. The whole atmosphere of this period was overwhelmingly philosophical. The change in the outlook of medicine from the magico-religious to the physical causation and theories, could very well be the result of the neo-philosophical concepts of the Nyāya - Vaiśeṣika and the Sāmkhya on which the theoretical structure of the Āyurveda is based.

References

1. *ṚV.*, X. 90.
2. *A.V.*, Whitney-Lanman translation, p. 22.
3. *A.V.*, XI.8.
4. *A.V.*, XI.4.
5. Zimmer H.R., *Hindu Medicine,* Baltimore, pp. 119-132, 1948.
6. *A.V.*, II, 1-8.
7. *S.B.*, XII. 2.4.9-14.
8. *S.B.*, XII. 3.2.3-4.
9. *S.B.*, XII. 2.4.13; VIII, 6.2.8-10.
10. *S.B.*, XII. 2.4.12-14.
11. *A.V.*, X. 8.43.
12. *Birih. Up.*, IV.2.4.

13. *Kath. Up.*, II.3.16; Chh. Up. VII.6.6.
14. *Birih Up.;* II.2.19.
15. Vijasaneyism; 39.10.
16. Roy, Mira, *Anatomy in the Vedic Literature,* I.J. *His. Sc.*, 2.40, 1967.
17. *Birih. Up.*, IV.2.3.
18. *Chh. Up.*, VIII.6.6.
19. *Māndukya Upaniṣad*, II.2.6.
20. *A.V.*, I. 36.
21. *A.V.*, VI. 90.5.
22. *A.V.*, X. 2.11.
23. *A.V.*, V. 11.
24. *ṚV.*, VIII. 18.8.
25. *ṚV.*, VIII. 22.10.
26. *A.V.*, VII. 53.1.; T.B. III.2.11.
27. *ṚV.*, I. 116.25; VIII. 8.13.
28. *ṚV.*, I. 116.10; S.B., IV. 1.5.21.
29. *ṚV.*, X.39.8.
30. *ṚV.*, I. 112.5; 116.11; 117.5; 118; X. 39.8.
31. *ṚV.*, I. 116.16; 117.17.18.
32. *ṚV.*, I. 112.8.
33. *A.V.*, II. 28.
34. *Kausika Sūtra*, 48, 23-26.
35. *A.V.*, VI. 37.
36. *A.V.*, VII. 83.
37. *Kaūsika sūtra*, 32, 14-16.
38. *A.V.*, VI. 90.
39. *A.V.*, I. 25.
40. *A.V.*, VII. 116.
41. *A.V.*, I. 3.7.
42. *A.V.*, I. 171.
43. *Kausika sūtra*, 26.10-13.
44. *A.V.*, I. 22.
45. *A.V.*, II. 31.

46. *A.V.*, I. 23.
47. *A.V.*, I. 23.
48. *A.V.*, I. 23.
49. *A.V.*, II. 9-10.
50. *A.V.*, II. 33.
51. *A.V.*, VI. 3.
52. *A.V.*, VI. 15.
53. *A.V.*, VI. 21.
54. *A.V.*, III. 2.
55. *A.V.*, IV. 6.
56. *A.V.*, VI. 81.
57. *A.V.*, VII. 35.
58. *A.V.*, III. 23, VI.11.
59. *A.V.*, VI. 17.
60. *A.V.*, I. 11.
61. *A.V.*, VII. 42.
62. *A.V.*, XIX. 47.
63. *R.V.,* X. 97.
64. Zimmer, H.R. *Hindu Medicine,* p. 26.
65. *A.V.*, VIII. 7.
66. Zimmer, H.R., *Hindu Medicine,* p. 15.
67. Majumdar G.P., *Vanaspati,* University of Calcutta, 1927.
68. *A.V.*, I. 23.1., 4.
69. *A.V.*, I. 24, 2.
70. *A.V.*, V. 4.2, 3, 8, 10.
71. *A.V.*, II. 7.5.
72. *A.V.*, IV. 17.2, 7.
73. *A.V.*, IV. 37.4, 6.
74. *A.V.*, IV. 37.7.8.
75. *A.V.*, VI. 85.1.
76. *A.V.*, III. 23, 6.
77. *A.V.*, VIII. 6, 9.
78. *A.V.*, V. 5.4.5.

79. *A.V.*, VI. 109.1.
80. *A.V.*, VIII. 56.1.
81. *A.V.*, II. 27.3.
82. *A.V.*, II. 27.4.
83. *A.V.*, III. 5.4.
84. *A.V.*, III. 6.3.
85. *A.V.*, XI. 15.1.
86. *A.V.*, VI. 129.1.
87. *A.V.*, I. 34.5.
88. *A.V.*, III. 18.1.
89. *A.V.*, IV. 4.8.
90. *A.V.*, IV. 72.1.
91. *A.V.*, VI. 101.2.
92. *A.V.*, VI. 139.3.
93. *A.V.*, VI. 30.3.
94. *A.V.*, VI. 136.2, 3, 137, 3.
95. *Ṛ.V.*, IX. 67.28.
96. *Ṛ.V.*, V. 45.9; IX. 68.6, X. 114.5.
97. *Ṛ.V.*, I. 28.1-4.
98. *Ṛ.V.*, I. 92.1.
99. *Ṛ.V.*, IX. 107.10.
100. *Ṛ.V.*, I. 28.1-4.
101. *Ṛ.V.*, IX. 69.9.
102. *Ṛ.V.*, IX. 82.2.
103. *Ṛ.V.*, IX. 16; VI. 69; IV. 71.7.9.
104. *Ṛ.V.*, 1.4.7.
105. *Ṛ.V.*, VI. 47.3; IX. 8.4.4; IX. 95.5; IX. 97.52.
106. *Ṛ.V.*, VIII. 48.3.
107. *Ṛ.V.*, IX. 1.10.
108. *Ṛ.V.*, VIII. 68, 2; X. 25.11.
109. *Ṛ.V.*, I. 91.6; VIII. 48.4.7.
110. *Ṛ.V.*, IX. 80.4.49.
111. *Ṛ.V.*, IX. 114.2.

112. *A.V.*, II. 9.3.
113. *A.V.*, I. 12.3; XVII. 3.5.
114. *A.V.*, XVII. 3.5.
115. Das Gupta S.N., *History of Indian Philosophy*, III, p. 300.
116. *Ait. Br.*, II. 3.2.2; *Ait. Up.*; III. 5.3, *Kans. Ar*; VII. 2.2; *Tait. Up:* III. 2.1.
117. *C.S.*, 1.1.37-40.

5

Concepts of Universe and the Body Function

Man questioned the nature of the power determining all kinds of existence even in the time of the *Ṛgveda* (2500 BC). The two possible sources of the universe were traced to *prakriti* (cosmic energy —unmanifested) and *vishva jyoti* (cosmic light). In fact, the cosmic light was considered to be "the soul of all gods" and the "womb" of all creation. Reference was also made to *aditi* (pure, eternal, earth) which constitutes the primordial substance of the universe. Brahmā the creator was described as the light source for the rest of the creation. The cosmic light and the cosmic law (*rita*) were thought to determine the course of things. The cosmic law (*rita)* was the cuase of the orderliness of the universe according to the *Rig Veda.* This along with *veina* (sacrifice) was later considered responsible for preserving the cycle of cosmic events in harmony. At a later period *ap.* (water) was conceived as the "suprasensible first cause". It was believed to be the first element, without any mythological connotation, to be responsible for creation. These ideas of the origin of things and their relation to energy and motion, signified and determined the root cause of the origin of the world. Gradually, however a concept of *pañchabhūtās* (five elements), i.e. *prithvī, ap, tejas, vāyu* and *ākāha,* was postulated. According to *Sānkhya, Nyāya* and *Vaisheshika* schools of Hindu philosophy, *panchabhūtās* are the constituents of the world. whereas *Jaina, Buddhist and Chārvāka* schools of thought considered only the first four of these as the basic elements.

The mention of the above hypothesis is unavoidable in discussing the concepts of the biological functions as mentioned in the ancient Indian texts. The *Maitrāyanī Upanishad* also make a mention of *tanmātrās* subtle and primary elements which were considered to be invisible and eternal constituents from which different elements arose. But the elements in themselves were not eternal. The Table I gives the origin of *panchabhūtās,* their attributes and corresponding *tanmātrās.* The *Sānkhya* school believes the creation means becoming manifest from the unmanifest but potentially existing material. It essentially implies transformation or regrouping of five elements for production of gross things. The idea of *Āyurveda* and *yoga* philosophy have incorporated these concepts, and to a certain degree they have been reflected even in the *Tibbe-e-Unānī* (Greek system of medicine).

The universe according to *panchabhūtā* concept is constituted by the primordial energy (*prakriti),* which is believed to be in an unmanifested form so long as its associated three qualities (*gunās), i.e., satva, rajas* and *tamas* are in a state of equilibrium. These qualities in a way are conceived to be independent entities from the *prakriti* and *bhūtās.* Their concepts seems to define the state of a thing at a given time and in a given context. The changing manifestation of inorganic and organic material inolves interaction, and comination of *prakriti, bhūtas* and *gunās.*

The elements in different combinations are believed to be capable of giving rise to six types of *rasās* (tastes). These combinations bestow a new quality to the characteristics of the *bhūtās.* The *rasās* (tastes) and their corresponding *bhūtās* are : sweet (*madhura)* due to the presence of *prithvī* and *ap.* sour (*amla*) due to *tejas* and *prithvī;* salty (*lavana)* due to *ap.* and *tejas;* pungent (*katu)* due to *ākāsha* and *vāyu;* bitter *(tikta)* due to *tejas* and *vāyu;* and astringent (*kashāya*) due to *prithvī* and *vāyu.* Although in the constitution of the *rasās,* the predominant *bhūtās* are mentioned, the theory also envisages the participation of other three remaining *bhūtās,* although in much smaller amounts.

It may be in order to give a brief account of each of the five *bhūtās* as visualized by the *Vaisheshika* and *Nyāya* concepts. Four of the five *bhūtās* are considered to be existing in two forms. One in the shape of atoms which is an eternal form, and the other in a transient form which manifests itself in constituting living objects as well as organs of perception. The five qualities, *i.e.,* the number, dimension, distinction, conjunction and disconjunction are common to all the five *bhūtās* described (Table II).

Prithvī (Earth): *Prithvī* in its short lasting form constitutes the living organism, and its sense organs (*indriyās)* for olfaction, and for the objects which are perceived. Amongst the objects are included inorganic and organic materials as well as living beings. The predominant or specific quality of earth is odour; and it possesses fourteen charcteristics. These are colour, taste, odour, touch, number, dimension, distinctness, conjunction, disjunction, distance, proximity, gravity, fluidity and faculty. The earth is also conceived to exist in its eternal form as atoms.

Ap (water): The special quality of water is described as taste, and it has white colour. It forms part of the living beings, sense organs and different objects like rivers,

Table I

Different *dravya* (substances) which include *panchabhūtās*, their *gunās* (attributes) and *kamās* (actions)

Name of Dravya	*Constituent of Pancha-bhūtas*	*Primary Tammātrās*	*Forms of existence*		*Present in Object*		*Total number of quality*	*Specific quality (guna)*
			Permanent	*Temporary*	*Living*	*Non-living*		
Ākāsha	yes	*Shabda* (sound)	exists every-where	Permanent auditory sense	Principal of non-material	non-material	6	sound
Vāyu	yes	*Shabda* and *sparsha* (touch)	in astomic state	"	Body, sense organ, breath & motive force for secretomotor functions	motive force for clouds, etc.	9	touch
Tejas	yes	*Shabda, sparsha* and *rūpa* (visual perception)	"	"	Body, sense organs	Heavenly, earthly, mineral & stomachic	11	colour

Ap	yes	*Shabda, sparsha, rūpa* and *rasa* (taste)	”	”	Body, sense organs	Rivers, oceans, moon, etc.	14	taste
Prithvī	yes	*Shabda, sparsha, rūpa, rasa* and *gandha* (odour)	in atomic state	forms the ol-factory Organ	Body, sense organs, plants	Rocks, minerals, gems, stones, etc.	14	odour
Kāla	no		permanent all pervading				51	—
Dik	no	”					1	—
Manas	no	”					8	—
Ātman	no	”	—	—	in body		14	—

oceans, etc., the last ones being manifestation of its transitory form. In the eternal form it exists as atoms. It too has been assigned fourteen qualities which are colour, taste, touch, number, dimension, distinctness, conjunction, disjunction, distance, proximity, gravity, viscidity, fluidity and faculty.

Tejas (fire): The special quality of *tejas* is visual perception. It is classified as heavenly. earthly, digestive and mineral. In heavens it exists as sun, lightening, etc. In the earthly form it is the one which burns the things of the earth. The digestive fire relates to the digestion of food in the gestrointestinal tract; while the mineral fire exists in the form of gold and other metals. It also constitutes parts of the body the visual sense organs, and the different objects referred to above. The eleven qualities of *tejas* are colour, number orientation, distinctness, conjunction, disjunction, proximity, distance, faculty, touch and fluidity.

Vāyu (air): It constitutes a aprt of four types of things, i.e., the body tactile sense organs, the objects which can be perceived in the air by touch, and *prāna* which asigns motor functions to the different organs for the transport of various humours and secretions. It has the quality of motion which it can impart to the material objects in the air, like the coluds and rain. Its general qualities are touch, number, orientation, distinctness, conjunction, disjunction, proximity, distance, faculty.

Ākāsha (ether): It is all pervading, non-material and has a special quality of sound. Its sense organs is car. Its general qualities are sound, number, orientation, distinctness, conjunction, disjunction.

The *bhūtās,* as is clear from the above descrition, also have specific sensory modalities i.e., earth has olfaction, water has gustation, fire has vision, air has touch, and ether has sound. Possibly this relationship is conceived in view of the fact that gustation, for example, is felt by the tongue for which the participation of water is essential, and the form is perceived by the eye, which is generated by light (fire).

Another consideration which may be relevant is the concept of *dravya* (substance). The parts of five elements constitute *dravya.* In addition to substance (*dravya),* there are five other things (*padārtha),* which are considered essential for knowing the "reality". They are *guna* (attributes), *karma* (action), *sāmānya* (generality), *vishesha* (particularity), and *samavāya* (incoherence). *Dravya* is the most important of all these, because it constitutes the material basis of others. There are nine types of *dravya : prithvī, ap, tejas, vāyu, ākāsha, dik* (space), *kāla* (time), *ātmā* (soul) and *manas* (mind). Out of these the first four are material, next three are non-material, and the last two are rational inferences. This concept of *Nyāya-Vaisheshika* schools of philosophy, while considering the attributes to be part of a substance, propounds the substance to be separate from its qualities.

In the ancient Indian literature the concept of *panchabhūtās* forms the basis of informations relating to different aspects of knowledge about the universe the world and the living beings. The four *Vedās* (books of knowledge) twelve *Upanishads* (brief catechistical treatises) and various *Smritis* (canons of law) are the principle sources with regard to the idea of the microcosm and the macrocosm. The subsequent writings like the *Yoga Sūtrās* of Patanjali (second century BC.) give an account of the manner in which a healthy body can be prepared for higher states of mental function, like *samādhi* (meditation). This work on the *Yoga* however, was a compilation of the information already existing for several centuries before Patanjali, which was passed down orally from teacher (*guru)* to his pupils (*shishiya).* The Mohen-Jo-Daro excavations have revealed a seal dating 3000 BC., which depicts figure of a deity seated in a yogic posture. This indicates that the *yogāsānās* (yogic postures) and discipline of *yoga* itself are much older than the *Vedās* and the *Upanishads.* It may be added that the commentators of the Patanjali's *Yoga Sūtras* have included their own descriptions which reflect either the personal interpretations or experiences of these later authors. The first known commentator of the *Yoga Sūtrā* of Patanjali was Vyāsa : and a later author by name Svatmarama Suri wrote the *Hathayoga Pradīpikā* (*Yoga Samhitā*), the most authoritative text book on the *hatha yoga.*

Concepts of physical culture and body functions in yogic teachings

Although information about *yoga* is available from several sources, the main text on the subject is the *Yoga Samhitā (Hathayoga Pradīpikā).* The word *Yoga* is derived from the Sanskrit root *yuj,* which means to link, to join, to unite. The English work 'yoke' originates from the same root. The word *yoga,* it seems refers to the union of the embodied *prāna* (vital force) to the universal energy (*mahā shakti).* However Patanjali interprets it to mean stopping the fluctuations and disturbance of consciousness (*chitta),* which permits the *shakti* embodied in the individual to shine in its own pristine state. It may also mean achievement of inner equilibrium (*samatvam)* under various circumstances. According to the *Yoga Sūtrās* of *Patanjali, Yoga* restrains the consciousness from responding to different forms of stimuli (*yogashchittavrittinirodhah).* Among the various concepts of *yoga* pertaining to an individual, the foremost is the concept regarding the maintenance of normal bodily functions. For this purpose, the *yoga* system advocates the cleansing and purifying the inlets and the outlets of the body. This involves basically the practice of six types of exercise (*shatkarma).* These are : (*i*) *neti* (cleansing the nasal passages); (*ii*) *dhauti* (cleansing the stomach);

(*iii*) *vasti* (cleansing the rectum and colon); (*iv*) *trātaka* (cleansing the eyes by fixing the gaze on some object without blinking and keeping it fixed until the lachrymal secretion starts flowing freely). With this practice, according to the *Tāntrika upāsanā* (meditation according to the *Tantrās), divya drishti* (celestial vision) is acquired; (*v*) *kapālabhātī* (cleansing the nosopharynx and possibly also the nasal air sinuses; literally means shining the head, and involves incessant forced brief exhalations through the nasal passage.); and (*vi*) *Vajrolī* (cleansing the urinary passages by drawing in water through the penis into the urinary bladder by means of *naulī*—an exercise in which the wave-like rhythmic contractions along the length of the rectus abdominis muscles are produced, with the diaphragm remaining fixed. Some additional cleansing practices have been advocated, from time to time, by various authors, which include some variations of the above six yogic exercises, as well as, *gajakaranī, bagī* and *shankhaprakshālana.* The variations of the six yogic exercises are drawing in air, water, milk, animal fat, cotton thread, or cloth, and ejecting out the material after retaining it in the body for sometime. *Gajakaranī* involves drinking large quantities of water, and vomiting it like an elephant (*gaja*) ejects water under force through its trunk. *Bagi* is done by throwing up the remains of food after a lapse of about 3 hours after eating. *Shankhaprakshālana* means pouring water into a conch shell (*shankha)* which comes out through its other end. In the yogic exercise, thus, a large quantity of water is taken by mouth and passed out through the rectum, in a brief period of time. All these practises are suggestive of systematized awareness regarding the need for the controlled function of the viscera of the body.

After cleansing the body of impurities by these yogic means, *yoga* advocates the performance of physical moral and psychological practices. These are described under eight headings : (*i*) *yama* (abstention), (*ii*) *niyama* (observance), (*iii*) *āsana* (physical postures), (*iv*) *prānāyāma* (breath control). (*v*) *pratyāhāra* (control of sensory perception), (*vi*) *dhyāna* (fixed attention), (*vii*) *dhāranā* (contemplation), and (*viii*) *samādhi* (absolute concentration).

The individual who is purified by these practices and is read to be initiated into the disciple of *yoga,* is made to accept moderation in his activities in relation to the external environment as well as in eating and sensory gratifications. The self-imposed discipline is accompanied by the practice of different postures, eighty-four in number, with several variations. The practice of these postures essentially tends to exercise and relax almost all the muscles of the body, to prepare it for a prolonged steady stable and co-odinated activity without producing fatigue.

The yogic postures may be classified into three categories. One of these is meant only to relax the muscles of the body, along with the mental relaxation. The second type of postures are meant for an improved coordination as well as exercise of different groups of muscles for maintaining steady postures. In these a postures is steadily and slowly acquired and maintained as long as an individual can hold it. Then gradually the body is returned to the initial starting position. These *āsanās,* thus, have a static component as well as a dynamic phase of muscle action. Extreme emphasis is laid on avoiding fatigue and regular practice is very much recommended. Each posture has a counter posture which generally involves the participation of antagonist muscles, whose agonists are used in the preceding posture. The third variety of *āsanās* is primarily aimed at maintaining a stable position of the body for a prolonged period, to initiate and sustain some other activity. These are specific body postures for meditation *(dhyāna),* for breathing exercises *(prānāyāma)* and for awakening of the *Kundalinī shakti* (serpent power), etc. This methodical use of muscles of the body for the control of physical, mental, and even visceral functions, dipicts a highly specialised interest in kinesiology and related fields of muscle action.

Prānāyāma (Prāna means breath, and *āyāma* a pause) pertains to controlled breathing exercises, and in a broader sense, also implies control of the vital forces, *i.e., Prānās.* There are eight basic types of breathing exercises which were originally decribed in the ancient texts. These are, *ujjāyī;* to pronounce aloud), *sūrya bhedana* (inhalation through *Sūrya nādī* or the right nostil) *sīkārī* (producing charcteristic wheezing sound during inspiration). *Shītalī* (cooling procedure by inhaling with a protruded tongue and break like opening of the lips), *bhastrikā* (breathing like bellows), *bhrāmarī* (imitating humming of the bees during inhalation and exhalation), *mūrchchā* (capable of rendering the mind passive), and *plāvinī* (enabling the person to float on water). The breathing and its exercises were understood to consist of three parts. These are *pūraka* (inhalation), *kumbhaka* (pause) and *rechaka* (exhalation). The pause is further considered to occur at the end of either the inspiration (*Ābhyantara kumbhaka)* or the expiration (*Bāhya kumbhaka*). Until specified otherwise *Ābhyantara kumbhaka* (pause after inspiration) follows deep ispiration, and at that stage the lung volume consists of tidal volume plus varying amount of inspiratory capacity and only vey rarely may be initiated after tidal volume alone. *Bāhya kumbhaka* (pause after exhalation) on the othe hand is made to occur after breathing out varying amounts of expiratory reserve volume, and may even be initiated sometimes after breathing out the total expiratory reserve capacity. These breathing exercises combine different proportions of the components of a breathing cycle. Although much more importance is given to the pause, the ratio of the time taken for inspiration, expiration as well as for the pause, is also emphasized. Thus, in *Ujjāyī* the ratio is 1:4:2 for *pūraka, kumbhaka* and *rechaka* respectively. Some of these are practised with sharp, quick continuous expiration, others by breathing against resistance, or breathing directed at evaporation of saliva during inspiration. This seems to achieve the objective of exercising the respiratory and oropharyngeal muscles in different situations. In addition, in some types of *prānāyāma* the adoption of slow gradual inhalation and exhalation, with prolonged pauses, probably may be leading to a gradual adaptation for a relative anoxia and hypercarbia. The latter two together may be gradually introducing a possibility for the individual to reduce his metabolic activty as a result of prolonged practice of *prānāyāma.* At the same time the entire respiratory tissue complex, including the lungs, is exercised and put to additional functional activity. The procedure of concerntration and developing self-confidence is very much related to the practice of *prānāyāma.* The most suitable environment indicated is a cold climate with a pure atmosphere in natural outdoor surroundings. While some of the *prānāyāmas* are used as cleansing practices, as mentioned earlier, others form the basis for the subsequent excitation of internal organs, which may be required in procedures like awakening of the *Kundalinī shakti.*

Apart from the yogic procedures mentioned above, there are twelve *mudrās* (symbolic gestures), ten *mahāmudrās* (great gestures) and three *bandhās* (blocking of passages of certain organs by fixing their status with contraction of certain muscles). The most commonly used *mudrās* are, *jnāna mudrā* (symbolic gesture of knowledge), *simha mudrā* (symbolic gesture of a lion), *yoga mudrā* (symbolic gesture of yoga), *yoni mudra* (symbolic posturing of pelvic region), *khecharī mudrā* (positioning the bifid and frenulectomized tongue against the posterior nares to block the nasopharyngeal respiratory passage), and *mahān mudrā* (symbolic posturing of several regions of the body simultaneouly, indicative of massive effort). The three *bandhās* are, *uddayana* (raising of diaphragm), *jalandhara bandha* (chinlock, when chin is pressed against the chest) and *mūla bandha* (vigorous contraction of anal sphincters and the pelvic diaphragm).

One of the steps in yogic training in *pratyāhāra,* which literally means "gathering towards oneself or checking outgoing powers of mind". This involves reducing or elimination of sensory inputs and controlling the motor outputs as well as attention towards the external environment. The other three steps are more or less continuous, which involve the practice of *dhāranā* (holding the mind fixed on certain points), *dhyāna* (meditation, which involves fixing of attention), and finally *samādhi* (superconscious state). *Dhāranā dhyāna* and *samādhi* together are called *Samyama.*

The highest aim in *yoga* is to attain a state of *samādhi. Yoga* is referred to in several contexts. By and large all of these refer to one or the other form of mental activity, consciousness about the self in relation to the universe, and its causal sources. One of them, i.e., *rāja yoga,* involves the practice of *samādhi* primarily, and the *yogī* may or may not go through the routine practice of all the eight steps enumerated previously. *Laya yoga* involves getting absorbed in an idea as guided by a teacher. In *mantra yoga* the *yogī* attains the ultimate objective of *samādhi* by means of chanting a *mantra* (formula). In *abhāva yoga,* the self is meditated upon as cipher, or is treated as brieft of all qualities. In *mahā* yoga, the self is realized as full of bliss and as one with the universal power. *Brahma yoga* implies the indentification of the self and the universe with the Creator Himself.

The various forms of *yoga* relate to different states of consciousness and ideas relavant to them. *Hatha yoga,* for example, is primarily concerned with the information and practices relating to the somatic functions of the body. *Kundalinī yoga,* on the other hand expresses idea about the relationship of bodily functions and the mental activities with the cosmological phenomenon. Thus, we see that *yoga* visualises the need for a controlled function of somatic musculature, visceral organs, and mental activity. It tends to relate the activities of an individual as a whole to his immediate surroundings and universe at large. Since life is dependent on regular breathing, which according to the ancient Indian concepts supplies *prāna,* the ancients attached considerable importance to the control of *prāna* intake and its utilisation in the body through the practices of *prānāyāma.*

Background concepts relating to the yogic thought

The *Vedānta* school of philosophy considers that there are seven different planes or levels (*sapta bhūmikās)* of the existence of mind. These different planes (*bhūmīs)* are also known as vortices or centres (*chakrās).* The cranialmast of all these centres existing at the seventh (highest) plane is the thousand petalled (*sahasrāra)* centre, and the caudal centres are collectively known as the "six centres" (*shatchakrās).* These planes of existence of mind can be understood only by acquiring knowledge of these centres (*that chakra bheda).* It is believed that the supreme form of existence or 'being' is mindless and limitless, and its understanding leads to knowledge, bliss and revelation of absolute existence. The self (*chit)* is veiled by mind, and the matter (*prakriti*). *Prakriti* possesses power of veiling (*āvarana)* and projecting (*vikshepa)* which is does through previous exeriences (*samskārās).* The creator (*Brahmā)* and its creative power (*prakriti shakti)* are inseparable and indentical. However creating power participates in the creation and evolves as mind and matter. It consists of three qualities (*gunās)* of *satva, rajas* and *tamas,* which are the cause of creation. The *prakriti* remains in quescent form as long as these three qualities are in equipoise, when no creation take place. Their imbalance however, leads to the creation. If the highest of these qualities (*satva guna)* predominates the creative power manifests as *māyā* (materialistic qualities of universe), but with the predominance of the other two qualities (*rajas and tamas),* the creative power manifests itself as ignorance (*avidyā).* The *prakriti shakti* under the sway of three *gunās* reveals itself as the created being (*jīva). Prakriti shakti* has also been termed as vital power (*prāna),* primordial power, and even equated with the *Kundalinī shakti* (serpent power) in the body. The manifested energy proceeds from the power of *prāna* or *Kundalinī,* but the manifested matter from *ākāsha.*

Ākāsha is one of the gross forces into which primordial energy differentiates. The vibrations of *prāna* in the subtle *ākāsha tanmātrās* or atoms, produce the gross ether (*ākāsha).* From ether (*ākāsha)* comes air (*vāyu),* from air (*vāyu)* fire (*tejas),* from fire (*tejas)* water (*ap*), and from water (*ap*) earth (*prithvī).* From earth (*prithvī)* all forms of living and nonliving objects are produced. Ether (*ākāsha),* air (*vāyu),* fire (*tejas),* water (*ap),* and earth (*prithvī)* are called *Panchabhūtās* of five elements, all of which have three qualities (*gunās) i.e. satva, rajas* and *tamas.* From *satva* quality of the five elements (*bhūtās)* are evolved the five sense organs of man (*jnānendriyās), i.e.,* the organs of sound, touch, vision, taste and smell. These senses are the faculties of the living being (*jīva)* and not the physical sensory organs themselves. Also from the *satva* quality of the five elements is evolved the mind (*manas).* From *rajas* quality arise five organs of action (*karmendryās), i.e.,* tongue, hands, feet excretory and generative organs, and five *prānās* (vital forces). The functions of mind (*manas*) are intellect (*buddhi*), ego (*ahankāra*), will (*ichchā*) and self or mind stuff (*chit*). *Tamas* with the five elements creates the physical or gross body. Individual (*ātmā*) lives in all living bodies (*sharīra*), and in the spiritual heart (*chetas*) lying two inches above the pit of the stomach and a little below the right nipple (Table II).

Table II

Interaction of the *panchabhūtas* (five elements) and *gunās* (attributes) in the creation of the body

Name of element (bhūta)	*Interaction with its quality (gunās)*	*Formation of the parts of the body*
Ākasha, vāyu, tejas,	*Satva*	*Jnānendriyās* (sense organs) *and manas* (mind)
prithuī ap and		
-do-	*Rajas*	*Karmendriyās* (organs of action) and *prānās* (vital or motive forces)
-do-	*Tamas*	*Sthūla deha* (physical boyd)
Ākāsha alone	*Rajas*	*Jihvā* (organ of speech)
Vāyu -do-	"	*Hasta* (hands)
Tejas -do-	"	*Pāda* (feet)
AP -do-	"	*Guda* (excretory organs)
Prithuī -do-		*Shepha* (generative organs)

The five *prānās* and *vāyūs* perform various secretomotor function in the different parts of the body. Every individual possesses three bodies — gross, subtle and causal. The gross body functions in the state of wakefullness, and the individual (*jīva*) identifying itself with this is called *vishwa*, or *vaishvānara*. It recognises external objects. The subtle body functions in the dream state, and the individual is then called *tejas*. It recognises internal objects. The causal body functions in the dreamless state of deep sleep, and the individual is termed *prajnā*. This state of *prajnā* is considered to occur through thought. Even a fourth bodiless state of existence is visualized as *ātman* or *turya*. In this state the existence loses the cognisance of even sound. Individual (*jīva*) is enveloped by five sheaths (*koshās*) which are : (1) The first sheath is called *annamaya kosha,* and in the physical body is sustained by food (*anna*). This results from *Tamoguna,* and is dominated by inertness. (2) The second sheath is called *Prānamaya kosha.* It consists of subtle body with five gross and five subtle senses, as well as ten types of breath and air (five *prānās*) and five *vāyūs*). It results from *rajoguna* and *kriyā* shakti (power of action). (3) the third sheath is *manomaya kosha.* It consists of mind (*manas*) with five subtle senses resulting from *satvaguna.* It is inhabited by cognition. (4) The fourth sheath is *vijanānamaya kosha.* It consists of intellect (*buddhi*) with five subtle senses, and is produced by *satvaguna* mixed with *rajogouna* (5) The fifth sheath is *ānandmaya kosha* which consists of *jīva* with causal body. This sheath is produced by *satvaguna* and contains joys of various kinds (*priya, moda, promoda*).

Concept of Kundalinī shakti

Prāna, which is the driving force and basis of life is conceived to be reaching each part of the body through numerous *shirās* or *nādis* channels). The total number of these channels in the body is different according to different texts. Thus there are 72,000 of them in the body according to the *Bhūtashuddhi Tantra,* 300,000 as per the *Prapanchasāra,* and 350,000 according to the *Shiva Samhitā.* The chief amongst these channels are *idā, pinglā, sushumnā, sarasvatī, lakshmī* and *medhā.* The most important two of them are *sushumnā* and *medhā nādīs.* These channels function in relation to six main centres (*chakrās*) which are considered to perform certain specific functions in relation to somatic, autonomic and mental activities. A brief concept of these channels (*nādis*), centres (*chakrās*) and their relationship to primordial energy

(*Kundalinī shakti,* meaning coiled like a serpent) is as follows :—

Under ordinary circumstances only some of these channels and centres are in a functional state. These however can be made active from their potential forms by certain yogic practices. The *prāna shakti* in the individual (microcosm) is also related to the cosmic energy (macrocosm) through the mediation of these channels in the body. Ordinarily *idā* or *pinglā shirā* functions to transmit *prāna* to the body. *Pinglā shirā* is related to right nostril and is also called *sūrya nādi* (pertaining to qualities of *sūrya* or sun), while *idā* refers to the left norstril and is named *chandra nādī* (pertaining to qualities of *chandra* or moon). These work alternatively and the activation of *idā* stops *pinglā* and vice versa. These two channels connect to *mūlādhāra chakra* below, and through a spiritual course upwards around *sushumnā,* tend to meet at *ājnā chakra* in the space between the eye-brows, from where they separate out and establish connection with left and right nostril respectively. Some commentators represent these to be taking a bow-like course instead of spiralling around *sushumnā. Sushumnā nādi* starts from *mūlādhāra chakra* which is located at the place of the meeting of the *Kunda* (the root of all the *nādis* including the *sushumnā nādi),* between genitals and the anus. It is situated in the interior of the *meru danda* (the spinal column) and extends up to the *brahmarandhra* located in the corwn of the head where the vortex of the hair is situated. The *sushumnā nādī* has an outermost sheath *sushumnā,* and an innermost sheath *chitrinī,* and within the latter is the *brahma nādī.* It is the latter through which *prāna* or the *Kundalim shakti* courses through after it *(brahma nādī)* gets opened. Normally *sushumnā* is closed and the primordial energy or *kundalinī* lies coiled up at the *mūlādhāra chakra (mūla* means root, and *ādhāra* means support). With the opening of *sushumnā nādī* working of *idā* or *pinglā* is first diminished, and as the *prāna* enters along the *sushumnā nādī,* their activity stops completely. The directing of the passage of *Kundalinī shakti* along *sushmnā* involves its passage through six basic *chakrās* which are also the meeting point of several other *shirās.* The *idā* and *pinglā* lie on either side of *sushumnā.* Corresponding to *idā, pinglā* and *sushumnā* are *sarasvati, lakshmi* and *medha* in front. The latter three become functional only after prolonged practice. *Kundalinī* courses through *idā* and *sarasvatī, pinglā* and *lakshmī,* and *sushumnā* and *medhā.* When *idā* and *sarasvatī* are functioning the breath flows through left nostril, and when *pinglā* and *lakshmī* are functioning then through the right nostril. With the functioning of *shshumnā nādī* the breathing takes place through both the nostrils. *Medhā nādi* starts from *mūlādhāra* and runs through in front of the body, in the midline, to the head region, where it joins *sahasrāra chakra* (thousand petalled centre). This relates individual *prāna* with the universal *prāna. Sarasvatī* also originates from *mūladhāra,* courses along left side of the urethra to the side of testicle after touching the *svādhisthāna chakra.* It then crosses the testicle and courses on the left side of the root of the genitals upwards, passes about 1/2 inch left of the navel, reaching the physical heart *(hridaya)* to which it is connected. It also connects with the spiritual heart *(chetas)* located on right side of the chest from where it joins the *sushumnā nādi,* and courses up one inch on the right side of the left nipple, going along he left side of the neck and the temporo-mandibular joint of the same side, along the back of the left ear from where it turns and joins *ājnā chakra,* between the two eye-brows. At this *chakra* it meets the other *nādīs i.e. idā, pinglā, sushumnā* and *lakshmī.* It is concerned with the elaboration of thought.

Lakshmī nādī takes a parallel course to *sarasvatī nādi* and runs along the right side of the body, taking a symmetrical course to its counterpart to reach the *ājnā chakra.* These principal channels are in communication with several other channels in the body and are supposed to be related to certain levels of body functions, especially in relation to the conscious states.

Kundalinī shakti in the body exists in potential and dynamic form. *Mūlādhāra chakra* is described as the centre for dynamic form from where its gross manifestations are observed. For this reason, functioning of this centre is expressed to be the source of all bodily powers which function at unconscious plane of mind. *Kundalinī shakti* exists in its potential form in *sahasrāra.* In a way there are two centres of its polarization, in dynamic (kinetic) form at *mūlādhāra chakra* and in static (potential) form at *sahasrāra chakra.* The linking of these two forms involves its activation and direction at the root of the *mūlādhāra chakra* and the realization of different planes of consciousness as it is made to course upwards, along the other *chakrās* intervening toward *sahasrāra.* The realization of this process of the subtle locations in the form of *chakras,* and their characteristics involve the association of certain symbols related to the basic sounds and words originating from them as well as aassociated colours. Activation of these *chakrās* also leads to the manifestation of the qualities of some specific *bhūtās,* as well as gods and godesses. The individual is described to achieve the characteristics accompanying their symbolic forms and expressions. Each symbolic sound is described to represent a form of *prāna shakti* related to a *nādī* in a given *chakra.* An equal number of *bija mantrās* (primal sounds) are experienced from each *chakra.* Out of these, one is considered to be specific for each *chakra,* whose experience and realization is essential to activate the presiding deity of the *chakra* as well as its *shakti.* The sounds relating to all the fifty alphabets of Sanskrit language are heard in the process of activation of different *chakras;* but each *chakra* has its own specific number of sounds which also represent number of *nādis,* which meet at the *chakra,* each carrying the *prāna shakti* of its own. The general concept of the *shat chakra,* each element (*bhūta*) related to each *chakra,* its location in the body and its functions, are discussed below.

Each of the *chakrās* is represented in symbolic form of a lotus. The number of petals of a lotus signify the number of *nādis,* and the energies related to a *chakra,* so also the colour and other geometrical and figurative representations. Each of these constitutes a *yantra* (instrument), and the manner of its use constitutes the *tantra* (technique). Any one of these procedures, *i.e.,* utilizing a *yantra, a tantra or a mantra* (formula for chanting) alone, or in combinaion could be employed for activating the *Kundalinī shakti* for its ascent to different *chakrās.* All these *chakras* are situated one cranial to the other, in the order mentioned below :

The essential function of *mūlādhāra chakra* is the creative desire (*kāma).* The activity relating to procreation results from its function, and so also the experience of different types of pleasures. From the *mūlādhāra chakra* the next stage of activity is the activation of *svādhisthāna chakra.* It is situated at the root of the genitals between *mūlādhāra* and *manipūra chakrās.* Its *vrittis* (qualities) are expressed in credulity, suspicion, distrust, disdain. delusion, disinclination, false knowledge and pitilessness. *Manipūra chakra,* as its name implies, is lustrous like a *gem (mani)* because of the presence of fiery *tejas* in it. It is located at the level of the navel in relation to *meru danda* (spinal column). Its qualities are shame, fickleness, jealousy, desire, laziness, sadness, dullness, ignorance, aversion, disposition of granting boon, showering blessing and dispelling fear. It can also lead to invulnerable passion. *Anāhata chakra* lies in the region of the heart. Its qualities are hope, care, anxiety, endeavour, *mamatā* (sense of possession), arrogance, hypocricy, langour, conceit, discrimination, coverteousness, duplicity, indecision and regret. *Vishuddha chakra* lies at the lower end of the throat, and its qualities are production of seven musical notes, venom and ambrosia (*amrita). Lalan chakra* is close to *vishuddha chakra* near the palate. It carries qualities of faith, contentment, sense of error, self-command, anger, affection, sorrow, greed, defection purity, detachment, agitation, appetite and desire. *Ājnā chakra* is situated in the forehead between the two eye-brows. it has all the three *gunās,* and its characteristic (*tattva)* is mind (*manas).* Above this is located *manas chakra* which has six *nādis* which denote faculties of hearing, touch, sight, smell, taste and sensations initiated in the brain during dreaming and hallucination. *Soma chakra* is above the *manas chakra* and has sixteen virtues of mercy, gentleness, patience, composure, dispassion, constancy, cheerfulness, rapture, thrill, sense of propriety, humility, meditation, gratitude, restfulness, gravity, enterprise, effort, absence of emotion, magnanimity and concentration. Highest of all these *chakrās* is *sahasrāra* or thousand petalled centre. In this centre all the sounds and energies of the lower *chakrās,* manifest in their causal states and different forms. Here static and kinetic forms of *prakriti shakti* unite. In this reside all the letters of the alphabet in each petal of the *chakra.* It contains the qualities of all the lower *chakrās* in potential state. It is here that the energies of universe and the self merge completely along with mind intellect, ego and mind-stuff. At this *chakra* quiescent consciousness is realised, and so also the supreme consciousness. In one of the forms of *samādhi,* subject, object and the knowledge completely merge together. This state manifests by an intense awareness of the self in relation to the universal *shakti*.

It is apparent from the above description that the activity of each *chakra* manifests in the form of *vrittis* (qualities) which the individual experiences as moral qualities. The *vrittis* of lower tow *chakrās* are materialistic and glorify selfishness, whilst those of *anāhata chakra* are mixed. The *chakrās* above this are associated predominantly or exclusively with good qualities. The concept of hierarchy in the evolution of higher functions is depicted in the form of subjective illustration of the experiences. Since the realization of this concept is based on the subjective analysis of sounds, especially those pertaining to the Sanskrit alphabet, a large number of letters of such alphabet is indicative of the magnitude of the development. Thus the total number of fifty letters of the Sanskrit alphabet is multiplied at least twenty times to constitute the thousand petals of the highest *chakra*. The ancients further realized that apart from expressive manifestation of consciousness in sound, a state of emptiness or void *(shūnya)* also exists, wherein even sound is not expressive. The supreme *bindu i.e.* the primal energy, is seen here in the void of the space relating to the supreme light, which is formless and decayless. It is here that one can function even without bringing in the concept of his own physical body.

There have been some attempts in the modern literature on *yoga* to compare some anatomical structures and their function as known to the modern science, with the practices of *yoga* and the concepts of *chakrās* and *nādis*. For example, to the vagus nerves are attributed the functional characteristics of *kundalinī* (Rele 1927), to the afferent and efferent nerves those of *idā* and *pinglā nādis* (Vivekananda 1914), and to the autonomic ganglia the functions of various *chakrās* (Avalon 1958). Such an attempt, however, cannot account for several attributes which do not fit in with the functional correlates of the proposed anatomical structures. In the present exposition of ancient concepts of *yoga,* therefore, an attempt has been made to give a brief account of the salient features of the original concept only, without referring to their possible correlation to any of the known aspects of the bodily function according to modern physiology.

The yogic concept of the bodily functions was primarily evolved from introspection, whereas the modern approach to elucidation of bodily function is experimental, in which the function is recorded in one or more physical parameters. While manipulating different functions of the body through breathing exercises and muscular activities, the *yogīs* describe mainly their subjective experiences accompanying such physical practices. Introspection being close to philosophy, they also relate the functional aspects of *yoga* to their religious experiences.

"The belief begins where science leaves of, and ends where science begins."

Composition of Human Body

Āyurveda is probably the earliest medical science that laid stress on positive health, a blending of physical, mental, social, moral and spiritual welfare. The main aim, if not the entire theme of *Āyurveda* is well expressed by Charaka, when he states "it is that knowledge of life which deals elaborately and at length with conditions beneficial or otherwise to the humanity, and to factors conducive to the happiness, or responsible for misery or sorrow, besides indicating measures for healthful living for full span of life". This stresses the need for a balanced living to ensure normal health or a disease free state (*ārogya).* All the ancient scriptures also lay emphasis on healthy living as a prerequisite for achieving the four supreme ends of life, *i.e.,* righteousness (*dharma),* wealth (*artha),* cultural and artistic values (*kāma)* and spiritual freedom (*moksha).* While emphasising the above aspect, however, the Āyurvedic system does not ignore information regarding the disease and its prevention as well as therapeutic measures.

Āyurveda defines life (*āyu)* as the union of body (*sharīra),* senses (*indriyās),* mind (*satva)* and soul (*ātmā).* The living man, the man of action (*karma purusha)* is a conglomeration of three humors (*tridoshās),* seven basic tissues (*sapta dhātūs)* and tree excretions (*trimalās) i.e.,* feces, urine and sweat. These constitute the body matrix (*deha)* and therefore, form basic doctrine of *Āyurveda.*

The body has been termed as *sharīra* and *deha.* Etymologically, the term *sharīra* means the place where destruction or destructive processes take place, and in modern parlance this may mean katabolism or the katabolic processes the term *deha* signifies the idea of growth and development, and is quite akin to the anabolic processes. Thus, the metabolic activity of the organism is indicated by the usage of these terms. The teaching of *Āyurveda* also emphasises that the body is the outcome of nutrition. The normal health or otherwise is largely dependent on ingestion, digestion, absorption, assimilation and metabolism of food. The digestive fire (*agni),* therefore, has a relevance in this regard along with the *doshas, dhātūs* and *malās.*

According to *Āyurveda,* a healthy person (*swastha)* is one in whom there is an equilibrium of the humours and the body tissues, with normal digestive as well as excretory functions, associated with the gratification of the senses, mind and soul (*prasannātmendriyamanah).* The disease is due to an imbalance of the equilibrium of either or all of the above. Of these constituents soul (*ātmā)* is the cause of animation, the mind (*manas)* constitutes the psychic or mental component, and the equipoise or otherwise is dependent on the inherent qualities of these constituents (*trigunās, i.e., satva, rajas and tamas*). A person with predominance of *satva* quality possess mental equipoise, clarity, purity of thought and ideas, pleasure, etc.; one with *rajas* quality is full of activity and energy; and one with *tamas* quality possesses in abundance inertia, passivity, bewilderment, delusion and ignorance. All these depict states of mind, and as such it is appropriate to state that *satva, rajas* and *tamas* are the qualities (*gunās*) of mind (*manas*). Just as there are three qualities of mind, there are three components connected with the body whose equilibrium or otherwise decides its state. They are the three humours, *vāta, pitta* and *kapha*. The Āyurvedic *Samhitās* also sum up the composition of man as a union of mental, spiritual and physical factors.

The physical body is composed of five elements or substances (*panchabhūtās*) namely *prithvī, ap, tejas, vāyu* and *ākāsha;* and so are all the parts of the body. There is a condensation of these elements in different proportions to suit the needs and requirements of different structures and functions of the body. The growth and development of the body depends on its nutrition, *i.e.,* on food. The food, in turn, is composed of the above five elements (*bhūtās*), which replenish or nourish the like elements (structures formed out of them) of the body.

Man is a microcosm, within the macrocosm or universe, since all the particulars which occur in universe are also present in him. The universe has also the five elements (*bhūtās*) which go to form the human body. The knowledge to these five elements (*bhūtās*), thus, helps in classifying substances on the basis of their generic properties. In man, they are also correlated to the five senses that enable man to have subjective contact with the objective universe.

Basic Humours of the Body

Vāyu, pitta and *kapha* are the three basic humours (*dhātūs)* of the body, which are susceptible to imbalance and vitiation, and in turn, capable of vitiating other structural and functional elements of the living body, thus causing the morbidities of different kinds. They are termed *dhātūs* since they sustain and support the body, when within proper measure and when in a state of equilibrium. This is a phenomenon observed in a state of *arogatā* (disease-free state). But when they are in imbalance and cause disease they are also called *doshās*. The three *dhātūs,* therefore, are basic humoural factors concerned with the healthy or the diseased condition of the body. This is the fundamental doctrine — *tridhātu* or *tridosha siddhānta* of *Āyurveda*. Sushruta, however, includes blood (*rakta)* along with the other three humours and considers the four *doshās* instead of three determining the origin, preservation maintenance, integrity and dissolution of the body. Blood was possibly given equal importance with the other humors by Sushruta since his main field was surgery. The basic qualities of the three humours and their role in the human body have been already outlined in another chapter of this text; and the seven basic tissues of the body have also been dealt with in detail.

The seers of *Āyurveda* have clearly indicated that the human body is the product of food. The health or disease has definite and distinct relationship to the ingestion of the type of food, *i.e.,* wholesome or unwholesome agreeable or otherwise. Meticulous care has been taken to indicate food substances that are wholesome and agreeable for normal functioning of the body. The mental and spiritual development are also equally influenced by the type of diet. In spite of mentioning the dietetic regimen and rules relating to the intake of food, the *Charaka Samhitā* (or more appropriately the *Agnivesha Samhitā)* makes it abundantly clear that a number of diseases, difficult to cure or incurable, arise out of lapses and indiscretions regarding dietary habits. The concepts of nutrition found in more recent works on physiology are also reminiscent of the ideas of the ancient physicians of India and their recognition of role of diet in the maintenance of health and causation of disease.

The foods are classified into four varieties based on their consistency, and on their mode of ingestion as *ashita* or solid foods, *pītta* or liquids that could be drunk, *līdha* or those that are licked, and *khādita* or those that are chewed. All these have the five basic elements present in them ; and have six different tastes, as stated in the earlier chapters, and other qualities which along with the taste, determine the anticipated physiological effects of each food.

Āyurveda lays stress on the study of *prakriti jnāna* (physiological knowledge) as this helps in thorough understanding of *vikriti jnāna* (pathological knowledge). The study of the various physiological functions attributed to the basic humors is therefore very essential. The *tridhātu siddhānta* declares that three *doshās* or *dhātūs* are responsible for vital biological processes that take place in the human organism. The mechanics of the body as well as its integrity are based on this concept. This approach of *Āyurveda* thus dispenses with the elaborate classification of systems such as the digestive, circulatory, respiratory, locomotor, nervous, endocrine, reproductive, excretory, etc. The cellular component of the human organism is indicated in the *Charaka Samhitā* which states that there are countless atoms (*paramānūs)* which are subtle and beyond the range of sensory perception. These may be considered the ultimate units of biological activity or life process and may be termed as "biological atoms". The *tridoshās* are ubiquitous and move throughout the body which is constituted by the *paramānūs.* It is this organisation that determines and is observable in the biological activity.

The term *vāta* is derived from the root *vā* which means to move, to enthuse, to make known and to become aware of. *Vāta* is an initiator and promotor of biological activity, is incorporeal and unstable.

The functions and role of *pitta,* the second member of the *tridhātu siddhānta.* in the maintenance of health could be appreciated if its very derivation from Sanskrit root, *tap-santāpe* (to heat, burn or warm up) is taken into consideration. *Pitta* is said to be predominantly constituted of *agnibhūta* (element of fire) and therefore, *agni* (fire) is almost taken as its synonym. *Pitta* in general is responsible for the generation of the body heat and certain psychological attributes of the individual. Like *vāta, pitta* also has five dividsions. They are : (1) *Pāchakapitta,* which is mainly concerned with digestion and metabolic activities; (2) *Ranjakapitta,* the one that imparts colour to the plasma (*rasa);* (3) *Sādhakapitta,* which is an instrument for achieving higher mental faculties; (4) *Ālochakapitta* connected with visual perception; and (5) *Bhrājakapitta* which is connected with the lustre of skin. *Pāchakapitta* is located between the stomach (*āmāshya)* and the large intestine (*pakvāshaya).* This *pitta* assists in augmentation of functions of other *pittās* present in the body; and the digestion of food and the metabolic activities are largely due to this *pitta.* The physical quality attributed to this *pitta* is liquidity (*dravatva*). *Rajakapitta* is located in the liver (*yakrit),* the spleen (*plihā)* and stomach (*āmāshaya)* and plays a vital role in the formation of blood (*rakta).* *Sādhakapitta* is located in the heart and is responsible for intelligence, memory, intellect, enthusiasm, and for the capacity to enable one to achieve one's aspirations. From the perusal of the attributed functions it is considered that this is associated with higher psychological and mental activities. *Ālochakapitta* is located in the eyes and is responsible for visual perception. Two aspects of this as *chakshuvaisheshika* and *buddhivaisheshika* are described. The former functions after correlation of soul (*ātmā)* and mind (*manas)* when the object has made its contact with it, leading to the perception and discrimination of its form, colour, size, etc. *Buddhivaisheshika ālochakapitta* is located between the two eye-brows, and is concerned with concentration, response and cogitation. *Bhrājakapitta* is located in the skin and is responsible for its colour, lustre and temperature.

It will generally be observed that this *dhātu* is mainly responsible for a variety of biochemical and biological activities, just as *vāta* is responsible for biophysical and biomotor activities. Any study on *pitta* calls for a particular reference to specific fires such as *bhūtāgni* and *dhātvagni.* The splitting of the food ingested into distinct physico-chemical moieties related to *pancha-bhūtās,* and subsequent biochemical events are due to the action of these specific fires. The utilisation of the food components for energy, structural synthesis and storage are, to a great extent, related to *pitta.*

Kapha, also known as *shleshma,* is the third member of the *dosha*-trinity and is constituted by the element water (*ambu)* and elemental earth (*prithvī). Kapha* is so named because it is the product of water. This may mean that *kapha dhātu* is concerned with the body fluids, and glandular function. The other term *shleshma* is derived from the root *'Shlish Ālingane'* which means to keep together or to cohere. The physical characters and qualities of *kapha* are heaviness, coolness, softness, viscosity, stability, sweetness and sliminess. These qualities are responsible for functions like keeping structures together, promoting unctuousness, contributing to body stability, promoting bulk of the body, providing strength as well as the necessary resistance to disease and decay. It also provides patience and fortitude. The general functions of *shleshma* are lubrication of the joints of the body (*sandhi samshleshana);* promotion of unctuousness of the body (*snehana);* promotion of healing and reparative process (*ropana);* filling up and participation of activities of coservation and storage (*pūrana);* promotion of body strength and improving body resistance to combat disease and decay (*balakrit);* soothing (*tarpana);* and conferring stability to the body (*sthiratva). Kapha,* like the other two humours is present throughout the body but is predominantly present in the chest lungs, stomach, and joints.

The different types of *shleshma (kapha)* are (1) *avalambaka-shleshma (2) kledaka-shleshma (3) bodhoka-shleshma (4) tarpaka-shleshma* and (5) *shleshka shleshma. Avalambaka-shleshma* is located in the chest, supports the sacro-coccygeal joint (*trikasthāna)* by its inherent potentiality, and the heart (*hridaya)* by the conjoint potentiality of its own and that of the other nutrient elements located in the heart. It also supports other places where phlegm is lodged (*kapha-sthānās). Kledaka-Shleshma* is located in the stomach (*āmāshaya),* and plays an important role in moistening, disintegrating and liquefying the ingested food. The base of the tongue (*jivāmūla)* is the site of *bodhoka-shleshma* and is concerned with gustatory function. The site of *tarpaka-shleshma* is the head, and it keeps the sense organs (*indriyās)* soothed and nourished. *Shleshaca shleshma* is present in the joints, and helps in keeping them properly united and plays a role in their smooth mobility. The five divisions of phlegm have been suggested to bear resemblance to the functions of extracellular fluid system, particularly the cerebrospinal, synovial, pleural and pericardial fluids, as well as the vitreous humour, glandular secretion and endolymph. *Kapha* also has an important role to play in the body immunity.

The seven basic tissues of the body (*sapta dhātūs)* exist as formed entities and exhibit changes in their formation and destruction depending on the metabolic processes involved. The replenishment of these tissues takes place constantly by *poshaka dravya* (nutrient substances). There are two kinds of these tissues, the nutrient (*poshaka dhātūs)* also known as *asthāyī dhātu* (unstable tissues), and *sthāyī dhātu* (stable tissues) which are nourished by *poshaka dhātu.*

The seven tissues are formed and nourished by the chyle *āhāra rasa).* The heat (*ūshmā)* in the tissues successively transforms one *dhātu* to the other in a specific and definite order. The essence (*sūkshmabhāga)* from the small intestines is driven by the motive force of *prāna,* along a main trunk, first to the heart, which is a great receptacle of chyle, and thence to the liver and spleen. In the liver, the colouring substance in the bile acts on the chyle, imparts to it a red pigment transforming it into blood; but the grosser part (*sthūlabhāga)* of chyle proceeds along other vessels (*dhamanīs),* driven by the motive force of *vyāna* all over the body. When the blood has been formed, the chyle in the blood acted on by the motive fires (*vāyu*) and the flesh forming fire (*māmsāgni),* forms the flesh with the earth (*prithvī)* part of the food substance specially contributing to its bulk. Of the flesh tissue thus formed, the grosser part goes to replenish the flesh tissue all over the body. The finer essence of flesh in the blood, left over in the chyle, is again acted upon by the motive force, and the fat-forming fire which imparts viscosity and whiteness to it and produces the adipose tissue, the earth and water (*ap)* parts of the food specially contributing to the product. The grosser part of the fat in the blood replenishes the adipose tissue of the body. The finer essence of fat remaining in the chyle is acted upon by the motive forces and the marrow-forming fire, and becomes hard or crystalline, and forms bony tissue; with the earth and fire parts of the food contributing principally to the product. The essence of the fat fills the hollow channels of the bones, and acted on by motive forces and marrow-forming fire, becomes transformed into the marrow. The marrow is similarly transformed into semen. The finer essence of the semen and all the other tissues give off *ojas* (tissue fluid), which returns to the heart, which is also the receptacle of chyle (*rasa*) and blood (*rakta),* and again floods the body and sustains the tissues thus completing the circle of metabolism.

Thus, the progressive metamorphosis of the tissues (*dhātūs)* as postulated in *Āyurveda* is that *rasa* forms *rakta; rakta* forms *māmsa; māmsa* forms *medas; medas* forms *asthi; asthi* forms *majjā,* and *majjā* forms *shukra.*

The commentators of the ancient medical treatises have advanced various hypotheses to explain the mode of production, specificity in the pattern of supply of the nutrient homologues, and the pattern of distribution of metabolically processed nutrients. The various channels (*srotasās)* do not transport *sthira dhātūs,* which already exist in a stable form and as concrete entities, which are nourished through the internal transport system by way of plasma (*rasa).*

Bala (power) is synonymous with *ojas* (tissue fluid) which is considered as *sāra* (extract) of the seven basic tissues. It can be said as quintessence of the seven tissues. *Ojas,* located in the heart (*hridaya)* mixes with plasma (*rasa*), circulates through and permeates the whole body. The presence of *ojas* is the essence of life activities, and a potential source of strength and power which resists decay and disease. "It is verily the seat of life" (*Sushruta Samhitā).*

Besides the seven tissues of the body, there are also supplementary tissues (*upadhātūs).* The table III shows at a glance the *upadhātūs* of the body.

The term *'mala'* (excretion) etymologically means 'to purify'; 'to clear out'. Excretions are produced in the body during digestive and metabolic activity as the by-product of the ingested food. Feces *(shakrit)* and urine *(mūtra)* serve as an index of this Feces represents to some extent the undigested residue left over after the nutrient portion *(prasāda)* is separated and absorbed.

Certain other *mālas* formed during the metabolic activity are mucus. 'bile' excretion of eyes, sweat, sebum, hair, beard and nails.

Table III.
The Upadhatus of the body

Basic tissue		*Supplementary tissue*
1.	*Rasa dhātu*	*stanya* (milk)
2.	*Rakta dhātu*	*rajah* (menstrual flow)
3.	*Māmsa dhātu*	*kandarās* (tendons)
		shirās (vessels)
4.	*Medas dhātu*	*vasā* (fat)
		shad twachās (six layers of skin)
		snāyu (sinew)

Upadhātūs are considered to be identical or similar to *dhātūs* but these do not undergo any further transformation. They do not support the body nor nourish it.

Srotas which means a channel, is defined by Charaka as a structure through which fluids flow *(sravanam)*. The etymological background of this term provides scope for knowing the functions which this structure is associated with. There is a long list of synonyms for this word, such as *dhamanī sirā, nādī, rasāyanī, mārga,* etc., which points out the subtle differences, from the functional as well as structural point of view, that *Āyurveda* ascribed to its various synonyms. The *Charaka Samhitā* makes a clear statement that "no structure in the body can grow and develop, or waste and atrophy, independent of these channels which transport nutrients of body tissues that are constantly being metabolished. Numerous types of these channels are present in the body, with specific function, ascribed to each type. When these functions are impaired they lead to *srotorodha* (blocking of the channel which is characterised by either excessive flow or retention, venous congestion or transportation of fluids to the channels other than the normal ones.

Abundant references to the heart and blood vessels are also found in the *Vedās* and *Upanishads*. The understanding of classification of the vessels into *sirā, dhamanī* and *nādī* is a puzzle in the anatomy of *Āyurveda*. Despite this, the works on *Āyurveda* provide considerable information about the functions of each of these vessels and the heart. The heart is the main receptacle for *rasa, rakta* and *ojas,* and an organ for distribution of the vital fluids to remote parts of the body. *Sirās* seem to possess property of contractility and expansibility. The pulsation of *dhamanīs* was also recognised. And *sirās* and *dhamanīs* are described to carry the vital fluids. The scheme of circulation can well start with the formation of *āhararasa,* and its subsequent sojourn after its reaching *hridaya.* The formation of *rakta dhātu* and other metabolic substances is also connected with the internal transport system. Nourishment and sustenance of body is intimately related to this.

The *Charaka Samhitā* states that "a person who takes suitable diet and practices self-control lives a full span of 100 years or 36,000 nights without illness". The aphorism has in it two components — physical and mental. In other context, the *Charaka Samhitā* states that the food, sleep and self control are the three pillars that support life. The body constituted of *panchabhūtās* like the food that goes to nourish it, has also in it the same constituents. The physical body is thus nourished by the similar physical constituents of the universe present in the food.

The food has physical or physico-chemical and mental properties, the classification of foods is made with reference to their *gunās* (properties or qualities), *rasa* (taste), *vīrya* (innate potency), *vipāka* (effects of the end of digestion), and also with reference to preponderance of elemental constituents. Another classification is made on the basis of the consistency of food. The substances are also grouped as those that are *sātvika, rājasika* or *tam̐asika,* based on such qualities of their constituents. Thus one finds a reference to physical and mental qualities of the body as a whole being affected by the food.

The well-balanced diet, according to *Āyurveda* should contain good rice procured from the paddy that has been harvested in sixty days, green gram, rock salt, embelic myrobalan (*āmalak),* barley, milk, properly collected rain water, *ghee,* flesh of animals living in dry zones, and honey. Careful and critical look into these food items indicates that the food items prescribed provide the body with the necessary carbohydrates, proteins, fats, minerals and vitamins.

Āyurveda commands that none shall eat food without washing hands, feet, and face, and cleansing the mouth. It also recommends that the food should be swallowed only after it has been properly chewed. The 'ten commandments' of Charaka with regard to the healthy food habits are :

1. Eat food when it is hot.
2. Eat unctuous food.
3. Eat in a suitable measure.

4. Eat after the digestion of the previous meal.
5. Eat food which does not contain items with antagonistic properties.
6. Eat in a congenial and agreeable place.
7. Do not eat hurriedly.
8. Do not eat slowly.
9. Eat with concentrated attention; do not talk or laugh while eating.
10. Eat according to individual constitution. Eat what is wholesome and agreeable to the temperament.

The dietary items having attributes indentical to those of particular tissues (*dhātu vridhi)* increase them, and are called homologous (*tulya);* and those that have opposite qualities decrease them (*dhātu (kshya)* and are called heterologous (*vishishta).* The dietary articles are also classified according to their substance, quality and action, in general, corresponding to the tissues they will nourish in the body, and accordingly the choice of the food substances has to be made by an individual.

The maintenance of health and alleviation of suffering in the afflicted one is the object of *Āyurveda.* It is, therefore, mandatory to follow the rules of health as enunciated in *Āyurveda,* and diligently strive to alleviate the suffering of the diseased. The various therapeutic measures propounded by *Āyurveda* are the result of the observations and investigations of the sages and seers, who have declared that "those alone are wise who act after investigation".

"It is easy to sneer at our ancestors" states Thomas Huxley. ". . . but it is much more profitable to try to discover why they, who were really, not one with less sensible persons than our excellent selves, should have been led to entertain views which strike us as absurd". India has suffered in the estimation of the world, more through the world's ignorance of her achievements rather than due to the absence or insignificance of her achievements. This is as much true of *Āyurveda,* as of any other sciences of ancient India.

Neurophysiology

Our ancestors in medicine practised methods of treatment for various diseases long before they understood the functions of the organs of the body. The contemporary philosophers offered vague interpretations of life processes on which our primitive knowledge of medicine was built. For example, due to the erroneous ancient concept of birth, the cult of phallic worship (*liṅga-pūjā*) engendered, which is a clear example of ignorance regarding the physiology of procreation.

The term 'neurophysiology' is of very recent origin even though the ancient medical men of India had their own ideas about the anatomy and physiology of the nervous system. The Hindu socio-religious restrictions on the study of practical anatomy by dissection of the cadaver was an obscurant policy which was solely responsible for our deficient knowledge of anatomy in general and neuroanatomy in particular.

To the medical historians the Aryan civilisation is of prime importance. Various historical facts derived from the treatises on the same are still of profound scientific value. It is certain that the Aryans of the oldest order lacked in modern methods of instrumentation and facilities of proper documentation. But their metaphysical ideas were so potent and rational that we cannot still refute some of their primitive concepts. Sushruta (?600 B.C.) was a greatest surgeon of ancient India, and Charaka (? 1st Century A.D.) was the greatest physician. The large volumes of literature on ancient Indian Medicine and Surgery left behind by these two stalwarts are still our best source of ancient Indian medical sciences.

Sushruta defined the human body thus: "the animate body is said to be composed of five *mahābhūtās* (principal elements) and the soul". (S.S.III. 1.16); whereas Charaka considered the body as the seat of *chetanā (*consciousness) and an evolute of the same *panchamahābhūta* (C.S. VI.3).

Later on another Indian medical scientists, Vāgbhatta (? 7th century A.D.) rationalised the ideas of Sushruta and Charaka, after expunging a good deal of metaphysics from their writings.

The ancient Indians developed all sciences to their contemporary optimum, including the science of healing or prolonging life, known as *Āyurveda.* This science of healing reached its zenith during the reign of Emperor Ashoka (Acc. 273-232 B.C.). The Indian knowledge of medicine was propagated to the countries of the West through Persia, Arabia, Egypt, Greece and Rome. The close philologic similarity of Sanskrit with Latin and Greek greatly facilitated the said propagation. The medicine practised by the Moors in the Southern provinces of Spain was nothing but a variation of Arabian Medicine with prior Indian influence. It would not be an exaggeration to say that Ippocrate Ieraclide (Hippocrates, 460-377 B.C.), the father of Western medicine was also influenced by Indian medical teachings through the School of Medicine in Cnidia, where he had part of his medical education.[1] (Bagchi). Hoernle[2] states that the extent and accuracy of ancient Indian anatomical knowledge was very much anterior to that of contemporary Egyptians and Greeks.

A considerable amount of material is available in *Āyurveda* regarding the anatomy and physiology of the nervous system. But one must have a fundamental knowledge of the very confusing array of glossary used by the same or different writers at various places of their descriptions for meaning a particular organ of the body. The Western medical science is also not very free from such an ambiguity. In Latin "*myelon*" means bone-marrow, and the same word is also used to mean spinal cord even to-day. Possibly, the ancient Western anatomists considered every object anatomically encased inside a body canal as bone-marrow. To cite a similar example in *Āyurveda* one must refer to *Shiras* or the head which was recognised as an important organ of the human body and its content brain has been variously termed as *mastishkam, mastulungam* or *ghritam.* Strangely enough the physiological functions attributed to the above trinominal object did not consider the brain as the centre of neural activity. But the functions of *hridaya (hrit, hritpindam* or the anatomical heart) have been described mostly as those of the brain. According to Charaka, "the part of the body in which the life stays, to which all senses are said to belong and which is the most important of all organs of the body is *Shiras*". Sushruta, was also of the opinion that "head was the most important organ of the human body". In *Sushruta Samhitā* it is clearly indicated that *unmāda* (insanity) and *apasmāra* (epilepsy) originate from the *Shiras.* Strangely enough everywhere in *Āyurveda,* the word *hridaya* is used as the seat of the mind, intellect, centre for sleep, consciousness and other similar faculties. It indicates that though the anatomy and physiology of the nervous system was not prevalent according to our modern concepts of medicine we had our own ideas about neural functions. Bhela (6th century B.C.)[3] when he stated that the seat of mind lay between the head and the palate, must have meant the brain. In spite of the abundance of confusing ideas and metaphysical overlay, the neurophysiologists of the twentieth century will be astounded at the precise fundamental knowledge that the ancient Indian scientists had about the nervous system even five to six hundred years before the birth of Christ.

As has been previously mentioned, the word *hridaya* does not refer to the heart in all cases, but it also means the brain. The present day medical scientists also attribute some sort of emotional factor to our heart knowing fully well that heart has nothing to do with emotions. To quote a famous contemporary heart surgeon, "A kidney is necessary for life. But a heart, many felt, meant not only life but soul". If a medical scientist of this century could utter the above statement, there is no wonder that the ancient Indian medical scientists could have also confused ideas about the brain and the heart. The function of *hridaya* (meaning the brain) are : knowledge (*jnānam),* regulations of five special senses (*panchendriyam),* and regulation of thought process (*chintā).* It is also said to be the seat of soul (*ātmā)* which controls desire (*kāmanā),* malice (*īrshā*), happiness (*pulaka),* sorrow (*dukkha)* and various other worldly human instincts.

In a chapter on *"Arthedasha mahāmōōlīya",* Charaka states that if the *hridaya* is injured, unconsciousness occurs and if it is destroyed the limbs are paralysed and death follows. It is interesting to note that the Latin synonym of *hridaya* is *"cordis"* or *"cor"*. The word *cordis* (Greek-*kardia*) has originated from the Sanskrit root *"Shradh",* *"Shraddhā"* or *"Shrāddha"*. All those words mean respect, which is a quality of the mind and not of the heart. According to Charaka the body consists of six limbs, knowledge, five senses, soul and thoughts emanating from the *hridaya* (C.S.I.30). Therefore, it can be assumed that most of the functions attributed to the *hridaya* are functions of the brain. The functions of the brain stated in various texts of *Āyurveda* can be summarised as:

1. It is a place of *ātmā* (soul).
2. The centre of *chetanā* (consciousness).
3. The seat of *panchendriyam* (special senses).

4. Store-house of *buddhi, medhā* (intellect).
5. The seat of *chitta* (consciousness).
6. Store-house of *smriti* (memory).
7. Centre of *jīvana* (life).
8. Regulator of *nidrā* (sleep).
9. Seat of *rajas* (emotion and passion).
10. It is the *snāyu kendra* (nerve centre).

The nervous system was referred to as *Vāyu,* which is one of the three humours of life (*tridhātu)* according to *Āyurveda.* The *Vāyu* is said to be the regulator of the physical mechanism of the body. According to *Shārangadhara* (14th century A.D.), *pitta* and *kapha* are dependent on *vāyu* "which drives them all as a cloud is driven by wind."

Five kinds of nerves are described in *Āyurveda,* namely *prāna, apīna, samāna, udāna,* and *vyāna.* Those nerves carry out physical functions like mascular contraction, perception of senses as vision, taste, smell touch and hearing. They also help in strengthening the elements of the body and activate speech, sound and hearing, and are the main factors involved in the perception of touch. It is through these nerves that man can perceive pleasure and pain. These nerves also help in digestion and elimination of the waste products of the body (C.S.1.12.7). The *prāna* nerves (cranial nerves) are located in the brain, thorax, ears, tongue, face and nose. The acts of spitting, sneezing, vomitting and digestion are the functions of these nerves (knowledge of these functions simply denotes an idea about a nerve which is comparable to the vagus nerve of modern neurophysiology). The *apāna* nerves are akin to the autonomic nerves and are located in the testis, bladder, genital organs, abdomen and anus. These help in the elimination of faces, urine, semen and ova, and in the delivery of the foetus. The *samāna* nerves are the regulators of the glands (*granthi*) and the lymphatics (*ambu*). The *udāna* nerves are located in the navel (*nābhi*), thorax (*vaksha*), and neck (*grīvā*). The *vyāna* nerves are comparable to the motor nerves. These help in walking and other motor activities (C.S. 6.28.4).

Charka is also of the opinion that man goes to sleep when his organs cease to operate, and explains how the memory is produced. These functions today are attributed to the temporal lobe by the modern neurophysiologist.

One could spend his whole life-time in searching and researching the concepts and interpretations of the functions of the nervous system as understood by the ancient Indians. Those with scientific and patriotic fervour must continue to research into our literature and history for revealing many forgotten facts which are equally rational as our modern concepts of science, particularly in respect of biological sciences.

Bibliography

Arthur Avalon (Sir John Woodroff): *The Serpent Power,* sixth edition, Ganesh and Company, Madras, 1958.

Arthur Avalon (Sir John Woodroof): *Introduction to Tantra Shāstra,* Sixth edition, Ganesh and Company, Madras, 1973.

Bose, D.M., S.N. Sen, B.N. Subbarayappa, (Editors): *A Concise History of Science in India.* Indian National Academy, New Delhi, 1971.

First All-India Yoga Health Seminar: Proceedings — Papers — Decisions, compiled by Yoga Health Department, Bharat Sevak Samaj, New Delhi.

Gopi Krishna: *Kundalinī*-Evolutionary Energy in Man. Shambala Publications, Berkeley, U.S.A., 1971.

Gopi Krishna: *The Biblogical Basis of Religion and Genius.* Harper and Row, New York, 1972.

Gopi Krishna: *The Secret of Yoga.* Turnstone Books, London, 1972.

Kuvalayānanda: *Āsanās*, (Part One), Kuvalayananda Kaivalyadhama, Bombay, 1949.

Kuvalayānanda: *Prānāyāma*, (Part One, Kaivalyadhama, Bombay, 1950.

Shri Yogendra: Yoga, *Personal Hygiene,* The Yoga Institute, Bombay, 1952.

Swami Anandanand: *Health and Yogasanas*. Sanskrit Prakashan Yogasadhana Ashram, Jaipur, 1972.

References

1. Bagchi, A.K. Yug hate Ygantae Chikitsa Shastra, (Medicine through the Ages). Serialised in Amtra, Calcutta — 1963.
2. Hoernle, A.F.R. Indian und die *Dewtschen,* by Leifer, W. *Erdmann,* Tuebingen, 1969.
3. Bhela Samhita; Published by the University of Calcutta, 1921.

6

Pneuma (Vāta) in Vedic Medicine

The lore of pneuma *vāta,* wind, airs or breath (*prānās)* dates back to early Vedic times. Closely similar theories about pneuma are found in the common literature of the early Indo-Iranians. The ideas in the earlier *Vedās* are reflected also in the *Avesta* the earliest religious text of the Parsis.

According to the Ayurvedic theory the three essential principles, *i.e.,* water, fire and wind are common to both the animal kingdom and the cosmos. Among these three principles again, it is the wind that is considered the most active element of the body and regarded by the Indo-Iranians as the motive force par excellence. The *Vedās* have used two words for wind, *vāyu* and *vāta.* The former word has generally been used for the god of winds and the latter for the element wind. The *Avesta* also uses the words *vāyu* and *vāta* with similar connotation as *vāyu* and *vāta* respectively have in the *Vedās.*

The hymns of the *Rg Veda* do not seem to give much importance to the wind as they do to the fire and waters.

But the cosmic importance of the wind is clearly recognised and highly proclaimed. The hymn X. 168 of the *Rig Veda* describes *Vāta* as the "king of entire universe", "the first born", "the soul of gods", "The embryo of the universe", etc. The *Vedās* ascribe to the wind the role of motive power, which regulates the heavenly bodies. The concept of reciprocal relations between the universe and the body is quite clearly shown. The cosmos is sometimes represented in the image of a huge human being (*purusha*) in standing position with his head represented by the skies, the navel by the atmosphere and the feet by the earth (*Ṛig Veda,* X, 90, 14). Among the other cosmic elements, the sun is born of his eye and the wind of his breath.

According to *Brihadāranyaka Upanishad,* however, the cosmos is in the form of the body of a horse (*ashwa),* which has been compared limb by limb with the universe. This *Upanishad* explains further that the world is conceived as the figure of a horse because the sacrificial horse must represent the world in miniature. Here also the wind has been called the breath of this cosmic horse.

In the *Atharva Veda,* Twashtri and Vāyu are the gods who bring breath (*ātman)* into the celestial bull (*rishabha),* which also is an animal of sacrifice. The *Atharva Veda* (X.4.15) decisively affirms the identity of the breath (*prīna)* with the wind (vāta). It is stated that the breath is Mātarishvan (god of wind), it is the wind which is called the breath; it is on the breath that all that was and all that is, all is based.

The *Avesta* of the early Iranians does not push the speculations regarding the wind as far as the *Vedās* do, but undoubtedly recognises the role played by the wind, which in a number of traits ascribed to it by the *Avesta,* resembles what the *Vedās* have given to the wind, with greater emphasis. Although one may admit that the *Avesta* could have borrowed certain data from the Brāhmanic

India, it is also possible that the importance accorded to the wind in the *Avesta* goes back to the pre-Vedic Indo-Iranian period.

The wind in the *Vedās* was conceived simultaneously as an organic as well as cosmic force. The plurality of the organic wind, which were distinguished from one another, shows that the pneumatology which dominates the physiology of *Āyurveda,* was already in the course of formation at that remote period. To understand the extent to which the Vedic texts contain, either in germ or in full form, the concepts of Āyurvedic medicine with regard to *vāta* (wind), one has to critically analyse those passages in the *Vedās* which deal with the vital winds — the *prānās.*

Ewing has very patiently collected all the references to these breaths in the entire Vedic literature. In his critical study he has not only compared the various translations of the *Vedās* by the learned sanskrit scholars, but also the interpretations of various philologists. He opens his discussion with the analysis of the word *'prāna'* and declares that it means the "breath in general". The bifurcation of respiration into inspiration *(prāna)* and expiration *(apāna)* is a very old idea and it appears as a dual compound *"prānāpānau"* in the earliest Vedic texts. The ancient Hindus, keen observers that they were, must have closely watched the phenomenon of respiration when they state that there is always an interval between respirations. They, therefore, created an altogether different term for the breath remaining within the body even in the absence of the above mentioned *prāna* and *apāna.* This was named as *"vyāna".* To these types of breathing other two were again added and by suffixing the root *ān* on to the preverbs *sam* and *ud,* new terms *samāna* and *udāna* were created besides *prāna, apāna* and *vyāna. Udāna* superseded *apāna* in the sense of expiration which etymologically also appears to be more convenient to denote the expiration.

Later on similarities were established between the different members of *prāna* series, and the bricks of the altar at *yajana* (sacrifice) which was prepared in the form of the animal sacrifised. The *Upanishads* explain the exact location of these *prānās* in the various parts of the sacrificial animal and correspondingly in the parts of the altar. The *apāna* for example was placed in the tail of the altar, that is why alter on *apāna* has been localised in the intestines and the urinary tract. Similarly the *samāna* is placed in the middle portion of the altar, so it later became an agent responsible for digestion.

The deductions made from the localisation and function of the different *prānās* have thus contributed to the Indian ideas of anatomy and physiology or the human body, although by themselves these *prānās* do not seem to have any significance. The translation of these words denoting various *prānās* is an extremely difficult task since they are more than individual phenomenal entities.

The word *'prāna'* has been used in the *Rig Veda* as the generic designation of all the *Vātās*. The *Atharva Veda* has also used it in the same context but sometimes it has been used in the plural form. The *Chhāndogra Upanishad* (1.2.9) states that "the *prana*" is *"mukhya"*, which means both "the mouth" as well as "the principal one"; "because therewith one eats, one drinks, one supports the other breaths".

The *vyāna* has been recognised as a 'diffused wind' all over the body. In the *Ṛig Veda,* it is an element of function, and the *Chhāndogya Upanishad* (1,3,3) calls it a joint (*sandhi)* between the *prāna* and *apāna.* If the *prāna* is the breath of the upper part and *apāna* of the lower part of the body, therefore, the *vyāna* which is supposed to circulate in the middle of the body is exactly the one which unites the two.

The *samāna,* along with three other *prānās* has been mentioned once in a verse in the *Atharva Veda* (10,2,13) : "Who has created all the things in the cosmic body ? Who has woven *prāna?* Who has woven *apāna?* Which god has founded the *Samāna* in the man ?" In this passage the significance of *samāna* however, cannot be gauged.

The fifth breath of the classical list, namely *udāna* is mentioned twice in a hymn (11.8.4 and 26) of the *Atharva Veda* which like the other hymns gives a "catalogues of the man". Here also there is no clue to give the correct sense of the word *udāna* but the mention of its name does suggest that the Atharvans already knew the breaths of the classical series.

The *Yajur Veda Samhitā* also explain the series of breaths like the *Atharva Veda* does. The *Vājasaneyī Samhitā, Kāthaka Samhitā* and *Maitrāyanī Samhitā* all make invocation of all the five *prānās,* but the order in which the five *prānās* are put differs from text to text.

To conclude, the essentials of the Vedic physiology are based on the belief that multiple breaths circulate inside the organism. There are exists a system of internal canals with which this concept of circulation is associated. This concept has become a fundamental in the classical medicine. The Medicine of Charaka and Sushruta, while explaining the psychic activity in terms of the interplay of *prānās* has followed the original tradition of Vedic antiquity. If the Vedic *Samhitās* do not offer a systematic explanation of the pneumatic theory, they at least give the technical vocabulary, which, later on has been fully developed in the classical texts of Charaka and Sushruta.

Theory of Pneuma

The fifth *mandala* (book) of the *Rig Veda* has many hymns attributed to a sage Atri or Ātreya. At the famous medical school in Takshashila (Taxilla) also, a medical teacher by name Ātreya, according to many Buddhist texts, is known to have been the preceptor of the famous Jīvaka, who became the personal physician to Gautam Buddha. Ātreya Punarvasu of the *Charaka Samhitā,* who was son of Chandrabhāgā (*Sūtrasthāna* 13,99) does not seem to be either of the above personages, because neither external nor internal source mentions Taxilla as the place of residence of Ātreya Punaravasu. On the other hand in *Vimānasthāna* 3,3 of the *Charaka Samhitā,* he has been described as taking a walk in Kāmpilya, which is a city on the bank of the river Ganges. The word Āgreya which is derived from Atri, means a descendant or follower of Atri.

Years back, in the valley of the holy Himalayas, a conference of sages was held with the common object of removing the suffering of mankind and assuring a long healthy and contented life to everybody (*Charaka Samhitā, Sūtrasthāna* 1). One of the sages whose name was Ātreya Punarvasu requested his six disciples to compile his teachings. Among the treatises which were compiled by Agnivesha, Bhela, Jātūkarna, Pārāshara, Hārīta and Kshārapāni, the one compiled by Agnivesha was considered to be the best. The *Samhitā* of Agnivesha, as it was known later on, was revised by Charaka, and this was the basis of Dridhabalā's edition of the *Charaka Samhitā.* The major portion of the *Charaka Samhitā* is presented in the form of questions and answers between the disciple Agnivesha and his teacher Āteya Punarvasu. That is why *Charaka Samhitā* claims to report the very words of Ātreya Punarvasu.

Many of the physical and metnal phenomena ascribed by modern physiology, primarily to the activities of the central, autonomic and peripheral nervous system, can be identified with the functions ascribed to *vāta* in the classical Hindu literature. The Greek system of medicine also contains a similar physiological concept of pheuma which is known as *Peri Phuson* of Hippocrates. According to A.

Gotze, the concept of breath during the period of *Brāhmanās* had undoubtedly influenced the Greek theory of pneuma.

In the *Charka Samhitā* (*Sūtrathāna,* 12), a scientific symposium at which discussion between the learned sages (*rishīs)* who had gathered from all parts of the world, is reported. On opening the discussion, its chairman Punarvasu Ātreya says "We are now going to contemplate on the functions and disorders of the *vāta."* The great *rishīs* who were desirous of knowing the opinions of one another regarding the knowledge of the functions and disorders of *vāta,* sat together and asked each other "What are the qualities of *vāyu ?* Which are the causes that excite it ? Or which are the objects that calm it ? How do the exciting or alleviating factors, as they are unable to come in contact with *vāta,* which is incorporeal (or formless) and unstable (or unsteady), either excite or alleviate it? And which are its functions when, either in excited or in its natural form it circulates inside the body or outside the body?"

At this moment Kusha, of the family of Sānkritya said, "Dry, light, cold, violent, or causing hardness, roughness and smoothness are the six qualities of *vāta."* After hearing this Kumārshirā Bhardwāja supported the view of Kusha Sānkrityāyana, and said, "It is just as the gentleman has observed. These are the properties of *vāta.* The *vāyu* is excited by the repeated use of such substances and actions which have similar properties. This is based on the principle that an increase in *dhātus* (tissues of the body) takes place by bringing into play the (substance of) homologous properties." Kānkāyana, the physician of Bactria, when he heard these words, said, "It is really the same which the gentleman has told. These are exactly the things which excite the *vāta.* The things which have properties contrary to it alleviate it, because the anatagonist of the exciter is the cause of alleviating the body tissues."

At this Vadisha Dhāmārgava said, "I agree to what has been told by the gentleman. These are only (the things) which excite or alleviate the *vāta*. Now I am explaining to you how do the exciting or the alleviating factors, unable, as they are, to come in contact with *vāta* which is incorporeal (or formless) and unstable (or unsteady), either excite or alleviate it.

"Really speaking, the factors which produce roughness, lightness, coldness, hardness, sharpness, inconsistency and hollowness (in the body) excite the *vāta*. The *vāta* having taken up residence in such and such organism, grows and gets excited. (On the contrary) the factors that promote unctuousness, heaviness, heat, smoothness, sliminess, stickiness and condenseness alleviate *vāta*. The *vāta* circulating in the body when comes into contact with such and such organism, it is alleviated."

The royal sage Vāryovida, when he heard the right statement of Vadisha being approved by all the sages, said, "undoubtedly, it is exactly the same as has been told by your honour; and after adoring the *vāyu,* we will prove by the means of observation, inference and comparison, and explain, to the best of our knowledge, the functions of *vāyu* when either in excited or in its natural form it circulates inside the body or outside the body.

"*Vāyu* is the support of the machinery of the body, it has five forms, *i.e. prāna, udāna, samāna, vyāna,* and *apāna,* it inspires all the senses and carries all the sense impressions to the mind, it holds together the various elements of the body in their proper form and maintains the cohesive unity of the body as a whole, it is the promoter of speech, it is the basis of sound and touch, it is the origin of joy and enthusiasm, the kindler of *agni* (fire), the drier of the *doshās* (elements of trouble), expulser of the *malās* (waste products), it divides *sūkshma* (microscopic) and *sthoola* (macroscipic) vessels of the body it is the maker of the form of embryo (in the womb), and it stands as an evidence of the existence of life when it is not excited.

"But when it is excited in the body, it inflicts on the body all sorts of derangements as a result of which the strength, the lustre, the well-being and the longevity of the person gets a setback, the mind is perturbed, all the sensory pathways are blocked; it either kills the embryos or causes malformations in them, or keeps them in the womb for a longer duration; it causes fear, chagrin, infatuation, depression and delirium and also the respiratory failure.

"While in natural state, when it circulates in the world its functions are in this way : It supports the world, causes fire to burn, governs the positions, movements and the orbits of the sun, the moon, the constellations and the planetary systems (gravitational and electromagnetic field), forms clouds, drops rains, causes rivulets to flow, produces flowers and fruits, sprouts the plants (*aubdhidās),* divides the seasons and various elements of the body determines the quantity and the appearance of the elements of the body, grows the grains, promotes growth and dehydration and final drying up of the crop, and produces transformation of these things which have not transformed so far.

"But when it circulates in the cosmos in its excited state, its functions are as follows : It shakes up the summits of mountains, uproots the trees, causes tides in the oceans, produces waves in the lakes, pushes back the currents of rivers, produces earthquackes, swells up the clouds, gives birth to mist, thunder, dust, sand, fish, frogs, serpents, alkalies, blood, stones and lightning, destroys the six seasons, does not allow the crops to grow, brings about calamities to human beings, destroys the existence, produces such clouds, sun, fire and winds which bring to an end the four eras (*yugās)* of the world.

"It is the source god of being, it is imperishable, it brings the beings into existence and is responsible for their exist, it is the originator of well-being and of trouble, it is death, it is the god of death (Yama), it is (overall) regulator, it is the Lord of creatures, it is the Eternal One (Aditi), it is the one which does everything, it has got universal forms, it goes everywhere, it is the director of each and every action, it is the atom between existence, it is penetrating, it is all pervader (Vishnu), it traverses the worlds, yes, it is the adorable *vāyu* (which does this all)."

After listening to the ideas of Vāryovida, Marīchī said, "Whatsoever has been told in alright, but how is it going to be applied in the doctrines or the science of medicine? Does it, in any way, concern the science of medicine?"

Then replied Vāryovida, "If the medical man does not consider that the wind *(pavana)* possesses extreme force, it is so violent, it acts so promptly, it never causes any delay in any action when forcefully excited, how will he prepare himself thoroughly to take any precaution to protect a person from the very beginning, without losing any time? In this sense the praise of *vāyu* itself promotes health, adds to the strength and lustre of a person, makes him more energetic, provides him sound knowledge and supplies him with extreme longevity."

(At this) Marīchī said, "It is fire *(agni)* alone that is located in the bile *(pitta)* and accordingly as it is normal or abnormal, gives rise to beneficial or harmful consequences, *i.e.,* digestion or indigenstion, visual perception or its impairment, normal or abnormal heat of the body, normal or abnormal colour of the body, courage, fear, anger, cheerfulness, consusion, serenety and such other opposite traits".

Hearing these words of Marīchī, Kāpya (intervened and) said, "It is watery element *(Soma)* alone, which while present in the phlegm *(sleshma or kapha)* of the body, accordingly as it is normal or abnormal, gives rise to beneficial or adverse consequences *i.e.,* firmness or loseness; obesity or thinness; enthusiasm or lethargy; virility or impotence; knowledge or ignorance; intelligence or infatuation; and such other opposite traits."

After listening to these remarks of Kāpya the adorable Punarvasu Ātreya said, "Gentlemen, all of you have told the right thing, only your remarks are exclusive. All the three, air *(vāta),* bile *(pitta)* and phlegm *(kapha),* when they are in their normal state make the faculties of a man intact, provide him with good health, amicable lustre and happiness, and thus add to his long life in the same way as the morals, interests and pleasures, rightly practised make man attain the utmost happiness in this world and the world to come. But, if they are abnormal, they put the man into the adverse abyss, in the same way as the three seasons when they become abnormal lead the world to calamity in their respective periods."

All the sages at this, approved the discourse of the blessed Ātreya and were very glad.

This symposium of the sages represents clearly the various ideologies that had been hovering over the ancient physio-cosmological speculations of the Hindus. Vāryovida credited the wind, Marīchī the fire the Kāpya the waters, like the ancient Ionian physiologist-philosophers who in their course of search for primordial element found the same answer; Thales (640-546 B.C.) in water, Anaximenes (611-546 B.C.) in air and Heraclitus (540-475 B.C.) in fire.

Bibliography

Atharva Veda : Translated in English by Ralph T.H.Griffith, 3 Vols., E.J. Lazarus and Co., Benares, 1916.

Brihadāranyaka Upanishad : From the Sacred Boks of the East, translated by F. Max Muller, Vol. XV, Part II. Motilal Banarsidass, Delhi, 1965.

Charaka Samhitā : (A Scientific synopsis), P. Ray and H.N. Gupta. Published by the National Institute of Sciences of India, New Delhi, 1965.

Charaka Samhitā : (In Sanskrit), with the commentary by Chakrapānidatta and Jajjata, edited by Haridatta Shastri, 2, Vols., 2nd Ed., Motilal Banarsidass, Lahore, 1940.

Charaka Samhitā, The : Edited and published by Shree Gulabkunverba Ayurveda Society, 6 Vols., with translations in Hindi Gujarati and English, Jamnagar, 1949.

Charaka Samhitā The : With the commentary of Chakrapānidatta, edited by Vaidya Bhushan Vaman Kesheo Datar of Nasik, 1st edition, Nirnaya Sagar Press Bombay, 1922.

Chhāndogya Upanishad, The : Swami Swahananda, Published by the President, Sri Ram Krishna Math Maylapur, Madras, 1956.

Dwarkanath, C.: *Digestion and Metabolism in Āyurveda,* Shree Baidyanath Ayurveda Bhawan Private Ltd., Calcutta, 1967.

Dwarkanath, C.: *Introduction to Kāyachikitsā,* Popular Book Depot, Bombay, 1959.

Ewing Arthur, H.: *The Hindu Conception of the Functions of breath* — A Study in early Hindu Psychophysics, JAOS, Vol. XXXII, 1901.

Filliozat, J.: *The Classical Doctrine of Indian Medicine,* translated by D.R. Chanana, Munshi Ram Manohar Lal, Delhi, 1964.

Ishādivinshottarashatopanishad : (in Sanskrit), compiled by Narayan Ram Acharya, Nirnaya Sagar Press, Bombay, 1948.

Rig Veda Samhitā : Edited and published by Manmatha Nath Dutt (Shastri), Society for the Resuscitation of Indian Literature, Cacutta, 1906.

Rig Veda Samhitā : Translated by H.H.Wilson, 6 Vols., Ashtekar and Co., Poona, 1925-28.

Shende, N.J. : The Religion and Philosophy of the *Atharva Veda.* Bhandarkar Oriental Research Institute, Poona, 1952.

Sushruta Samhitā : (in Sanskrit) with the commentary by Dalhanāchārya, edited by Jadavji Trikumji Acharya, Nirnaya Sagar Press, Bombay, 1915-915.

Sushruta Samhitā; The : Translated and Edited by Kaviraja Kunjalal Bhishagratna, 3 Vols., 2nd Ed., Chowkhamba Sanskrit Series Office, Varanasi, 1963.

Vājasaneyi Samhitā : (The Texts of white *Yajur Veda)*, Translated by Ralph T.H.Griffith, 3rd Ed., P. 409, E.J. Lazarus, Benaras, 1957.

7

The Science of Prophylactics and Cures

According to the Western school of thought, the *Atharvaveda,* which was known as *Brahmāveda* in the oldest Indian traditions, has been interpreted as the veda of spells and charms, a veda which contains a "whole series of magic, incantations and exorcisms." Prof. Winternitz thus makes his observations on this veda:

"The Brahmanas, however, were from the beginning too practical a people to have used the magic charms always only in the interests of kings or other people, and not also for themselves. Among the magic incantations belonging to the "king's rites", we already find a few lines which are concerned more with the purohits, the indispensable family priest of the king, than with the latter himself. And although attacks on witchcraft and exorcisms are not lacking in brahmanical literature, yet the lawbook of Manu (XI, 33) says clearly and distinctively: 'without hesitation, the Brahmana shall make use of the sacred texts of the Atharvaveda, the word, indeed, is the weapon of Brahmana, therewith may he kill his enemies.'

Thus also in the *Atharvaveda* we find a whole series of magic incantations and exorcisms in the interest of the Brahmanas. In these hymns, the inviolability of the Brahmanas and their possessions is repeatedly emphasized in the strongest manner and the heaviest curses are pronounced against those who assil the property and lives of the Brahmanas." (*History of the Indian Literature,* p. 147)

According to Prof. J.N.Farquhar, "We have already seen that a number of spells for use in magic are contained in the Rik. The character of these poems proves that the old-world incantations which the Aryans, in common with other Indo-European peoples, had been accustomed to use had in the main at least, given way before a new type of spell, written in polished language and metre, on the model of the hymns to the gods. Doubtless, hundreds of these were being used by sorcerers, exorcists, and magicians, although only a few found their way into the hymn-books of the priests; and the process of composition continued after the canon of the Rigveda was closed. The incantation priest had no lack of wealthy clients ready to pay well for his magic acts and poetical charms instinct with supernatural power. Hence, numerous hymns from the Rigveda were turned to these purposes; philosophic poems were perverted to more mysterious uses, their sounding phrases and incomprehensive concepts rendering them most formidable to the ear; and many new incantations were composed to fit into the detailed ritual of magic, both black and white. The man who muttered charms was usually summoned also to do the priestly duties in the domestic ceremonies, which were observed at the time of birth, marriage, death and such like.

Then, during the period of the Brahmanas, a school was formed for the training of this class of priests and quite naturally a great collection of these incantations was made the text-book of the school. This text-book is the *Atharvaveda.* It has come down to us in two recensions, named Saunakiya and Paippalada."

(*An outline of the Religious Literature of India,* p. 23)

According to Prof. Macdonell, "the hostile charms it contains are directed largely against various diseases or the demons which are supposed to cause them. There are spells to cure fever (takman), leprosy, jaundice, dropsy, scrofula, cough, opthalmia, baldness, lack of vital power, fractures and wounds, the bite of snakes or injurious insects, and poison in general, mania and other ailments." (*Sanskrit Literature,* p. 196).

Before dealing with the distorted interpretation that has been placed on certain terms, which actually imply germs and microbes, but which are wrongly taken to imply demons and spirits, we may quote Morris Jastrow and appreciate what he says about these demons and spirits and the incantations of the priests to drive them out.

Dr. Osler quotes him thus in *The Evolution of Modern Medicine* (p. 17), "These demons, invisible to the naked eye, were the precursors of the modern 'germs' and 'microbes' while the incantations recited by the priests are the early equivalents of the physicians' prescriptions. There were different incantations for different diseases, and they were as mysterious to the masses as are the mystic formulas of the modern physician to the bewildered, yet trusting patient. Indeed, their mysterious character added to the power supposed to reside in the incantations for driving the demons away. Medical remedies accompanied the recital of the incantations, despite the considerable progress made by such nations of hoary antiquity as the Egyptians and Babylonians in the diagnosis and treatment of common diseases, leading in time to the developmenf of an extensive pharmacology. So long as the cure of disease rested with the priests, the recital of sacred formulas, together with rites that may be conveniently grouped under the head of sympathetic magic, was regarded as equally essential with the taking of the prescribed remedies."

A. The significance of the term कृत्या in the Atharvaveda

The word is often used in the *Atharvaveda* but it has nothing to do with magic spells as it has long been erroneously believed. कृत्या is an appliance to kill the enemy कृभ, हिंसायाम् the verb कृ, used for 'killing'. In his *Arthashastra,* chapters 150-152, Kautalya has made a reference to कृत्या, saying that the learned advisors of the king should urge the king to make use of कृत्या *i.e.* weapons to kill the enemy and अभिचार *i.e.* weapons which pierce through the body of the enemy and consume him (cf. चर भक्षणे).

Chanakya says :

पुरोहितपुरुषाः कृत्याभिचारब्रूयुः

Keeping in view this *modus operandi* as adopted in the *Atharvaveda,* we shall now exmine some of the terms which have been unfairly interpreted by a group of scholars.

All references to कृत्या in the *Atharvaveda* should be interpreted in the light of the above implication. Compare also :

ते मे देवाः पुरोहितः प्रतीचीः
कृत्या प्रतिसरैरजन्तु।।

(*Atharvaveda.* VIII, 5.5)

So may these gods whom I have set before me oppose with Kritya and banish enmity!

These कृत्या weapons contain powder, stones, and knives.

अभी कृत्या पाष्प्रानं।। यस्तेनान्यं जिघांसति।।
अइमानस्तस्यां दग्धायां।
बहुलाः फट क्ररिक्रति।।

(*Atharvaveda* IV, 18, 3)

"With the sharp sound of many stones, the weapon cracks down upon the enemy to kill him."

The कृत्या are like the fire-missiles

याः कृत्या आङ्गिरसोर्याः

कृत्या आसुरीर्याः।

कृत्या स्वयं कृताया चान्येभिरामृताः।।

(*Atharvaveda* VIII, 1.1)

Compare अङ्गिराड हृग्निः (Shatapatha Brahmana I, 4, 1,25) with आसुरी कृत्याः those which proceed in a gaseous form unseen.

***B. The significance of the term* अभिचार**

अभिचार relates to food poisoning or to the weapons which pierce through the body of the enemy. A caution is indicated in *Atharvaveda,* VIII 2, 26, to guard against poisoned food served by relations.

परित्वा पातु सामानेभ्योभिचारात् सम्बन्ध्युभ्यः . . . .

'Let it preserve thee from thy equals and from food-poisoning by thy relatives; though Griffith translates "food-poisoning" as "incantation".

The *Atharvaveda* X, 3.7 provides a remedy against such poisoning of food, by suggesting वरणमणिबन्धन what is वरण? This is no magic spell nor does it imply use of any gem. Let us examine the mantra:

अरात्यास्त्वा निर्ऋत्या अभिचाराद भयाद्।

मृत्योरोजीयसो वधाद् वरणो वारयिष्यते।।

(*Atharvaveda* X, 3, 7)

Grifith translates it so:

From mischief, from malignity, from incantation, from alarm, from death, from stronger foeman's stroke, Varuna will guard thee well.

वरण means 'Protection', for example the remedy against food poison suggested in *Sushruta.* I, 18 is

हृदयावरणं नित्यं कुर्याच्च मित्रमध्यगः

and so in *Charaka,* 23, 44, on food poisoning

आदौ हृदयंरक्ष्यं तस्यावरणं पिवेद्यथालाभम्।

It is abundantly clear, therefore, that western scholars have not done justice to the interpretations of the few words like Apsara, Gandharva, Yatudhana, Rakshasa etc. Which are actually various technical terms for germs or radiations and which have been assumed to refer to demons and ghosts. There are no charms, and there is no magic, implied in these terms.

C. *The significance of the terms, Yatudhana and Kimidin*

Commenting on *Atharvaveda* 1, 7, Prof. Griffith writes: "The hymn is a prayer to Agni and Indra for the direction and destruction of evil spirits." (1, 8) " is a continuation of Hymn VII. The sacrifice has proved effectual, and a *Yatudhana* or sorcerer has been forced to come forward and confess".

इदं हविर्यातुधानान् नदी फेनमिवावहत्
य इदं स्त्रीं पुमानकरिह सस्तुवतां जनः
अयं स्तुवान आगमदिमं समप्रति हर्यत।।

Hitney gives the heading of this hymn as "Sorcerers" holding, that this hymn is a prayer to Agni to exorcise black magic.

The two hymns refer to यातुधान Yatudhana, (which according to Griffith is one of the class of evil spirits, demons of sorcerers) what Sayana refers to as Rakshasas.

स्तुवानमग्न आ वह यातुधानं किमिदिनम्
त्वं हि देव वन्दितो हन्ता दस्योर्वभूविथ।।

(*Atharvaveda. 1, 7,1*)

'Bring the Kimidin hither, bring the Yatudhana self-declared. For Agni, God, thou, lauded, hast become the Dasyu's slaughter. (Griffith)

The correct meaning is actually quite different.

The *Kimidin* is one of the class of malignant spirits, *Nirukta* VI, 11 explains it to mean 'one who moves about crying "किम इदानीम्" Kim Idanim, or what now ? or किमइदम what this ? यातु: is one who inflicts pain, and its destortion (अपभ्रंश) is जादू hence, this word has been wrongly connected with magic.

यातुधानाः यातना दुखं तं दधति ते यातुधानाः which inflict pain.

राक्षस is a kind of worm that moves at night and kills the lonely man. One should beware of it.

रक्षो रक्षितव्यमस्माद्

रहसि क्षणोति इति वा

रात्रौ नक्षत इति वा (*Nirukta* IV, 18)

किमीदी = किमिदानीमिति चरते (*Nirukta* VI, 11)

"moving with a will to sting."

The derivation of other words is similarly simple. For example, गन्धर्वः = गां वाणीं धारयतीति "worms which sing, as it were like mosquitoes".

अप्सरा = अप्सारिणी भवति (*Nirukta* V, 13) *i.e.* germs which breed in water.

D. Terms such as the Bhuta, Preta and Rakshasa explained

Atharvaveda IV, 37, is full of what have been known as ghosts and demons. But the error becomes apparent when we examine that the words भूत, प्रेत, राक्षस, गन्धर्व mean only the "poisonous germs" which cause disease. They are destroyed by the disinfectant fumes of हींग, सरसों, तुलसी, गुग्गुल. These medicinal herbs are also mentioned in the

Atharvaveda. According to *Raja-Nighantu,* हींग is called रक्षोघ्न "killer of demons" and *Dhanwantri Nighantu* gives a synonym of हींग as जन्तुघ्न 'killer of germs'. हींग is also called भूतनाशिनं हिड़गु 'killer of spirits'. The ayurvedic Nighantus are full of references and classification of these medicinal herbs, that kill the germs, that go by the name राक्षस, भूत, प्रेत, गन्धर्व of etc.

The Germs called Rakshasas

The राक्षस is surely not a demon as is misinterpreted by some.

असृग्भाजानिह वैरक्षांसि–

(*Kaushitaki Brahmana* 17, 4) the blood sucking germs are called Rakshasa.

रक्षो रक्षितव्यमस्मात्

(*Nirukta* IV, 18)

Rakshasa is a germ from which one has to protect oneself. It is the disinfecting Sun alone which can kill these Rakshasas. As the *Shatapatha Brahmana* 1, 3, 4, 8, puts it : सूर्यो हि नाष्ट्राणां राक्षसामपहन्ता.

These rakshasas can be killed by *fire,* too. अग्निर्वै ज्योति रक्षोहा (*Shatapatha Brahmana* VII, 4, 1, 34) अग्निर्वै रक्षसामपहन्ता (Ibid 1, 2, 1, 6)

The *Kaushitaki Brahmana* of the *Rigveda* in VIII. 4, 10, 3 confirms this.

अग्निर्वै रक्षसामपहन्ता

Hydropathy or water hyper treatment also kills these germs. आपो वैरक्षोघ्नी (*Taittiriya Brahmana* III, 23, 12) आसुरा: are those germs which deprive the blood of vitality.

असुं प्राणान् राति आददाति इति

E. The word पिशाच (Pishacha) clarified

The word is derived as पिशित + अश meat eather and its dictionary meaning is 'meat eater,'

पिशितं मांसमश्नातीति पिशाचः one eating meat is called Pishacha (*Shabdakalpadruma*) and according to *Vacaspatikosha* पिशितं मासमाचामतींति पिशाचः *i.e.* "one who eats or licks meat."

Internal evidence from the *Atharvaveda* will make clear that the *Pischacha* is no other than a worm.

यदस्य हृतं विहृतं यत् पराभृतमात्मनो जग्धं यतमत् पिशाचैः

तदग्ने विद्वान् पुनराभरत्वं शरीरे मासमसुमेरयामः।।

(*Atharvaveda* V, 29, 5)

This is prayer to Agni, to restore that part of the body which has been consumed by flesh-eating germs or skin diseases, Griffith has translated it thus : "Whatever of his body hath been taken, plundered, borne off or eaten by Pisachas, this Agni, knowing it, again bring hither! We give back flesh and spirit to his body." (*The Atharvaveda,* p. 237)

The invocation to Agni as protector has been made, because Agni is known to be the germ-killer. (*Ṛgveda* X, 118, 1).

अग्ने हंसि न्यत्रिणां दीद्यन्

Agni refulgent among men, thou slayest the devouring fiend (germs). Agni kills the germs called *Rakshas. (Rigveda X, 118, 7)*.

अदाभ्येन शोचिषऽग्ने रक्षस्त्वं दह

O Agni, burn the Rakshasas with thine unconquerable flame ! (Griffith) सर्वेषाञ्च क्रिमीणां . . . . दहाम्यग्निनामुखम्

(*Atharvaveda* V, 23, 13)

'I destroy all germs by means of fire'.

प्रति दह यातुधानान् प्रतिदेव किमीदिनः
प्रतीचीः कृष्णवर्त्तने सं दह यातुधान्यः।।

(*Atharvaveda* 1. 28, 2)

O Agni, burn these germs called यातुधान these called किमीदिन Kimidiana; burn all female Yathudhana germs.

F. *The term 'Durnama' (दुर्णामा) explained*

Atharvaveda VIII, 6 makes specific mention of Rakshasa and Pishacha. Let us examine the first verse of this hymn wherein we find the word *durnama* दुर्णामा mentioned.

यौ ते मातोन्ममार्ज जातायाः पतिवेदनौ
दुर्णामा तत्र मा गृध्दस्मिंश उत वत्सपः।।

(*Atharvaveda* VII. 6, 1)

"Let neither fiend of evil name *Durnama, Alinsa, Vatsapa desire thy pair* of husband wooers which thy mother cleansed when thou wast born." (Griffith) Now what is दुर्णामा ?

According to Yaskacharya it is a kind of worm which lives on raw flesh.

दुर्णामा क्रिमिभर्वति पापनामा
क्रिमिः क्रव्ये मेद्यति

(Nirūkta *VI, 12*)

G. *The word Apsara (अप्सरा) explained*

This word does not denote any nymph, but it is the name given to these insects which live on fragrant flowers, and are called रोगोत्पादक क्रिमि

गन्ध इत्यपसरस उपासते

(*Shatapatha Brahmana* X, 5, 2, 20)

H. The word Gandharva means

The *Shatapatha Brahmana* clarifies it as those insects which are attached to beautiful thigs. Therefore, speaking for both, the *Shatapatha Brahmana* holds that the *Apsaras* are worms of fragrance and *Gandharvas* are worms of beauty.

अथो गन्धेन च वै रुपेण च

गन्धर्वाप्सरसश्र्चरन्ति

(*Shatapatha* IX, 4, 1, 4)

According to one view अप्सरस् is a class of those malarial germs which flourish on water in marshy places and गन्धर्व 's' refer to the singing mosquitoes. So both the apsaras and gandharvas are mosquitoes of malaria which dirty water breeds.

I. The term कश्यप Kashyapa

In *Atharvaveda* II, 33,7, we read

यक्ष्मं त्वचस्यं ते वयं कश्यपस्य वीवर्हेण विश्वञ्च चिवृहामसि

"We, with the exercising power of Kasyapa drive far away consumption settled in thy skin."

What is कश्यप ?— it is a type of a deer.

कश्यपः मृगविशेषः (वैद्यक शब्द सिन्धुः)

The deer skin is known to cure so many ailments.

According to the *Shatapatha Brahmana* VII, 5, the word *Kashyapa* means 'vital breath'.

कश्यपो वैकूर्मः प्राणो वैकूर्मः

J. Magic Spells

इन्द्रजाल is the name for magic. We find it mentioned in *Atharvaveda* VIII, 8, 17 and VIII, 8, 18.

वृहत् ते जालं वृहत् इन्द्र शूर

सहस्त्रार्धस्य शतवीर्यस्य।

तेन शतं सहस्त्रमयुतं न्युर्बुदं
जघान शक्रो दस्यूनांममिधायसेनया।।

"Great is thy net, brave Indra, thine the mighty match for a thousand; Lord of Hundred Powers" (Griffith)"

इन्द्रदूवक्षजालाभ्यां शर्व सेनाममूं हतम्

(*Atharvaveda* VIII, 8, 18)

"With your entangling snares and nets Sarva and Indra, slay that host. (Griffith)

This contrivance of इन्द्रजाल is used for creating confusion in the army by the use of electric mechanism, lightning etc. There is no illusion or fraud. The effect is also not brought about merely by the chanting of a mantra as is erroneously understood, *Indrajala* is a particular type of electric mechanism used in warfare. *Tantra*— This is a scientific method of controlling the various faculties and thereby curing ailments. The *Mantra* is connected with psychotherapy and is perfectly scientific. Under this category fall hypnotism and mesmerism.

K. *Psycho-therapy* मन्त्र विद्या

(*a*) The *Atharvaveda* abounds in references to curing of diseases by the exercise of will-power; because according to *Atharvaveda* XIX, 52. 1, will-power is the very essence of the mind.

(कामस्तदग्रे समवर्तत मनसो रेतः . . .)

This is scientific approach to the problem of disease. It is truly said, 'a peaceful mind generates power.' The mind has to be enriched with vital thoughts, to ensure to rich and strong body.

"The influence of the mind and brain," says Combe, "over the action of the heart and lungs is familiar to most persons, as sighing, palpitation and fainting, so often witnessed as consequences of emotions of mind, are evidences which no body can resist, and death itself is not a rare result in delicately organised persons."

James Coates observes, "In cases of self-healing by auto-suggestion, it is the diversion of the mind from unpleasant and unhealthy subjects which arrests the course of disease and brings about the immediate cure, this change affecting the internal direction of the vital or nervous force."

(*Human Magnetism,* p. 111)

Let us examine some of the verses in the *Atharvaveda* in which this method of will-power is applied in overcoming ailments.

परो पेद्दि मनस्पाप विमशस्तानि शंसति. . .

(*Atharvaveda* VI, 45.1)

Sin of the mind, avaunt begone! why sayest thou what none should say.' (Griffith)

And again, कृतं मे दक्षिणे हस्ते जयो मे सव्य आहित:

(*Atharvaveda* VII, 50.8)

My right hand holds my winnings fast and in my left is victory." (Griffith)

To acquire valour by increasing one's will power is enjoined in a verse of the *Rigveda.*

वृषा ह्यसि राधसे जज्ञिषे

वृष्णि ते शव:

(*Rigveda* V. 35, 4)

"Mighty to prosperus wast thou born and mighty is the strength, thou hast." (Griffith)

अग्ने यन्मे तन्वा अनन्तन्मऽआपृण

(*Yajurveda* III, 17)

Is a prayer to Agni to supply all that is wanting in me. (*Wilson)* which is the same as

अपेहि मनसस्पतेपक्राम परश्चरः

(*Atharvaveda* XX, 96,24)

"Avaunt, thou Master of the Mind ! Depart and vanish far away." (Griffith)

(*Atharvaveda* III, 22, 1.)

हस्तिवर्चसं प्रथतां वृहद्यशो अदित्या यत्

तन्वः सम्बभूव –

This mantra corresponds to Patanjali's *Yoga-Sutra* IV, 24, बलेषु हस्तिबलादोनि which assures the yogi, the power of an elephant, through concentration and identification with the might of an elephant.

(*b*) **Healing by Touch.** This is a part of the science of Mesmerism which was introduced in Europe by Mesmer, but the sages knew this science since the age of the vedas. We have a reference to this application in *Atharvaveda* IV, 13, 6.

अयं मे हस्तो भगवानयं मे भगवत्तरः

अयं मे विश्वाभेषजोऽयं शिवभिमर्शं नः

"Felicitous is this my hand, yet more felicitous is this. This hand contains all healing balms, and this makes whole with *gentle touch.*" (Griffith)

Again दक्षं त उग्रमाभारिषं परा यक्ष्मं सुवाँमि ते

(*Atharvaveda* IV, 13, 5)

"I bring the mighty strength, I drive thy wasting malady away." (Griffith)

Referring to the power of healing by touch, the *Atharvaveda further holds*

हस्ताभ्यां दशशाखाभ्यां जिह्वा वाचः पुरोगवी

अनामयित्नुभ्यां हस्ताभ्यां ताभ्यां त्वाभि मृशामसि

(*Atharvaveda* IV, 13, 7)

The tongue that leads the voice precedes

Then with our tenfold branching hands,

With these two healers of disease; we

Stroke thee with a soft caress, (Griffith's translation).

A strange experience of this phenomenon of "touch" is narrated in the life of Vivekananda. He once said to Swami Ramakrishna, "Even if millions of men were to believe in God, I would not say, I believe, if I have not proved it myself." But Ramakrishna never wavered in his love for him and in a mood of semiconsciousness he *touched* Narendra. As T.L. Vaswami puts it : "A sudden change came upon him. The effect on him of western *rationalism* was overcome. Naren no longer denied God. Naren passed through a series of mystic experiences, crying again and again, Siva, Siva". (*The voice of Vivekananda,* p. 21)

As Dr. Mitra puts it, "The success of psychotherapic treatment depends on an exhaustive and careful study of subconscious cerebration, the cornerstone of psychotherapy. Europe and America recognized this all-important mental function as late as 1876. Western scientists have had scarcely time enough during the last fifty years to build up anything like a science of psychotherapy; whereas the Hindus who discovered subconscious cerebration about thirty centuries ago, have practised drugless mental healing even since that distant age."

(*Some Aspects of Hindu Medical Treatment,* p. 23).

Theory of Vedic Medicine

The longevity of man's life to hundred years जिजीविषेत् शतं समाः—(*Yajurveda XL, 2)* or even more, जीवेम शरद; शतम्-भूयश्च शरदः शतात् can be maintained according to vedic teachings.

And how that span of life can be attained is given in the Ayurveda, the science of life, with all its therapeutical hints and prescriptions given in the *Atharaveda* (in a nucleus form). The extent and object of introducing medical knowledge, therefore, in the *Atharvaveda* is abundantly clear.

The sage Dhanvantari tell Sushruta that this science of medicine should be studied for the sake of affording relief from suffering to humanity in its pursuit of happiness, for the sake of prolonging our own lives and for the sake of the general good of the people.

According to sage Kashyapa, 'medicine should be studied by the Brahmana for the sake of the knowledge to truth, to acquire spiritual merit for himself and so as to extend help to humanity; by the Ksatriya for he sake of safeguarding the health of the people; by the Vaisya for the sake of a livelihood; and by the rest for the sake of service. All may study it for the sake of living the good life.'

(*Kashyapa Samhita* 42)

The Origin of Medicine

Medicine arose out of the primal sympathy of man with man, out of the desire to help those in sorrow, need and sickness.

— Osler

Dr. Payne, the eminent medical historian, remarks, "The basis of medicine is sympathy and the desire to help others and whatever is done with this end must be called medicine."

Tracing the origin of medicine Zimmer writes that "out of the sphere of time-less existence — medical wisdom steps into the range of man's vision in the garb of historical tradition."

(*Hindu Medicine, p. 88*)

The starting point of this tradition is the intuitive insight "realized through an introverted awareness of the elements and laws that constitute the fact of life and the characteristics of living beings, the interrelation of the many and various data of the life-process" (*Ibid.,* p. 89).

को ददर्श प्रथमं जायमानं
अस्थन्वन्तं यदनस्था विभर्ति।
भूम्या असुर सृगात्मा क्व स्वित्
को विद्वांसमुपगात् प्रष्टुमेतत्।।

(*Rigveda* I, 164, 4)

"Who beheld life, when it first arose? — Life that formless in itself, fills all forms. From earth are fashioned blood and breath but whence the spirit that informs these? Who has gone to the ultimate Knower of all things to put the question ?" (Griffith's translation)

Yet, the empirical link of ideas, with vigilant observation followed widening experience.

Tracing the source of medicinal knowledge, Sir William Osler observes, "The first lessons came to primitive man by injuries, accidents, bites of beasts and serpents, perhaps for long ages, not appreciated by his childlike mind, but little by little, such experiences crystallised into useful knowledge. The experiments of nature made clear to him, the relation of cause and effect, but it is not likely, as Pliny suggests that he picked up his earliest knowledge from the observation of certain practices in animals as the natural phlebotomy of the plethoric hippopotamus, or the use of emetics from the dog, or the use of enemata from the ibis."

(*The Evolution of Modern Medicine,* p. 7)

Edward Berdoe in his *Popular History of Medicine* refers to the instinctive use and knowledge of valerian by the cats, antidotal herbs for snake-poison by the mongoose, of plantago major by the toad, of salt by the cow, buffalo, horse and camel. In the *Atharvaveda* we have a mention of the animals and birds from whom the use of healing herbs and drugs could be learnt.

वराहो वेद वीरुधं नकुलो वेद भेषजीम्

सर्पा गन्धर्वा या विदुस्ता अस्मा अवसे हुवे।

(*Atharvaveda* VIII, 7, 23)

"The boar knows the plant, the mongoose knows the remedial herb. What the serpents, the gandharvas know, those I call to aid."

And in the *Atharvaveda* VIII, 7, 24,

याः सुपर्णा आङ्गरसीर्दिश्व या रघटो विदुः

वयांसि हंसा या विदुर्याश्च सर्वे पतत्रिणः

मृगा या विदुरोषधीस्ता अस्मा अवसे हुवे।।

"The herbs of the angirasas that the eagles know, the heavenly ones that the Raghatas know, those that the birds, and the swans know, and what all the winged ones know, these herbs that the wild beasts know — I call them to aid." Again,

यावतीनामोषधीनां गावः

प्राश्नन्तिऽध्न्या यावतींनामजावयः

तावतीस्तुभ्यमोषधीः शर्म यच्छन्त्वाभृताः।।

(*Atharvaveda* VIII, 7, 25)

"Of how many herbs, the inviolable kine partake, of how many the goats and sheep, let so many herbs, being brought, and extend protection to thee."

It is in such associations, that we find the origin of rational medicine, of the healing art, with a fourfold classification of vedic therapy which is alluded to in the *Atharvaveda* XI, 4, 16.

Four kinds of remedies are considered to protect life :

1. The drugs of the Angirasas (Juices of plants and herbs)

2. The drugs of the Atharvans (a part of the mantra-therapy.)
3. The divine drugs in the form of prayers and mental yoga.
4. The drugs of human artifice and contrivance.

In the growth and development of medicine, by observation, knowledge, reason, and self-consciousness of man, free — associational suggestion also has played a guiding role. As Sir Osler puts it, "The association of ideas was suggestive — the plant eyebright was used for centuries in diseases of the eye because black speak in the flower suggested the pupil of eye. The old herbals are full of similar illustrations upon which indeed the so-called doctrine of signature depends."

(*The Evolution of Modern Medicine,* p. 7)

The colour, texture of the shape or things in plants or animals were taken as the guiding factor in indicating the relevance of those plants or animals as remedies or as replenishing agents. In other words, those substances which could tinge the fluids bright red, were utilized as blood tonics or in checking haemorrhages.

Milk and milk-coloured liquids were utilized in the promotion of the body elements of a similar colour, for example, the semen or the protoplasmic cell fluid.

The *Atharvaveda* mentions turmeric (हल्दी) and yellow birds into which jaundice is induced so as to relieve the human patient of that disease. उरो मत्वा क्षतं लाक्षां पयसा मधुसंयुताम् सद्य एव पिबेज्जीर्णे पयसा उद्यात् सशर्करम्।

In the days of Hippocrates, it was believed that dryness could be expelled by moisture; cold by heat and so on from this *doctrine of contraries* later developed the *doctrine of similars* on which is based the mode of treatment known as *homoeopathy*. This is close to the doctrine of signature according to which, the use of eyebright is advocated in diseases of the eye and cyclamen in diseases of the ear because of parallel physical resemblance. The Egyptian or ganotherapy had the same basis — spleen would cure spleen, heart, heart.

Atharvaveda and the History of Medicine

The history of medicine in India is shrouded in mystery. There is, therefore, very scanty material available. Chronology is unsure, and there is little or no information about the great sages, seers, surgeons and acharyas who have played eminent part in contributing to the knowledge on Indian medicine.

Max Muller's observations on the History of Philosophy in India apply equally well to the History of Medicine.

"From the actual works themselves written by the poets, philosophers and scientists of India, very little is to be had pertaining to the life and work of the author. Most often even the name has to be learnt from the colophons or such other appendages to the originals contributed by the editors, commentators and such others. The difficulties in computing the dates are augmented by the prevalence of different eras in vouge in the various parts of India."

It is equally true that foreign domination and invasions have thrown much of the literature on *medicine* into oblivion and although a great help has been rendered by the explorations of Harappa and Mohenjodaro revealing the civic and domestic life of ancient India, the system of drainage, sanitation, and roads, the inscriptions and tablets leading to the evidence of knowledge of drugs and minerals, still much remains to be discovered and integrated.

And yet "The Atharvaveda is the compendium of medicine in its various stages of evolution and contains the most primitive as well as highly advanced stage of therapy. . . It is a record of psychosouratic technique of healing by a combined procedure of charms, prayers, incantations, amulets and drugs."

(*The Caraka Samhita* published by Shri Gulab Kunverba Ayurvedic Society, Vol. 1, p. 19)

That the Indian medicinal system had reached a degree of sophistication in such early times cannot be doubted.

Surgery certainly was a well developed art.

According to the great historian Sir William Hunter, "many centuries ago at the monastic medical university at Nalanda, near modern Gaya, Hindu surgeons successfully performed the operation of rhinoplasty and other feats of surgical skill. In old Hindu medical book one may find the description of that branch of surgery which deals with the improvement of deformed ears and noses and the forming of new ones, one of the scientific additions to surgery in great hospitals in the large modern cities in Europe at the present time." (*Soma Aspects of Hindu Medical Treatment.* p. 7)

In the domain of surgery, it is true that the knowledge of instruments and the operations performed by old Indian physicians has become dim with the passage of time, but there are strange similarities still observable in the names of the some of the surgical instruments used now. For example, सिंह मुख and मकरमुख स्वस्तिक 's' are the prototypes of Lion and the Crocodile forceps of the modern physicians.

Surgical Instruments of the Hindu by G.N.Mukerjee, (a Griffith prize volume of the Calcutta University), researches sub questions in detail.

यदान्त्रेषु गवोन्योर्यद्वरतावधि संश्रितम्
एवा तेमूत्रं मुच्यतां वर्हिवालिति सर्वकम्
प्रते भिनद्मि मेहनं वर्त्रवेशन्तिआइव
एवा ते मूत्रं मुच्यतां वहिर्वांलितिसर्वकम्।।

(*Atharvaveda* I, 3, 6, 7, et. seq).

Here we have a mention of a certain tubular instrument to relieve the retention of urine and modern surgery continues to employ the catheter and tubal instruments for the dilation of urethral system. An Indian surgeon is proud of the fact that "*Susruta Samhita,* although it is available only in fragmentary form, is the world's first book of surgical knowledge." (*Nagarjun* Vol. II, p. 19)

"In the reign of Asoka the Great, the hole of India was studded with hospitals not only for men but also for the animals." (*Ibid.,* p. 18)

The eight branches of Ayurveda were taught in all the famous universities of ancient India viz. Nalanda, Vikramshila, Odantapuri, Valabhi, and Taxila. The dissection of human bodies was used to teach anatomy and surgery. There were three famous schools of medicine at that time : the Atreya School of Medicine, the Sushruta School of Surgery, and the Kashyapa School of Pediatrics and Obstetrics. Brahma was the first to promulgate the medical science and from him the science was learnt by Daksa, from him by Aswins and from the Aswin twins it went to Indra and then to various sages, Dhanvantri and Divadas (one view) to Kasyapa, Vasistha, Atri and Bhrigu (second view) and to Bharadwaja. (third view).

"The recent discovery at Boghaz Koyi in Cappa-docia of the names of Nasatyas and other vedic gods in Cuneiform character, and the occurrence of the name Naunghaitya in the Zend Avesta clearly directs us to search for the medical knowledge as taught by celestial

Asvins not solely in India, but also in Persia and Mesopotamia." (G.N. Mukerjee, *History of Indian Medicine,* Vol. I, p. 7)

The professional abilities of four famous physicians of ancient India have been handed down to us.

निदाने माधवः श्रेष्ठः सूत्रस्थाने च वाग्भट्टः

शारीरे सुश्रुतः श्रेष्ठः चरकस्तु चिकित्सिते।।

Madhava is unrivalled in actiology and diagnosis, Bagabhatta in principles and practice of medicine, Sushruta in anatomy and surgery and Charaka in therapeutics.

The Injection of Solutions was popular in vedic times. The Sanskrit word for injection is अन्तःक्षेप or सूचीबेध We have a reference to this in *Rigveda* X, 97, 12.

यस्यौषधीः प्रसर्पथाङ्ग मङ्गं परुष्परः।

ततो यक्ष्मं वि वाघध्व उग्रो मध्यमशीरिव।।

The word प्रसर्पसि (penetrates) is thus derived : प्रविश्य अन्तः शिरामुखे व्याप्नोषि referring to the needle entering the body and spreading the medicine.

Long before Jenner had discovered vaccination, Col. King had evidenced the frequent use of vaccinations in India. This is confirmed by a statement recorded by Har Bilasa Sharda in *Hindu Superiority,* p. 260.

Dr. Huillet of Pondicherry holds the view that actual vaccination itself was known to the Hindus. (G.N. Mukerjee, *History of Indian Medicine,* Vol. III, p. 11)

The following list of the noted physicians of the vedic time may be interesting particularly from the perspective of the history and growth of Indian medicine, which later developed into the European system of allopathy, with the use of same herbs and roots and decoctions but with a different system of nomenclature. The oldest Hindu physicians are :

Agni (अग्निः)

Vata (वात – the wind-god)

Vrhaspati (वृहस्पतिः)

Ushana (उशना) or शुक्राचार्य

The theory of Hindu Medicine and the Doctrine of Tridosa (त्रिदोश)

It was Paracelsus who said "Man is his own doctor, and finds proper healing herbs in his own garden, the physician is in ourselves, in our own nature are all things that we need."

The *Ayurveda* is essentially the science of life and as Charaka holds it, the entire suffering of the mind and the body, responsible for shortening man's life is rooted in his ignorance, and the only source of happiness is a clear-cut and scientific knowledge of things.

समग्रं दुःखमायत्तमविज्ञाने द्वयाश्रयम्।
सुखं समग्रं विज्ञाने विमले च प्रतिष्ठितम्।।

(*Charaka XXX, 84*)

This knowledge of the physical laws of health in the triad of Vata, Pitta and Kapha, is essential for a seeker of health, just as the knowledge of the *three fold misery* — mental, physical and metaphysical in the universe is essential to ensure happiness to man according to the Sankhya School of Thought.

दुःखत्रयाभिघाताजूजिज्ञासा तदपिघातके हेतौ।

(*Sankhya-Karika I*)

The scope of Ayurveda, the science of life, is splendidly defined by Charaka as under :

हिताहिते सुखं दुःखमायुस्तस्य हिताहितम्।
मानं च तच्च त्रयोक्तमायुर्वेदःस उच्यते।।

"That is named as the *Science* of life which lays down the good and the bad, the happy, and unhappy elements and what it wholesome and unwholesome in relation to life as also its measure."

It was Descartes who said that we could be freed from an infinity of maladies both of body and mind if we had sufficient knowledge of their causes and of all the remedies with which Nature has provided us.

For centuries together, the cardinal doctrine of Tridosha त्रिदोष in India or the humoural theory of Hippocrates in the West, has been a guiding doctrine regarding man's health and maintenance of the life currents of his psycho-somatic constitution. There are classical principles of modern medical thought, which trace out the cause and prevention of the disease in the individual and his environment, and affirm the existence of three Doshas or essential principles which pervade all the tissues, secretions and excretions and determine health and disease. These three principles are called *vata, pitta and kapha* — the fundamental functionaries of the man's constitutional pathology.

Harmonious working of these three functions, is health, and any discordance and disharmony will result in disease.

The five elements in matter have been grouped into three, in this way :— air and ether being combined into *vata,* fire turned into *pitta* and water and earth combined into *kapha.*

वाय्वाकाशधातुभ्यां वायुः।

आग्नेयं पित्तम्

अम्भः पृथिवीभ्यां श्लेष्मा।।

They refer to the fluid balance, the thermal and the vital force in human organization.

Kapha is derived (from क water, फ which is synonymous with पूलेष्मा and सोमं)

फलति इति सोम एव शरीरे श्लेष्मान्तर्गत:

(*Charaka*)

This stresses at the necessity of maintaining a fluid balance in the body, *Kapha* is that cohesive force which is responsible for holding the joints together and fulfils all cohesive, nutritive and stabilizing functions and supplies living waters to the roots of life.

Pitta derived from तप्त to heat, gives an idea of the thermal force and that specific heat which is essential to be maintained in the body of digest and assimilate materials.

अग्निरेव शरीरे पित्तांतर्गतः।

Vata, derived from to move, refers to the dynamic force in maintaining that vital force which is essential for the progress of the vital processes in the body.

As charaka testifies : Vata, pitta and kapha sustain a physical condition of normalcy till they are disturbed.

सर्वशरीरचरास्तु वातपित्तश्लेष्माणः

सर्वस्मिन् शरीरे कुपिताकुपिताः

शुभाशुभानि कुर्वन्ति।।

(*Charaka,* Sutra XX, 9)

Hippocrates (460 B.C.), the father of Western medicine, whose keen observation has dominated the profession for twenty-five centuries, writes in *The Nature of Man,*

"The body of man contains in itself blood and phlegm and hellow bile and black bile, which things are in the natural constitution of his body and the cause of sickness and of health. He is healthy when they are in proper proportion between one another as regards mixture and force and quantity and when they are well mingled together. He becomes sick, when one of these is diminished or increased in amount, or is separated in the body from its proper mixture, and not properly mingled with all the others."

What happens when this pathological *vata* is disturbed ? Charaka holds,

कुपितस्तु खलु शरीरे शरीरं नानाविधैः
विकारैरुपतपति बलवर्णसुखायुषामुपघाताय मनोव्याहर्षयति
सर्वन्द्रियाण्युपहन्ति विनहन्ति गर्भान् विकृतिमापादयात्यकालं
वा धारयति भयशोकमोहं हैन्याति
प्रलापंजनयति प्राणां चोपरुणद्धि ।।

(*Charaka* Sutra XII, 8)

"When however, *vata* is disordered in tne body, it afflicts the or iganism with different ills; it tends to impair its strength, compiexiun, well-being and life, it depresses the mind, impairs all the senses, destroys the foetus in uterus, or deforms it or unduly prolongs the period of gestation; it gives rise to fear, grief, stupefaction, depression of the spirits and finally delirium; so obstructing the vital functions."

The Indian concept of the three-dosha originated the humoural theory amongst the Greeks and Romans. As Dr. Cyril Edwood observes, "Ths doctrine was taught in unmistakable terms in the holy books of the Hindus. From India it was carried to the Greeks by way of Persia." (*Medicine in Persia*)

It is inaccurate to say that this theory of three humours in the Hindu system of medicine is borrowed from the Greeks. As Sir Sinhjee observes, "The humoural theory of the Hindus is extraordinarily like that of Hippocrates, as may be seen by a more detailed description, but as it is spoken of in the *Rigveda,* the theory that it was derived by the Hindus from Hippocrates in untenable."

(*A short History of Aryan Medical Science,* p. 191)

Who is the Greatest Physician?

The greatest physician recognised in the vedas is God.

उन्नो वीरां अर्पय भेषजोभिर्भिषक्तमं त्वा भिषजां शृणोमि ।।

Brahma is the physician.

(*Rigveda* II, 33, 4)

Do thou with strengthening balms incite our heroes; I hear thee famed as best of all physicians.

The *Yajurveda* XVI, 5, also states the same thing.

अध्यवोचदधिवक्ता प्रथमो दैव्यो भिषक्।

The Advocate, the first Divine Physician, hath defended us.

The Ashvini Kumars are considered to be the physicians of the gods. As we read in the *Aitareya Brahmana* I, 18.

अश्विनौ देवानां भिषजौ

and there is a prayer in *Rigveda* VIII, 18, 8 to these physicians to protect us.

उत त्या दैव्या भिषजा शं नः

करतो अश्विना युयुयातामितो

रपो अप स्रिधः।।

And may Ashvins, the divine pair of physicians, send us health. May they remove iniquity and chase our foes.

(Griffith)

Who are these Ashvins ?

Nirukta XII, I gives a clarification in these words :

अथातो द्युस्थाना देवताः

तासामश्विनौ प्रथमागामिनौ भवतः

अश्विनौ भद् व्यश्नुवाते सर्व रतेनान्यो ज्योतिषान्यः

अश्वैरश्विनावित्यौर्णवाभः

तत कावश्विनौ द्यावापृथिव्यावित्येके

अहोरात्रावित्येके। सूर्याचन्द्रमसावित्येके। राजानौ

पुण्यकृतावित्यैतिहासिकाः।।

About the surgical and therapeutic skill of the Ashvin twins, the physicians of the gods, it is stated that they worked miracles, they could replace the head of a man with that of a horse. They successfully treated Pusan when his teeth had become loosened. They treated Bhaga when he had lost his eye sight and restored the hand of Indra when it had become wittered. They cured Soma of consumption. When sage Cyavana, the son of Bhrigu had become paralysed with old age, and lost his voice it is the Ashvini twins that made him young once again with the medicine, now popularly known as Cyavana-Prasha after the name of that sage.

वृद्धोऽपि च्यवनो युवा बभूव।

The *Atharvaveda* V. 29, I recites the qualfications of a good physician as:

1. one who knows the preparation of medicines भेषजस्य कर्त्ता,
2. one who can understand diagnosis and prescribe the remedy readily क्रियमाणं अग्रेवेत्ति।

It is such a physician who is expert in all ways, has good contacts with specialists and cures the ailment in its entirety.

विश्वेभिः देवैः संविदानः अस्य परिधिः पताति।।

(*Atharvaveda* V.29, 2)

A physician has, by virtue of his medicines, the power to increase the longevity of a person who is क्षितायु : *i.e.* debilitated by age.

यदि क्षितार्युयदि वा परेतो यदि मृत्योरन्तिकं नींत एव

तमा हरामि निर्ऋतेरुपस्थादस्पार्षमेनं शतशारदाय।।

(*Atharvaveda* III, 2, 2)

"Though his days are ended, though he is almost departed, though very near death already, I bring him out of destruction's lap, and save him for life, to last a hundred autumns, and so with the person who is nearing death."

Such was the demand laid on the vedic physician.

Sushruta, who was the exponent of the science of medicine in his age, insisted on six kinds of basic knowledge before the physician could arrive at a correct diagnosi of the patient's condition and behaviour. According to him,

संचय च प्रकोपं च प्रसरं स्थान संश्रयम्
व्यक्तिं भेदं च यो वेत्ति दोषाणां सः
भवेद भिषकू।।

(*Sushruta Sutra* 21, 36)

He is entitled to be called a physician who knows the various stages of pathogenesis — accumulation, संचय; provocation, प्रकोप; diffusion प्रसर; location, स्थानसंश्रय; manifestation, व्यक्ति; and termination, भेदः।

***Atharvaveda* as a Monument of Indian Medicine**

Prof. Macdonell says, "The *Atharvaveda* is the oldest literary monument of Indian Medicine."

(*Sanskrit Literature,* p. 196)

The *Atharvaveda* consists of twenty section called Kandas and has come to us in nine recensions. Two recensions are extant : the शौनकेयः (which is the only popular recension) and the पैप्पलादः also known as the kashmiri recension. The 18th Kanda is not found in the पैप्पलाद शाखा and is, therefore believed to be of a later date. It is also believed that the 20th Kanda is completely borrowed from the *Rigveda*.

The Kandas 19 and 20 are ignored in the प्रातिशाख्य of the *Atharvaveda*. Of the nine recensions of the *Atharvaveda,* seven have been lost.

114 hymns in this veda are devoted to medical subjects, in which some of the outstanding topics like fever,

consumption, various wounds, leprosy and poisoning are mentioned. It is on these foundations that the later sages made researches in Ayurveda, with its eight branches and three fundamentals.

The eight branches of this science, as taught and practised in ancient India, are :

1. Medical therapy,
2. The science of the diseases of the eye, ear, nose, throat *i.e.* of supra-clavicular parts.
3. Surgery शल्यापहर्तृकं
4. Toxicology विषगदवैरोधिकप्रशमनम्
5. Psycho-therapy भूत विद्या
6. Paediatrics कौमारभृत्यकम्
7. Rejuvenation रसायनम्
8. Virilification वाजीकरणम्

Sushruta observes that a doctor of medicine should not only be well read but equipped with versatile understanding it he wishes to arrive at the correct diagnosis.

एकं शास्त्रमधीयानो न विद्याच्छास्त्रनिश्चयम्

तस्माद् बहुश्रुतः शास्त्रं विजानीयात् चिकित्सकः।।

Human Physiology and Anatomy in the Vedas

The Atharvaveda X, 2 mentions 121 different parts of the body. The *Yajurveda,* also contains a long list of the several analyseable parts of the body, including:

Teeth	Nostrils
Gums	Upper lip
Tooth Sockets	Head
Tongue Tip	Frontal Bone
Palate	Lower Neck

Jaws
Mouth
Foot
Rectum
Entrails
Arms
Belly
Rib Cartilages
Neck Tendons
Knees
Shoulders
Large intestines
Testicles
Chest
Kidneys

In a nutshell we quote *Atharvaveda* X, 2 verses 31, 32 describing all outlets — the dight chakras or ganglions and the nine gates of the human body.

अष्टचक्रा नवद्वारा देवानां पूरयोध्या
तस्यां हिरण्मयः कोशः स्वर्गो ज्योतिषाकृतः।।
तस्मिन् हिरण्ये कोशे त्र्यरे त्रिप्रतिष्ठिते
तस्मिन् यद् यक्ष्मात्मन्वत् तद्वै ब्रह्मविदो विदुः।।

(*Atharvaveda* X, 2, 31, 32)

This fort of gods, (human body), impregnable with circles eight and portals nine, contains a golden treasure chest, celestial, begirt with light (31).

Men deep in the lore of Brahma, know that Animated Being, which dwells in the golden treasure chest that hath three spokes and three supports.(32).

(*Portals nine* refers to the orfices of the human body, seven in the head and two below.)

Hydropathy in the Vedas

The *Atharvaveda* VI, 7, and VI, 57, are full of references to diseases which are curable through the various uses of water and vaporisation.

शं चनो मयश्चनो मा चनः किं चनाममत्
क्षमा रपो विश्वं नो अस्तु भेषजं सर्वं नो अस्तु भेषजम्।।

(*Atharvaveda*, VI, 57, 3)

"Let it be health and joy to us. Let nothing vex or injure us. Let water be the universal medicine — Let all to us be balm".

The *Atharvaveda* I, 4, I, 5 and I, 6 have copious references to water therapy, declaring the efficacy of water in so many words.

शिवतमः रसः	(I, 5, 2) water is the 'Essence'.
अपो मयोभुवः	(I, 5, 1) water is beneficial.
अप्सु अमृतम्	(I, 4, 4) water contains nectar.
अप्सु भेषजम्	(I, 4, 4) water is medicinal.
अप्सु विशवानी भेषजानि	(I, 6, 2) water contains all medicinal properties.

(*i*) The *Rigveda* 1, 23, 9 says: अप्स्वन्तरमृतमप्सु भेषजम् and again in *Rigveda* I, 32, 20, we have,

(*ii*) अप्सु मे सोमो अब्रवीत् अन्तर्विश्वानि भेषजा।

"Within the waters, Soma thus hath tole me dwell all balms". (Griffith) and in the next verse,

(*iii*) आपः पृणीत भेषजम्

O waters, teem with medicine to keep my body safe from harm; and

(*iv*) आपः पृणीत भेषजं वरूथं तन्वे मम

(*Rigveda* I, 23, 21)

Water destroys the diseases of the internal organs.

(*v*) याः शुचयः पावकास्ता आपो देवीरिह मामवन्तु

(*Rigveda* VII, 49, 2)

Bright purifying, let those water goddeses, protect me.

(*vi*) अयक्ष्मा अनमीवाः नाअगसः (*Yajurveda* IV, 12)

May the water, that we have drunk, become auspicious, make us free from all sin and malady and sickness.

(*vii*) *Rigveda* X, 9,1 states : आपो हि ष्ठा मयोभुवस्ता न ऊर्जे दध
ातन। महे रणाय चक्षसे।।

You waters are beneficient, so help us to energy, that we may look on great delight. (Griffith)

(*viii*) यो वः शिवतमो रसस्तस्य भाजयते हनः उशतीरिव मातरः
(*Rigveda X, 9, 2)*

Ye waters, give us a portion of your lap, O most Auspicious, like a mother in affectionate love.

(*ix*) ईशाना वार्याणां क्षयन्तीश्चर्षणीनाम्
अपो याचामि भेषजम् (*Rigveda* X, 9,5)

I beg to the floods to give us balm, these queens who rule over precious things, and have supreme control over men.

In a certain prayer in the *Yajurveda* VI, 31 water is invoked.

(*x*) मनो मे तर्पयत प्राणं मे तर्पयत चक्षमे तर्पयत
श्रोत्रं मे तर्पयतात्मानं मे तर्पयत।।

Content my mind, content my speech, content my breath, content mine eye. Content my ear, content my soul etc. (*Rigveda,* VII, 104, 21)

(*xi*) *Atharvaveda* XIX, 2, 8 is full of references to the healing power of water.

शंत आपो हैमवतीः शमु ते सन्तूत्स्याः
शंते सनिष्यदा आपः शमु ते सन्तु वर्ष्याः
(*Atharvaveda* XIX, 2, 1)

Blest be the streams from hills of snow, sweet be the spring waters into thee. Sweet be the swift running waters, sweet to thee be rain-water.
(Griffith)

(*xii*) Rain and the water from waterfalls has electric power in it that makes the body elastic like that of a horse.

अपामह दिव्यानामपां स्त्रोतस्यानाम्
अपामह प्रणेजनेऽश्वा भवथ वाजिनः।।

(*Atharvaveda* XIX, 2, 4)

The Different kinds of water are distinguished in the *Atharvaveda*

(*i*)	देवीः आपः	(I, 4, 3)	Water received from clouds.
(*ii*)	वार्षकीः आपः	(I, 6, 4)	Rainy water.
(*iii*)	सिंधुः	(I, 4, 3)	Sea water.
(*iv*)	अनूप्याः आपः	(I, 6, 4)	Water obtained in watery regions.
(*v*)	धन्वन्याः आपः	(I, 6, 4)	Water obtained in desert or regions of scanty rains.
(*vi*)	खनित्रिमाः आपः	(I, 6, 4)	Water obtained from wells which are sunk.

The *Atharvaveda* XIX, 2 gives a composite list in terms of usage

(*vii*)	हैमवती	Water from mountains.
(*viii*)	अत्स्याः	Fountain water.
(*ix*)	सनिष्यदा;	Water form streams and canals which flow throughout the year.
(*x*)	वर्ष्याः	Rainy water.
(*xi*)	धन्वन्याः	Water in desert area
(*xii*)	कुम्भेभिरामृताः	Water stored in pitchers.

Homoeopathy is based on the "Law of Similars" and its medicines are potencized in 3,6,30,200,1000, etc.

While discussing the Doctrine of Signature, we have already referred to the Law of Similars in Nature, which forms the bsis of Homoeopathic treatment.

The *Atharvaveda* IV, 17, 1 describes how to increase the potency in medicine by a 100 times.

ईशानां त्वा भेषजानामुज्जेष आ रभामहे
चक्रे सहस्रवीर्यां सर्वस्मा ओषधे त्वा।।

(*Atharvaveda* IV, 17, 1)

"We seize and hold thee, Conquering One, the queen of medicines that heals. Plant, I have endowed thee with a thousand powers for every man." (Griffith)

Homoeopathy and Allopathy

Homoeopathy is based on Hahnemann's doctrine of "*Similia Simibilus Curentor*". A homoeopathic drug is given to cure a disease that has symptoms similar to the physiological effects of that drug. This procedure is contrary to the principle of allopathy in which there is no direct relationship between the symptoms of the disease and the physiological effects of the remedy. For instance, it is well known that strong decoction of coffee at night causes sleeplessness. In homoeopathy Coffee is a drug given to cure insomnia and so on with Arsenic, Ipecac, Lachesis, or Apis, An allopathic cure for fever might be a purgative or diaphoretic mixture by which, the entire system is stimulated to increased activity in the hope of relieving the morbidity present in some particular parts. The ultimate result of such artificial stimulation instead of curing the disease, increases constipation or indigestion or other morbid conditions of the body and sometimes even produces toxic effects in the system.

Hippocrates, the father of modern medicine, foresaw that "Disease is produced by similars and by similars administered, the patient is restored to health, thus, that which produces strangury cures strangury and that which causes vomiting, cures vomiting."

'Likes are to be removed by likes and not by contraries' is the basic axiom in Homeopathy.

Homoeopathy is careful to classify its degrees of potency Lower Potencies 1x, 3x, 6x, 12x, 3, 6:

Medium Potencies 12, 30.

Higher Potencies 200, 1000 (M) 10,000 (D. M.) 1,00,000 (C.M.), 1 million (M.M.)

Increasing the potency is a graduate process of succession, by which the operative power of the drug usually styled "nuclear energy" is enhanced. The *Atharvaveda* IV, 17, 1, as we hve noticed alludes to 1000th of a certain herbal cure.

Homoeopathy recognises three basic substances — Sulphur, Mercury and Salt — the three *Soras,* the necessary ingredients of all bodies — organic or inorganic — which correspond to three doshas of the Ayurveda or the "three humours" or the Greeks.

Chromopathy in the Vedas

References to treatment of diseases of heart, kidney, liver etc., by means of sun's rays are found in *Atharvaveda* I, 22 and in *Atharvaveda* VI, 83.

(*a*) In *Athrvaveda* IX, 8, it is mentioned that the rays of the sun absorb the toxic elements of the body which explains its effectiveness in curing disease.

शीर्षक्तिं शीर्षामयं कर्णशूलं विलोहितम्
सर्व शीर्षण्यं ते रोग वहिर्निर्मन्त्रयामहे।

(*Atharvaveda* IX, 8, 1)

(*b*) *Sunlight kills germs.*

(*i*) उत् पुरस्तात्सूर्य एति विश्वदृष्टो अदृष्टहा

(*Rigveda* I, 191, 8)

Slayer of things unseen, the sun, beheld of all, rises.

(*ii*) उद्यन्नादित्यः क्रिमीन् हन्तु (*Atharvaveda* II, 32, 1)

Uprising, let the sun destroy the worms.

(*iii*) ये सूर्यं न तितिक्षन्त (*Atharvaveda* VIII, 6, 12)

These worms cannot bear sun.

(*iv*) हृद्रोगं मम सूर्यं हरिमाणं च नाशय

(*Rigveda* I, 50, 11)

Sunlight is efficacious regarding heart-diseas and jaundice.

(c) *Colour Therapy*

Colour therapy has recently made a very great progress in modern medicine. It is now well-recognized that all colours which emanate from the sun, affect not only the physical health of a person but also his state of mind and feelings. Today's psychologists know how colours can help to calm disturbed mental conditions and this factor is made use of in industries too, to ensur a happier and healthier condition of living for the workers.

The Solar spectrum contains seven primary colours, (1) Violet, (2) Indigo, (3) Blue, (4) Yellow, (5) Green, (6) Orange and (7) Red. Within these seven colours there are as many as 378 visible colour combinations. Inapt colour combinations can caus depression. "If you are a bundle of nerves, cannot relax, and feel depressed, why not try a dose of colour?" is rightly said.

Red and orange are warm, green is relaxing and blue is the best for quietening nerves. In the radio studios of the National Brodcasting Company of America, one finds the walls and ceiling painted in two shades of blue. This has been found an effective antidote for the feelings of anxiety of those waiting to broadcast.

The restful harmony which the sun's rays produce through the combination of colours was recognized by the vedic seers and the *Atharvaveda* presents in a nucleus form, this aspect of chromopathy.

Fever Therapy in the Vedas

The *Athavaveda* V. 22, mentions fevers and their cure.

(*a*) There are three types mentioned.

(*i*) सदहिन: that which occurs daily.

(*ii*) तृतीयक: that which occurs every third day.

(*iii*) वितृतीयक: that which occurs on the fourth day.

तृतीयकं वितृतीयं सदन्दिमुत शारदम्
तक्मानं शीतं रूरं ग्रैष्मं नाशय वार्षिकम्।।

(*Atharvaveda* V, 22, 13)

(*b*) Apart from these three types of periodical ague, there are seasonal fevers.

(*i*) ग्रेष्म: The fever that occurs during the summer season on account of excessive heat.

(*ii*) शारद: The fever that occurs during the winter monsoons.

(*iii*) वार्षिक: The fever that occurs during the rainy season.

(*iv*) शीत: The Malarial fever which is accompanied with fits of shivering.

(*v*) रूर: The fever that occurs due to dryness.

(*vi*) क्लास: The fever that arises on account of phlegm.

(*vii*) कास: Fever accompanied by bronchitis.

(*viii*) उत-युगं Where phlegm and bronchitis occur as parallel symptoms.

(*ix*) व्याल: High fever, as severe as a snake bite.

(*c*) *Atharvaveda* V, 22 verses 6,7,12 mentions the classes of people who suffer from attacks of fever.

(*i*) निष्टक्करीं The thin and lean or those who are dissipated.

दासी निष्टक्करीमिच्छ तां वज्रेण समर्पय

(*ii*) प्रफर्व्यम् : The obese. (V, 22, 6)

शूद्रामिच्छ प्रफव्य तां तक्मन् वीव धूनुहि (V, 22, 7)

(*iii*) अरणं जनम : The over-indulgent of voluptuary.

पाप्मा भ्रातृव्येण सह गच्छामुमरणैं जनम्।। (V, 22, 12)

(*d*) *Atharvaveda* V, 22, 9, holds that fever does not attack the self controlled individual.

अन्यक्षेत्रे न रमसे वशीसन् मृडयासि नः।

"One who is self controlled among us, fever does not give him pain but leaves him unaffected."

(*e*) Then in *Atharvaveda* V, 22, 2, V, 22, 4, Resistances against fever are suggested.

(*i*) The one who performs sacrifices will gain immunity. By havan yajna, the air is purified and there is no contamination of atmosphere by germs.

वर्हिः शोशुचाना समिधः

इतः तक्मानं अप बाधताम्।।

(*Atharvaveda* V, 22, 1)

(*ii*) The man who is regular in the care of his bowels will protect himself because according to vedic injunction, with no constipation, there will be no fever.

अधा हि तक्मन्नरसो हि भूया
अधा न्यङ्ङधराङ् वा परेहि।। (V, 22, 2)

(*iii*) Vegetarianism and moderation in eating are a protection against fever.

शकम्भरस्य मुष्टिहा पुनरेतु महावृषान्

(*Atharvaveda* V, 22, 4)

The metaphor is, that the vegetarian will strike the fever away, as if by a fist. (मुष्टि-हा)

(*f*) The vedic word for ague is तक्मा derived from तकि कृच्छ्र जीवने inflicting pain on the body. We have a reference to this in *Atharvaveda* 1, 25,1

यदग्निरापो अदहत् प्रविश्य
यत्रा कृण्वन् धर्मधृतो नमांसि।
तत्र त आहुः परमं जनित्रं स नः
सं विद्वान् परि वृङ्ग्धि तक्मन्।।

"When Agni blazed, when he has pierced the waters" (the idea is that fevers begin to be prevalent at the commencement of the annual rains, when Agni, the God of Fire, descends in the form of lightning from the waters of the firmament and falls with the rain into waters of the earth.) (Griffith)

According to their types and season, there are more than forty names listed.

(*g*) *The Three Herbs*

There are several remedies suggested in the *Atharvaveda* to counteract agues but there are three most popular herbs. They are जंगिडः

(*i*) Cf. आशरीकं विशरीकं बलासं पृष्ट्यामयम्
तक्मानं विश्वशारदमरसां जंगिडस्करत्।।

(*Atharvaveda* XIX, 34, 10)

"Lumbago and rheumatic pain, consumptive cough, and pleurisy and fever which each autumn brings, may *jangida* make powerless." (Griffith)

(*ii*) कुष्ट *Kushta* is another remedy given in *Atharvaveda* V, 4, I

कुष्टेहि तक्मनाशन तकमानं नाशयन्नितः।।

(*iii*) The third is आंजन

त्रयोदासा आँजनस्य तक्मा बलास आदहि।।

(*Atharvaveda* IV, 9, 8)

The three persistent hazards : fever, phlegm, and burn are controlled effectively by the herb known as *Anjana*.

(*h*) *Prayer for Heading of a Sick Person*

(*Atharvaveda* X, 6, 8)

यमबध्नाद् बृहस्पतिर्मणिफालं

घृतशचुतमुग्रं स्वदिरमोजसे

तेनोमाँ मणिना कृषिमश्विनावभिरक्षतः संभिषग्भयां महोदुहे।।

"The charm Brihaspati hath bound. . . the Asvins with the Amulet protect this culture of our fields. This may yield power and protection by two physicians."

The Chemistry of Metals

(*a*) In Vedic times, gold silver, copper, iron, lead etc. were used as medicines and we have a reference to this fact in *Yajurveda*, XVIII 13.

हिरण्यं च मे ज्यश्व मे श्यामं च मे लौहं च मे

सीसं च मे त्रपु च मे यज्ञेन कल्पन्ताम्।।

(*b*) Small amounts of Lead are mentioned as a general tonic

सीसेन हुह इन्द्रियम् (*Yajurveda* XXI, 36)

'with lead, yield strength and power!

इदं बाधत्तअत्त्रिण
जातानि पिशाच्याः

(*Atharvaveda* 1, 16, 3)

It kills the germs known as Atri. Pishacha, Yatu, Rakshasa etc.

(*c*) Mark the emphasis of its efficacy in *Atharvaveda* 1, 16, 4.

'Lead is a remedy against consumption in the cattle, consumption in men.'

यौगोषुयक्षमः पुरुषेपु यक्षमः तेन त्व साकयघराड् परेहि

(*Atharvaveda* XII, 2, 1)

Treatment in Snake Bites

Hypnotic Method.

(*i*) There is a mention of treatment by hypnosis called संवशीकरण In *Atharvaveda* V. 13 we have

चक्षुषाते चक्षुर्हन्मि विषेण हन्मि ते विषम्
अहे म्रियस्व मा जीवीः प्रत्यगम्थेतु त्वा विषम्।

(*Atharvaveda* V, 13, 4)

"I with this eye destroy thine eye, and with this position conquer thee. Live not, O Snake, but die the death, may thy venom return on thyself."

(Griffith)

(*ii*) *Atharvaveda* VII, 93, reads :

इन्द्रेण मन्युना वयमभिस्याम पृतन्यतः घ्नन्तो वृत्राण्यप्रति।।

"With Indra's and with Manyu's aid, may we subdue our enemie resistlessly destroying foes."

(Griffith)

(*iii*) *Atharvaveda* VII, 56, 2, refers to the same.

(*iv*) *Atharvaveda* V, 13, 5, is just a hypnotic way of exorcising *kairat* कैरात, snakes (पृश्न, उपतृण्य, बभ्रु and असित and अलौक), away from the courtyard.

कैरात पृश्न उपतृण्य बभ्र आमे
श्रृणुतासिता अलीकाः
मा मे सख्युःस्ताभानमपिष्ठाता
श्रावयन्तो निविषेरमध्वम् ।।

"Listen to me, Black-snakes, and hateful creatures, Lurkerin-grass, Kairat, and Brown and Spotted, Approach not near the house, my friend inhabits, give warning and rest quite with your poison."

(Griffith).

(*v*) *Atharvaveda* V, 13 refers to eighteen varieties of snakes as under :

कैरात	:	living in forests
पृष्नि	:	spotted
बभ्रु	:	of brown colour
असित	:	of back colour
अलीक	:	bad to look at
तैमात	:	living in wet places
अपोदक	:	not living near water
सात्रासाह	:	attacking any way-farer
मन्यु	:	extremely wrathful
उपतृण्य	:	living in grass
आलिगी	:	coiling round the body
विलिगी	:	remaining away from the body
उरुगुला	:	having large body

असिक्त	:	black female serpent
दद्रुषी	:	causing itch after bite
कर्णा	:	having ears
श्वाबित्	:	one whom the dog follows
खनित्रमा	:	snake emerging out from underground

The medicinal herbs suggested as cure for snake bite ताबुव are and तस्तुव. What these are compounded of remains yet a matter for research. It is conjectured that these may be some kind of stones, rubbing of which cures snake bite. The second method is to control the spreading poison by means of a constructive bandage tied in three places.

गृह्णामि ते मध्यमम उत्तमम्
अवमन् एतासु विषं अग्रमम्।।

(*Atharvaveda* V, 13, 2)

Gem Therapy in the Vedas

The Ayurvedic practitioners praise the efficacious use of gems in warding off disease. For example, in *Susharuta* chapter 46, we have

मुक्ताविद्रुमवजरेन्द वैदूर्यं स्फटिकादयः
चक्षुण्या मणयः शींता लेरवना विषेसूदनाः
पवित्रा धरणीयाश्च पाप्मालक्ष्मी मलापहाः।।

The gems are मोती, मूंग, हीरा, लहसुनिया, and स्फटिक.

Wearing of these gems improves eyesight, has cooling effect, purifies the mind, increases beauty, decreases ugliness and removes poison. Inspite of the fact that wearing of these gems in advocated in Ayurveda as curative for ailments yet, it is believed by certain researchers that references to मणिबन्धन (a list of which is given below) in the *Atharvaveda* relate not to gem therapy, but to knowledge of agricultural missiles and other scientific equipment. For example, फालमणिबन्धन in *Atharvaveda* X, 6, is considered to have nothing to do with the particular type of gem known as फालमणि but relates to a certain agricultural implement. The same view is held regarding the references to

आञ्जनमणि	:	in *Atharvaveda* IV, 9
शंखमणि	:	in *Atharavaveda* IV, 10
अस्ततृमणि	:	in *Atharvaveda* 1, 46
जंग्डिमणि	:	in *Atharvaveda* 11, 4
जंग्डिमणि	:	in *Atharvaveda* XIX, 34
पर्णमणि	:	in *Atharvaveda* III.5
शतवारमणि	:	in *Atharvaveda* XIX, 36
ओदुग्धमणि	:	in *Atharvaveda* XIX, 31
अभिबर्तमणि	:	in *Atharvaveda* 1, 29
प्रतिसरमणि	:	in *Atharvaveda* VIII, 5
दर्भमणि	:	in *Atharvaveda* XIX, 28/29/30
औदुम्वरमणि	:	in *Atharavaveda* XIX, 31
वरणमणि	:	in *Atharvaveda* X, 3

This is a matter for further research and precise clarification.

About the effectiveness of those gems, if we agree to call them so, Dr. Benoytosh Bhattacharya writes, "The seven principal gems are the inexhaustible mines of the seven cosmic rays contituting the cosmos or the universe. . . Like the planets, these sacred gems are nothing else but condensations of the seven cosmic rays." (*Gem Therapy*, p. 7). Gems continue to be used by men from time immemorial. Mostly gems have been used not only as a source of investment, but for their auspicious value in regard to longevity, power and popularity, and for averting diseases and misfortunes. Kings in ancient India were advised to collect the very best gems to protect themselves against emergencies. Astrologically too, people stuck by misfortune are advised to wear differnt kinds of gems in order to counteract the effect of malefic planets."

(*ibid.*, p. 2)

These मणि: circular, uncut and pierced gems, were taken from dried roots of herbs and used as medicines in the vedic times. Whether they were actually tied round the waist or the arms, as is a custom prevalent even now a days is not clear. Some scholars, however, infer from a word ग्रसते in *Atharvaveda* XIX, 34, 8, that these gems were tied on different parts of the body.

अथोपदान भगवोजगिंडामितवीर्य

पुरात उग्रा ग्रसत उपेन्द्रो वीर्यं ददौ।।

(*Atharvaveda* XIX, 34, 8)

Griffith translates this verse, thus :

Then when thou sprangest into life,

Jangida of unmeasured strength,

Indra, O mighty one, bestowed,

Great power upon thee from the first.

Veterinary Science in the Vedas

Veterinary science which has for its nucleus, the *Atharvaveda* VI, 59; 11, 26; 1, 11, 14; expanded under the attention of the postvedic teachers, and we have voluminous treatises, not only on botany and the vegetable kingdom (वृक्षायुर्वेद) but on horses (अश्वायुर्वेद) elephants (हस्त्यायुर्वेद) the cows (गवायुर्वेद) and even on hawks. (श्येनकायुर्वेद)

Charaka devotes chapter II verses 19 to 26 to this science and *Harit Samhita* has several references to this. Salihotra is known as the father of the veterinary science and in the Punjabi dialect, the word 'Salotri' means a veterinary surgeon.

Hindu veterinary science possesses a monumental compilation known as *"Hasti-Ayurveda"*, the sacred wisdom on the "Longavity of Elephants." This text has been edited by Mahadeva Apte and is a huge work consisting of 46 chapters and about seven thousand and seven hundred stanzas.

The *Matanga-Lilla* of Nilakantha and Fraklin Edgertons' book *The Elephant-Lore of the Hindus,* are remarkable contributions on elephant surgery and therapy.

Dairy-farming

We have reference to this in the *Atharvaveda* II, 26. It is essential for cows to roam about, to ensure healthy breeding. (cf. येषां सहचारं वायुः जुजोष *Atharvaveda* II, 26, 1) and that those animals that have wandered may return safely is indicated in :

ये पश्वः परा ईयुः ते इह आयन्तु (*Atharvaveda* II, 27, 1)

Atharvaveda III, 14 is an important hymn on cow breeding (गोसंवर्धन)

The most efficacious remedy in veterinary diseases is the herb known as अरुन्धती (*Atharvaveda* VI, 59)

It increases milk in the animals such as the cow.

अनडुद्भ्यस्त्वं प्रथमं धेनुभ्यस्त्वमरुन्धति
अधेनवे वयसे शर्म यच्छ चतुष्पदे।।

(*Atharvaveda* VI, 59, 1)

First, O Arundhati, protect our oxen and our milky kin, protect each one that is infirm-each quadruped that yields no milk. (Griffith)

The following mantras on cow-breeding are interesting.

(*i*) संजग्माना अबिभ्युषिरस्मिन्
गोष्ठे करीषिणाः

विभ्रतीः सौम्यं मध्वनमीवा उपेतन।।

(*Atharvaveda* III, 14, 3)

Moving together, free from fear with
Plenteous droppings in this pen,
Bearing sweet milk like Soma Juice,
Come hither free from all disease.

(*ii*) इहैव गाव एत नेहो शाकेव पुष्यत
इहैवोत अजायध्वं मयि संज्ञानमस्त वः।।

(*Atharvaveda* III, 14, 4)

Come hither, to this place, O Cows, here
Thrive as though ye were manured
Even here increase and multiply, let us
Be friendly, you and me.

(*iii*) शिवो वो गोष्ठो भवतु
शारिशाकेव पुष्यत इहैवोत प्र
जायध्वं मयावः सं सृजामसि।।
मया गावो गोपतिना सचध्वमर्ये

Auspicious be this stall to you,
Prosper like cultivated rice.
Even here increase and multiply,
Thyself do we bestow on you.

(*Atharvaveda* III, 14, 5)

(*iv*) वोपो गोण्ठइह पोषयिण्पुः।
रायस्पोषेण बहुलाभवन्तीः
जीवाजींकन्तीरुपवः सदेम।।

(*Atharvaveda* III, 14, 6)

Follow me, cows, as master of the cattle,
Here may this cow-pen make you grow and prosper,

Still while we live, may we approach you living,
Ever increasing with the growth of riches.

(*Griffith's translation*)

On Disinfectants

सर्वेषां च क्रिमीणां सर्वासाँ च क्रिमीणाम्

भिनद्याश्मना शिरो दहाम्यग्निना मुखम्।।

(*Atharvaveda* V, 23, 13)

Of every worm and insect, of the female and the male alike — I crush the head to pieces with a stone and burn the face with fire.

आमे सुपक्वे शबले विपक्वे

यो मा पिशाचो अशने ददम्भ।

तदात्मना प्रजया पिशाचा

वि यातयन्तामगदोऽयमस्तु।।

(*Atharvaveda* V, 29, 6)

If some Pishacha, in my food, raw, ready, thoroughly cooked, hath deceived me, let the Pishachas with their lives and off-spring atone for this and let this man be healthy (Griffith)

Surely these *Pishachas* in the food could not be demons or ghosts, but germs which cause food poisoning.

Hair Diseases

The falling of hair and premature grey hair, are treated in *Atharvaveda* VI, 136. The remedy is the use of the herbs called,

केश दृंहणी (*Atharvaveda* VI, 21, 3)

नितत्नि (*Atharvaveda* VI, 136, 1)

केशवर्धनी (*Atharvaveda* VI, 137, 1)

देदी देवयामधिजाता पृथिव्यामस्योषधे (*Atharvaveda*, VI, 136)

तां त्वा नितत्नि केशेभ्यो दृंहणाय खनामसि

दृंह प्रत्नान् जनयाजातां जातानु वर्षीय संस्कृधि

यस्ते केशोऽवपद्यते समूलो यश्च वृश्चते

इदं तं विश्भेषज्याभिषिञ्चामि वीरुधा।।

(*Atharvaveda* VI.136, 3)

Born from the bosom of wide earth, the goddess, godlike plant art thou : So we Nitatni, dig thee up to strengthen and fix fast the hair.

Make the old hair firm, make new hair spring, lengthen what has already grown.

Thy hair where it is falling off and where the roots are torn away, I wet and sprinkle with the place, the remedy for all disese. (Griffith's translation)

Insanity

देवैनसादुन्मदितमुन्मत्तं रक्षसस्परि

कृणोमि विद्वान् भेषजं यदानुन्मदितौसति

(*Atharvaveda* VI, 111, 3)

Insane through sin against the gods, or maddened by a demon's power, well-skilled I make a medicine, to free thee from insanity. (Griffith)

Eye Diseases

तिस्रो दिवस्तिस्रः पृथिवीः

षट् चेमाः प्रदिशः पृथक्

त्वयाहं सर्वा भूतानि

पश्यामि देव्योषधे।।

(*Atharvaveda* IV, 20, 2)

Through thee, O god-like plant, may I *behold* all creatures that exist, three several earths and these six regions one by one. (Griffith)

Herb for Beauty

इदं खनामि भेषजं माँ पश्यमभिरोरुदम्

परायतो निवर्तनमायतः प्रतिनन्दनम्।।

(*Atharvaveda* VII, 38, 1)

I dig this healing herb that makes my lover look on me and weep. That bids the parting friend return and kindly greets him as he comes. (Griffith)

Sterility

आ ते योनिंर्भ एतु पुमान् बाण इवेषुधिम्

आ वीरो ऽत्र जायतां पुत्रस्ते दशमास्यः।।

(*Atharvaveda* III, 23, 2)

यासाँ द्यौः पिता पृथिवी माता समुद्रो

मूलं वीरुधाँ बभूव

तास्त्वा पुत्रविद्याय दैवी प्रावन्त्वोषधयः।।

(*Atharvaveda* III, 23, 6)

(*i*) As arrow to the quiver, so let a male embryo enter thee. Then from thy side, be born a babe a ten month child, thy hero son. (Griffith)

(*ii*) May those celestial herbs whose sire was heaven, the earth their mother and their root and ocean. May those celestial plants assist thee to obtain a son. (Griffith)

Herb for Pregnacy

शमीमश्वत्थ आरुढ़ तत्र पुंसुवनं कृतम्

तद् वै पुत्रस्य वेदनं तत्स्त्रीष्वा भरामसि।।

(*Atharvaveda* VI, 11, 1)

Asvattha on the Shami-tree. There a male birth is certified. There is the finding of a son; this bring we to the women-folk. (Griffith)

Female Diseases

यस्ते गर्भमनीवा दुर्णामा योनिमाशये

अग्निष्ठं ब्रह्मणासह निष्क्रव्याद मनीनशत्।।

(*Atharvaveda* XX, 96, 12)

Agni concurring in the prayer, drive off the eater of thy flesh. The malady of evil-name (दुर्णामा) that hath attacked the babe and womb. (Griffith)

Contagious Diseases in the Atharvaveda VII, 65,3

श्यावदता कुनखिना बण्डने यत् सहासिम

1 2 3 4

अपामार्ग त्वया वयं सर्वं तदपमृज्महे।

If with the cripple we have lived, whose teeth are black and whose nails deformed with thee, O Apamarga the plant *achyranthes aspera* we wipe all that ill away, from us. (Griffith)

Leprosy

नक्तंजातास्योषधे रामे कृष्णे असिक्निच

इदं रजनि रजय किलासं पलितं च यत्।

(*Atharvaveda* I, 23, 1)

Plant, thou sprangest up at night, dusky, dark coloured black in hue! So Rajni, re-colour thou these ashy spots of this leprosy. (Griffith)

Haemorrhage

(*Atharvaveda* II, 3) This is checked by लाक्ष herb

अरुः स्राणमिदं महत् पृथिव्या अध्युद्भृतम्

तदास्रावस्य भेषजं तदु रोगमनीनशत्।।

(*Atharvaveda* II, 3, 5)

Mighty is this wound-healing balm, from out the earth was it produced. This is the cure for morbid flow this driveth malady away. (Griffith)

Skin Diseases

विद्रधस्य बलासस्य लोहितस्य बनस्पते

विस्लपकस्योषधे मोच्छिषः पिशितं च न।।

(*Atharvaveda* VI, 127, 1)

Of abscess, of decline, of inflamation of the eyes, O plant of penetrating pain! thou herb, let not a particle remain. (Griffith)

Sciatica सन्धिवात

दश वृत्र मुञ्चेमं रक्षसो ग्राह्या।

अधि यैनं ज ग्राह पर्वसु

अथो एनं वनस्पते जोवानां लोकमुन्नय।।

(*Atharvaveda* II, 9, 1)

Free this man Dasa Vriksha ! from the demon, from *grahi* who hath seized his joints and members.

And raise him up again, O Tree, into the world of living men. (Griffith)

Birth Control or Family Planning

Atharvaveda VI, 138 refers to birth control by rendering one impotent. The name of the herb is not mentoned but the entire hymn with five verses is worth examination.

त्वं वीरूधां श्रेष्ठतमाभिश्रुतास्योषधे

इमं मे अद्य पुरुषं क्लीबमोपशिनं कृधि।।

(*Atharvaveda* VI, 138, 1)

Plant, thy fame is spread abroad as best of all the herbs the grow. Unman for me to-day, this man that he may wet the horn of hair — make him a eunuch.

क्लीवं क्लीवं त्वाकर्र वध्रेबध्रिं

त्वाकरमरसारसं त्वाकरम्।

कुरीरमस्य शीर्षणि
कुम्बं चाधिनिदध्मसि।।

(*Atharvaveda* VI, 138, 3)

Yes, I have unmanned thee eunuch ! yes, impotent! made thee important, and robbed thee, weakling, of thy strength. (Griffith)

Incidentally it may be mentioned that perhaps for reason of obscenity, Griffith has not translated the verses 4 and 5.

Atharvaveda VI, 138. 4, perhaps refers to that operation by means of which the right testicle (seminal gland) is cut.

ये ते नाड्यौ देव कृते ययोस्तिष्ठति वृष्ण्यम्
ते ते भिनद्मि शम्ययामुष्या अधि मुष्कयोः।।

(*Atharvaveda* VI, 138, 4)

Wooing a woman

According to Macdonell, "there is a group of charms concerned with women, being intended to secure their love with the aid of varous herbs, potent herbs." (*Sanskrit Literature)*

यथेमे द्यावापृथिवी
सद्यः पर्येति सूर्यः
एवा पर्येमि ते मनो
यथा मां कामिन्यद सो
यथा मन्नापगा असः।।

(*Atharvaveda* VI, 8, 3)

As round this heaven and earth, the sun goes day by day encircling them. So do I go around thy mind that woman, thou shalt love me well and shall not turn away from me.' (Macdonell's translation). *Atharvaveda* III, 25, 2, is another instance.

आधीपर्णां कामशल्यामिषुं

सङ्कल्प कुल्मलाम्।

तां सुसन्नतां कृत्वा कामो

विध्यतु त्वा हृदि।।

That arrow, winged with loving thought, its stern desire, its meek resolve. Let Kama, having truly aimed shoot forth and pierce thee in the heart. (Griffith)

Scrofula

Scrofula or गण्ड माला is also known as अपचित् and is of eight kinds. It affects the neck. In *Atharvaveda* VIII, 76, it is called ग्रैव्य.

य ग्रैव्या अपचिथोतो या उपपक्ष्याः

विजाम्नि या अपचितः स्व्यं स्रसः।

(*Atharvaveda* VII, 76, 2)

Pustules that rise upon the neck. Pustules upon the shoulder joints, Pustules, that falling of themselves, spring upon every twofold limb. (Griffith)

For its remedy, the *Atharvaveda* VI, 83, advocates treatment by rays of the sun and the moon and *Atharvavead* VII, 74, 1, suggests surgical operation with instrument made with he root of a herb known as मुनिवृक्ष.

Reference to surgical operations by the Asvini Kumaras, or physicians of the gods is found in the *Rigveda,* as शल्यक्रिया.

Tuberculosis is known as जायान्यः (*Atharvaveda* VII, 76, 5), because it is caused by excessive sexual intercourse and consequent loss of vitality — a disease caused through the female sex. यज्जायाभ्योऽविन्दत् तज्जायेन्यस्या.

The *Taittiriya Samhita* II, 3, 5. 2 calls this पाप्मा (*Atharvaveda V, 22, 12).* Its remedy lies in the use of the herb known as आंजन (*Atharvaveda* XIX, 44, 2) and sacrificial homa which will kill germs. *Atharvaveda* VII, 76. 5 states the use of sacrificial homa as a remedy.

विद्म वै ते जायान्त जानं
यती जायान्य जायसे
कथं ह तत्र त्वं हनो
यस्य कृण्मो हविर्गृहे।।

We know thy origin, know whence thou art born. How hast thou then struck this man here, him *in whose house we sacrifice.* (Griffith)

Atharvaveda is thus considered as the moment of Indian Medicine.